"YE ARE GODS"

"Ye Are Gods"

By

Annalee Skarin

DeVorss Publications
Camarillo, California

Ye Are Gods
Copyright © 1952, 1979
by Annalee Skarin

ISBN: 978-0-87516-718-3
Twenty-third Printing, 2024

DeVorss & Company, Publisher
P.O. Box 1389
Camarillo CA 93011-1389
www.devorss.com

Printed in the United States of America

THE PRAYER OF DEDICATION

THIS WORK is dedicated to the glory of God, that His name might be magnified upon the earth forever.

It is dedicated to the honest-in-heart, to the humble and meek, to the distressed and suffering, to the learned and the great, and to all who seek for truth and to those who desire to live in righteousness, and to know God.

Lord God Almighty, in the name of Thy Beloved Son, Jesus Christ, let this work go forth to bring light to the earth, and peace into the hearts of men. May the divine vision it contains be revealed to those who will fulfill the law of "asking" that they might KNOW the Truth. And may Thy great and mighty promises be fulfilled unto all those who catch the vision and begin to fulfill it in their lives, that Thy name might be made known and Thy power be manifest in the lives of men.

So be it—*Amen.*

"God standeth in the congregation of the mighty; he judgeth among the gods."

PSALMS 82:1

Jesus answered them, "Is it not written in your law, I said, Ye are gods? If he called them Gods, unto whom the word of God came, and the scriptures cannot be broken; say ye of Him, whom the Father hath sanctified, and sent into the world, Thou blasphemest; because I said, I am the son of God."

—JOHN 10:34-36
PSALMS 82:1-6

"For as many as are led by the Spirit of God, they are the sons of God—the spirit itself beareth witness with our spirit, that we are the children of God: and if children, then heirs; heirs of God, joint-heirs with Christ . . ."

—ROMANS 8:14, 16, 17

"When I consider thy heavens, the work of thy fingers, the moon and the stars, which thou hast ordained; what is man, that thou art mindful of him? And the son of man, that thou visitest him? For thou hast made him a little lower than the angels, and has crowned him with glory and honor. Thou madest him to have dominion over the works of thy hands; thou hast put all things under his feet."

—PSALMS 8:3-6

"And when ye shall receive these things, I would exhort you that ye would ask God, the Eternal Father, in the name of Christ, if these things are not true; and if ye shall ask with a sincere heart, with real intent, having faith in Christ, he will manifest the truth of it unto you, by the power of the Holy Ghost.

"And by the power of the Holy Ghost ye may know the truth of all things."

—MORONI 10:4-5

CONTENTS

    I. HOW REAL ARE OUR REALITIES? 1

   II. HAVE YOU A SOUL? 9

  III. MAN, KNOW THY PLACE 15

  IV. IS FAITH A WORD OR A POWER? 24

   V. THE POWER OF VISION 34

  VI. THE PATHWAY OF GLORY 42

 VII. THE ATOMIC POWER OF THE SOUL 56

VIII. HOW THOUGHTS ARE PLANTED, AND HOW THEY PRODUCE 69

  IX. "SEEK AND YE SHALL FIND" 79

   X. THE STOREHOUSE OF ETERNAL KNOWLEDGE . . 93

  XI. "ABIDE IN ME AND I WILL ABIDE IN YOU" . . 101

 XII. THE POWER AND MAJESTY OF ALMIGHTY GOD . 110

XIII. THE POWER OF TRANSMUTATION 136

XIV. THE SUBSTANCE OF ETERNAL ELEMENTS . . . 144

 XV. THE THREE GREAT TESTS 160

XVI. LOVE, THE GLORY OF THE UNIVERSE 171

XVII. "THERE SHALL BE NO MORE DEATH" 181

XVIII. THE TRUE PATTERN OF EACH INDIVIDUAL LIFE . 198

XIX. "IN THE NAME OF JESUS CHRIST" 209

 XX. OIL FOR THE LAMPS OF ISRAEL 222

 XXI. "YE ARE GODS" 239

XXII. THE LAMB'S BOOK OF LIFE 266

XXIII. THE KEYS OF ALL POWER 275

XXIV. THE NEW AND EVERLASTING COVENANT . . . 303

XXV. "LABOR NOT FOR THAT MEAT THAT PERISHES" . 317

XXVI. THE SEAL 330

     INDEX 337

CHAPTER I.

HOW REAL ARE OUR REALITIES?

Do you have unanswered longings deep within your soul struggling for release, and does your heart sometimes speak louder than your mind? If you desire, if you yearn, if you hope, if you think and feel and aspire, then there is something dwelling within your little clay house that you must meet.

This day I would like to knock at the door of your earthly tabernacle, the body you have built, and reaching in, invite you to come and get acquainted with yourself—that you might know yourself, and that from now on, henceforth and forever, you might be free.

In order to do this it will first be necessary to compare man's realities with the things he considers unreal.

Can one suffer more from a broken leg or a broken heart? A broken heart leaves scars that never heal. The suffering can be so intense that many have died from it. Yet one cannot see a broken heart, touch it, or even describe it. But is the broken leg more real because it is more tangible than the broken heart? Not to those who have suffered from heartbreak, though eyes have never gazed upon a quivering brokenheart, nor hands ever touched one.

These tangible things that man has doted on, and lived by, let us examine them. The most real things in our lives are food, clothing, transportation and shelter. Let us take them one by one and give to each the test of durability.

What did you have for dinner two weeks ago this evening? That meal was such an important thing, yet you probably can not remember a single thing you ate, no matter how hard you try, that is, not unless it was a special occasion, you had guests, it was a holiday, or for some reason you had a poor, make-shift meal. The most important substance of life, that

1

for which we labor incessantly, is the most quickly forgotten. The thousands of meals consumed by each individual are the most unimportant things in our memories after we have eaten and digested them, unless we are very hungry or gluttons. Of course we still look forward to more meals; but they, too, will join with those of the forgotten past—realities that have become only vague dreams of intangible memories.

Clothing lasts longer than food; it is as vital. We enjoy dressing beautifully quite as much as we enjoy eating. We go to endless expense and effort to clothe our bodies becomingly. But what has become of all the suits of apparel we have worn in the past? A husband will struggle and scheme to buy his wife the gorgeous gown on which she has set her heart—and later pins her pride. She is so happy over it she hopes the house will not burn down and destroy it if she leaves home without wearing it. It is the most important thing in her existence, that is, for awhile. Her fingers caress its loveliness in happy enjoyment; yet a year or so later she looks at the delapidated "rag", declaring in disgust that she would not be seen in "that old thing" for all the world. She would rather stay home forever than appear before her friends in it—and the glamorous gown has become a repulsive thing, hated and despised. Its glory has vanished. It ends up at last in the incinerator, or for cleaning rags, taking its place among the dead, forgotten elements of the things that have been.

Shall we take a car next? Surely it is practical. It is one of the most substantial things one could possibly think of in this day of practicability. Even its paint is of hardened, baked enamel. Its softest substances are steel-reinforced cushions and hard rubber tires. It is so real it is the very life and joy of the whole family, from father down to baby Danny. It is the most worth-while thing in their lives. And while the family ride on the seats, their heads soar along in the clouds. Yet within a year or so this beautiful, practical thing of iron and steel begins to show signs of wear. Within ten years it has become such a "rattle-trap", the family, in shame, refuse to ride in it. So dad still drives it to work, nursing it, caring for it like a tender parent, though nothing will save it forever, for eventually it is dragged to the graveyard of cars, and there are none to mourn its passing. It has perished, this practical thing of earthly elements refined to their highest, most durable point of excellence.

The next most vital thing in man's life is his shelter. He may labor and save all his days to buy the home that will satisfy the desires of his heart. Yet no matter how, or where he builds, within a few years it will be in the slum district— his dream becomes outmoded, out of style, dilapidated. The most gorgeous homes of the past are the slums of the present.

The once beautiful palace of the Mexican Governor, Pico, still stands on North Main Street in Los Angeles. If one has imagination he can still see the glory that once resided there, and feel the pride that built this monument of stone to stand through generations, glorifying beauty and magnificence. But its splendor has passed away and perished. Its former grandeur stands leering down in mockery at the frail things men's hands have made. It is like a once beautiful woman, slouching along with hose lagging over unlaced shoes, hair unkempt, clothing soiled and dirty, face unwashed and hands begrimed with filth. The palace of past glory now houses the cast-off remnants of men's rags in a second-hand clothing store.

So these practical things man clings to in his substantial way through life are fleeting, transitory things. And if one thinks deeply, the question comes, how real are our realities?

Where is the child you used to be? That little child that was you? It did exist, but where is it now? It has gone, and will never live again—and the "YOU" that exists today will soon pass on, and there will be an older person walking in your shoes, bearing your name.

All the tangible things of earth are best described by the old colored gentleman who quoted his favorite passage of scripture, "And it came to pass." The war, the famine, the tempest came—to pass—and life went on again.

Are all things then passing and transitory? Are all these substantial, practical things we deal in and depend on only dreams of a night vision? Is there nothing vital or lasting in life?

Can one suffer more from a broken heart or a broken leg? One is physical, the other mental. Is it possible that the things we cannot see or touch are more powerful and lasting than these tangible things our eyes behold?

One cannot see electricity. Neither can one touch it, nor hold it in his hands. Electricity is a form of energy, yet who can describe it? Who can fathom it? What is the source of its eternal supply of vital, throbbing power? Where is its abiding place? Who constructed its habitation? How was it created? And why? No man would be foolish enough to deny its existence because he has not beheld it with his physical eyes, for he has only to see it in action to know that it does exist. By its strength our houses are lighted, cleaned and heated. In a thousand ways its mighty power is brought to serve us and do our bidding. It is a greater servant, more dependable, more obedient than the genie of Aladdin's lamp. Yet our eyes have never beheld it. Even the lightning in the heavens is only electricity in action—its forces at play—but no man can gather it in his hands and say, "I have it! Behold, it is mine!"

Neither can wind be seen, nor held in the hands of man, yet even small children know that the wind is a reality. No one knows where it was born or where it dies. Eyes have not seen its resting place. No one can hold it in his bosom, nor store it for use. The fluttering leaves tell of its presence, the trees bend and sigh with its melody; and there are times when it seems to lift the very earth in its strong arms, bearing tons upon tons of dirt aloft into the sky. The thousands upon thousands of tons of soil that are hurled aloft in every wind storm of the "dust bowl" would stagger the imagination of man if it could be computed. Whence came this limitless source of energy? Check your electric bill when running continuously an electric fan that stirs the slightest breeze in your room—measure the energy used in creating the slightest draft in kilowatts. Even the mighty deep, wrestling with the wind, is lashed into a raging fury of madness in order to hold its own. Then measure, if you can, the trade winds of a world and the eternal energy behind them. Oh, yes, wind is a definite reality though physical eyes have never beheld it. It was so real to the ancients that in the days of the great historian, Herodotus, it was believed that the wind blew the sun back and forth across the equator to cause the seasons.

Let your mind encompass the majesty of a storm, the power of the clouds. One thunder cloud drifting in floating splendor above the earth can release 300,000 tons of water in a few moments of deluge. Whence came the energy to lift these tons of moisture? Who has ever beheld the source of this unspeakable energy, or measured it?

And now, I would ask, what is thought? Has anyone ever beheld the thoughts of man, those illusive, intangible, transitory, invisible nothings? No. One cannot behold the thoughts of man any more than he can grasp the sunlight in his hand, but he can view thoughts in action. Every bridge, every car, every building has been constructed by the thoughts of man.

Hate, unseen, indescribable, destructive hate is a reality, a power, a force that can destroy individuals and nations. It can destroy worlds, yet hate itself is invisible. It is a subtle, intangible influence whose very breath brings wars, destructions, death. Have you ever had someone standing before you, hating you with an intense anger that sent vibrations against you that were so strong and overwhelming they almost unbalanced you, upsetting you, upsetting your whole nervous system and in turn you wanted to "haul-off" and strike back with all the strength and energy you possessed? Perhaps you did strike back by fist or word—perhaps you controlled the attack—no matter, you know of what I speak.

Love, on the other hand, brings life and glory and health and happiness. It is the most powerful force in existence. It is the binding and welding substance of souls, a cement stronger than any mortar manufactured by the ingenuity of man. It is eternal, for death cannot destroy it. Long after death has claimed a loved one and his body has rotted in the grave, love lives on, undimmed. It binds families together, churches, communities, states or nations. Without it there is no unity or strength. Yet this powerful force of love has never been looked upon by man, or held in his mortal hands. To deny love because it is not visible to physical eyes would be as wise as trying to deny one's own existence. One sees it in action when beholding the great drudgery and hardships a man will endure to provide for his wife and children. One sees it in action when witnessing that glorious thing of motherhood, that soul-searing sacrifice of birth—followed by its years of devoted service. One views it in courtship. One beholds it at death. But love itself, that glorious, ethereal substance that is impossible to describe or measure, is veiled from man's grubby eyes.

As love is an element of the soul, so, too, is music. Yet who can deny music? Where does it come from, and where does it go as it dies away? What became of those heavenly tones that held one so enthralled, causing the very universe to stand quivering in shivers of ecstasy? Could one ever deny music after feeling it vibrating through his soul? Yet can he take it in his hands? Can his mortal eyes gaze upon it? No one has ever seen the notes of melody ringing through the air, yet to deny them would be foolishness indeed, especially when we can gather them up with a tiny instrument from the four quarters of the earth in a few seconds of time. Even a deaf person can enjoy the strains of heavenly music, though his ears are sealed. Through the sensitive touch of his fingers, in every cell of his body it can vibrate. Helen Keller shuddered at the tones of "jazz" but enjoyed the masters' offerings with the keenest delight.

Could it be possible that this physical world of ours is the unreal? A thing that is a reality today, tomorrow has passed away. Is it possible that there is a spiritual existence within us that is the eternal part of man, more real than this body that changes so many times between birth and death? Could it be that this world of our mortal concept is the realm of "outer darkness" and that all mankind is dwelling in it? Could our conscious, mortal minds, ruled by our five muddled senses, have deceived us? Have we condemned ourselves to "outer darkness" by our physical concepts and hypnotized way of thought? Are we inhabiting a world of shadowy dreams, fleet and passing, seemingly very real, but impermanent and transitory? Are we ourselves only the phantoms of our own true greatness, the shadowy images of our divine reality that has been imprisoned within our mortal selves?

Is it wise to deny the spirit because we cannot see it? Could it be that the soul is represented in every act and in every thought? That great chemist that resides within each man, which has the power to take the conglomeration of food he eats, and create blood, bones, muscles, marrow, vision, hair, fingernails, and even keep life going could be the soul in action, could it not? Could the power to keep one's temperature at ninety-eight degrees in the freezing cold of Alaska, or the burning heat of the Sahara be the power of one's soul in action?

Could it be possible that thoughts are the conversation of souls?

Are these foolish questions? One cannot behold the spirit of man, but should it be denied because it cannot be seen? If one is going to deny the things his eyes cannot behold, he will have to deny the wind, electricity, hate, love and melody. He will have to deny joy, happiness and anguish. He will have to deny thought, ideals, hopes and aspirations. In truth, if he denies these things, then he will have to deny his own existence.

Does it prove that God does not exist because you have not seen Him? Is it possible that we have seen Him in action? Does He ride upon the storm? Is it possible that "The heavens do declare the glory of God; and the firmament sheweth His handiwork?" Every blade of grass, every flower, every leaf, every song coming from the throat of a bird, every ray of sunlight, every cloud and breeze could be manifesting the power and intelligence of God. Is not the very existence of man a demonstration of God in action? Could it be that the billions of living, active atoms that compose all matter, are receiving their co-operative intelligence and energy from God? Isn't energy itself the very proof of a governing intelligence and power so superior to mortals that it is incomprehensible to us unless we seek in deep humility to understand. Only by opening our small finite minds wide to the power of the infinite can we hope to comprehend any of the least of nature's wonders surrounding us. let alone those unspeakable mysteries of eternal energy and light, birth and death, life and eternity, power and glory.

What man traveling over the deserts or through the mountains, or over the forgotten highways or byways of life, on seeing a dwelling would not realize that at some time man had been there? Would not the building itself shout the fact with such power of undeniable evidence a fool would understand? Surely then, if some crumbling structure signified that man had been that way, and had lingered to build from the materials of the earth, surely the sun, the moon, the stars, the worlds, the grass, the seasons, the very clouds and rain must testify to the existence of a builder or a designer. No house ever put itself together. No world just happened. The very eternal circulatory system of the earth's blood-stream, the throbbing pulse of the world's arteries, its life-giving streams of everlasting supply coursing in their destined veins testify to creative intelligence in action. The very energy that pumps the earth's supply of living springs of water that turn into rushing streams, flowing rivers, ocean currents is a breath-taking mystery to the man who has learned to think.

Have we clung so desperately to our practical, substantial surroundings that we have failed to see the value of the unseen? Have we taken everything so much for granted that we have become spiritually blind and have eyes that see not, and ears that hear not—yes, and minds that think not? Perhaps, after all, our realities are the things that are unreal, who knows? Is there more power in a grain of sand, or a drop of water released to the invisible or atomic power than in the tangible particle? Could it be possible that spiritual energy released within one could remove mountains, raise the dead, heal the sick? If the spiritual power in a grain of sand is so potent, perhaps the spiritual energy contained within the breast of man, if released would be just as great in comparison.

> "Though man a thinking being is defined,
> Few use the great prerogative of mind.
> How few think justly of the thinking few!
> How many never think, who think they do."
>
> —JANE TAYLOR

Chapter II.

HAVE YOU A SOUL?

D ID YOUR PARENTS create you? Did your existence commence with your birth into this world? Or do you have an eternal soul, something beyond this physical body of flesh and bones your father and mother gave you?

If your parents created you, would they not know what makes you "tick?" And if anything went wrong with this strange human mechanism, surely they would be able to fix it. If I made a car I would be able to repair anything that broke down, it being my brain-child, I having created it, could most assuredly tear it down and then again rebuild it. At least I could replace the damaged, broken, marred part. Then why can't these parents mend and heal a little broken body? For the simple reason they do not know the first thing about it. They do not know until the child is born whether it is a boy or a girl. They look carefully over the outside and pronounce it normal, but what do they know about the inside? Every organ may be misplaced, every fibre working backward, the heart on the right side, the stomach upside down, a thousand irregularities, but do the parents understand that? Could they do anything about it if they did? Is the gift of creation given to human parents in its fullness? Or could it be that parents are only co-creators with the great God of souls? If parents, indeed, can create a child and unaided give it life, they are no longer mortals but gods.

Within each soul which comes to earth is a knowledge of chemistry greater than any living chemist ever possessed, or ever will possess on this earth.

Assume that you were handed a great tray of food; soup, salad, potatoes, gravy, vegetables, meats, desserts—and told to build yourself a body. Conceive, if you can, your utter bewilderment if you were commanded to portion so much to

9

marrow, so much to bones, blood, fingernails, hair, the color of your eyes, the liver, skin, nerves and energy. Yet within you is a knowledge that does just that very thing. Did your parents give you that knowledge? How is it that the tiny, new-born infant drinks of its milk, and begins to grow finger and toe nails, eye lashes, hair, larger bones, more flesh? And that very growth must come from within. No one teaches it, not here. Surely that knowledge is not an hereditary gift because no parents since the world began ever had that knowledge in their physical minds to hand down. You say it is instinct. Then tell me what is instinct? Where does it come from? How is it that the tiniest insect is endowed with this powerful force of knowing?

And for that matter, what are hunches? You have had them. Every man has had them. But what are they?

Anyone who has ever watched *birth* or *death*, and who has used his brain to think, cannot deny the existence of the soul. At birth the tiny infant is a little lump of inert flesh, then suddenly it spreads its tiny arms, opens its mouth, every muscle and fibre becomes imbued with life. A victorious cry issues forth, and as it breathes the breath of life, it becomes a living soul. Such is the miracle of life that is ours.

At death the vital, living, thinking, feeling, moving power departs. What was it? Where did it go? You may say, it died with the body. But how could that be? The body is still there in all its tangible, mortal reality—not one single cell of it has disappeared—all that is gone is the living, breathing, feeling, warming power of intelligence, energy and action—the great intangible, dynamic power to think—the soul of being. It is true that only the intangible, invisible part of being has departed. Yet that intangible part is the true reality of man. What is anyone without it but a lump of slowly, disintegrating, lifeless flesh? Yet that very power and reality of being has been denied, ignored and most shamefully neglected.

This magnificent thing which is man. Whence came he? Whither does he go? "Oh God, what is man, that thou art mindful of him? Or the son of man, that thou visitest him? For thou hast made him a little lower than the angels, and hast crowned him with glory and honor." (Psalms 8:4-5).

This glorious structure of man, how does it work? Was there ever anything more perfect than the human body that has the power to rebuild and heal itself? You scientists and inventors, could you create a man and give him breath, the power to think and feel and act? Could you create anything with power and knowledge to rebuild itself, to heal its wounds? Could you even create a heating and cooling system as perfect as that within a humble, mortal man? Your great porcelain refrigerators are automatic, unbreakable, efficient, but are they perfect? Is it not true that your little motors speed along on the electric current, burning energy sent out from the main source of supply, humming along for fifteen or twenty minutes at a time, then to keep the regulated temperature desired, it is necessary that they shut off completely for ten or fifteen minutes? However, man's temperature control never shuts off. In the blizzards of Alaska or the scorching desert heat, man's temperature sings along at ninety-eight degrees if he is normal. Oh, man, whence came this perfect plan to balance cold or heat, to control it in one small body of flesh and blood?

Of all the animal creation, man alone has the knowledge and power to clothe himself. All animal life is clothed with skin or scales, feathers, or hair; and each unfortunate beast wears his clothing without change except for falling or growing hairs, cells, or scales of his hide. Mankind can change his garb at will, from crisp clean cottons to silks, linens or velvets. He can bathe, dress, reason, build, tear down, explore or WILL.

Man is the only one of all animal creations that continually walks upright. He is perfectly balanced. He can dance, teeter on his toes, lean to or fro, whirl, stoop, or leap into the air. What stump the height of a man could keep its balance long if left to stand upon a foundation no larger than the feet of man? The first breeze would topple it over and leave it lying prone upon the earth. A man can brace himself against the wind. He can climb a mountain steep. Even more, with two-inch soles upon his feet he can reach down into the earth and cling to the ground, making himself a third heavier than his ordinary weight to lift. What is this power within man, this

WILL, that can reach down through solid wood or leather, or even metal and cling to the earth? Who can explain it? Yet with all this power of grace and balance, rhythm and motion, the moment a man dies, his limbs buckle beneath him and no power on earth can make him stand alone, unaided. He turns back to a lifeless lump of flesh. What becomes of the warmth, the life, the twinkle in the eyes, the breath, the energy, the desires, the power to love, to think, to feel? Oh, man, who is taken for granted by the foolish—but man, the majestic marvel of the wise.

Science tells us that anything a man can imagine, he can produce. Telephones, houses, sky-scrapers, bridges, electrical wonders, cars, airplanes, radios, television, atomic power, shoes, clothing, or furniture are all the mental dream-children man has brought into being. Anything a man can imagine is possible. This is an undisputed fact although everything that man has dreamed of has not yet been brought forth. In time it will be.

There is only one thing in all existence that man cannot possibly imagine. There is only one thing that you, individually, cannot imagine. And that one thing is: THAT YOU ARE DEAD! You may think you can, but can you? Is it possible to imagine yourself completely dead, or non-existent? Let us try it and see. Picture yourself laid out on a couch, a bed, or in a soft, plush-covered casket, your hands folded, your eyes closed, your breath gone, your whole body cold and still. You can even imagine your loved ones and friends grieving for you, you can see the flowers, the funeral procession, the grave. It is a simple thing to imagine this body dead because that is possible. But where are YOU? Are you not there watching, feeling, thinking, analyzing? Oh, yes, you are there, beholding it. Suppose we try it from another angle. Put yourself into that dead, lifeless corpse lying on the bed, your hands folded, your eyes closed, does that help? No. For YOU are still thinking, still alive. The only thing you cannot possibly imagine is yourself absolutely dead, this living, thinking, feeling part of you, because it is one thing that is utterly impossible. You can imagine the body dead. Surely. But never the eternal YOU that lives in the body you have built.

Let us now analyze this spiritual YOU. In order to do this it will be necessary to begin with the physical. Commence with your feet. Analyze them. Think of them. Feel them. Wiggle your toes. Become very foot-conscious. They are part of you, but they are not YOU. They could be cut off and YOU would still be there. Next, think of your legs, they, too, are part of you, but they are not YOU. Go on up to the intestines, the kidneys, the stomach, liver, heart, lungs—it is possible to examine each organ as you would examine the furniture in a room, they are there and earthly life needs them as furniture is needed in a home, but they are not YOU. Go on up into the throat, the ears, the eyes, their sensitive connections with the brain, they are part of you, or the furniture, but not YOU. Then if you know anything about human anatomy you can stand apart and analyze your own brain, that physical, tangible bit of gray matter, you can actually seem to caress it with your spiritual fingers, and as you do so, you discover that even the brain is not YOU.

Is it not then an easy matter to become acquainted with your own soul? The wisest teachers of the East have said, "Whatever you are looking for you must first find through yourself." We find that the flesh is not the real man, that the material brain is not the life-giving intelligence within him. We do not have to take the spirit out and handle it to know that it is there any more than we have to put our clumsy fingers within our skulls to be sure that there is a brain within.

Most people, however, in building their little clay houses from the elements of the earth have built them too solid and too compact. They have left no windows for the soul to look out and they dwell as prisoners locked in the dark confines of their physical selves. The word "personality" is from the Greek word, "persona" meaning a mask. The mask for most people has become the reality. It becomes the person and the individual behind the mask becomes buried. Open wide the windows, or if you have built none, then rebuild. Hew out openings and let light shine in—and vision will come and the eternal joys of everlasting value will begin to find a place in life for YOU. The physical body senses only the earthly, tangible, decaying substances of which it is composed—the spiritual senses the everlasting glory of light and hope, ideals and laughter, love and thought. It deals with that which is beyond decay. It deals with the eternal, indestructible elements of eternal energy, power and light. It deals with the substance of reality, for it is existence itself. It is the eternal.

CHAPTER III.

MAN, KNOW THY PLACE

IF YOUR earthly parents did not create you, then some greater power must have had a hand. Surely you did not create yourself. If you had, you would know how to keep yourself in perfect health, you would have the power to live without age leaving its marks and stooping your shoulders, dulling your sight, and making your hair white. You, having created all the intricate parts in the beginning, would know just what to do about it. But you did not create yourself because you know nothing more about this body of yours than your parents do. That is, not with the physical mind. If you did not create yourself, and your parents could not create you, then it must be assumed that some greater intelligence had a hand in this marvelous personage of YOU.

"Then shall the dust return to the earth as it was (the little clay body of earthly elements); and the spirit shall return to God who gave it." (Ecclesiastes, 12:7).

Then John, the Beloved, adds still another bit of information: "No man hath ascended up to heaven, but he that came down from heaven, even the son of man which is in heaven." In other words, even the Son of Man in order to get back into heaven had to come down from heaven in the first place— and NO MAN shall ever return who did not abide in heaven before he came to earth.

Job, in his grief and despair over the hardships and trials he was called upon to endure, at last lifted up his voice to God and cursed the day he was born. He gave it a "going-over" as only Job was capable of. "And Job spoke, and said, let the day perish wherein I was born, and the night in which it was said, there is a man child conceived. Let that day be darkness; let not God regard it from above, neither let the light shine

upon it. Let darkness and the shadow of death stain it; let a
cloud dwell upon it; let the blackness of the day terrify it. As
for the night, let darkness seize upon it; let it not be joined
unto the days of the year, let it not come into the number of
the months. Lo, let that night be solitary, let no joyful voice
come therein. Let them curse it that curse the day, who are
ready to raise up their mourning. Let the stars of the twilight
thereof be dark; let it look for light, but have none; neither
let it see the dawning of the day; because it shut not up the
doors of my mother's womb, nor hid sorrow from mine eyes."
This is only part of it. There is a whole chapter given over to
Job's grief for having been born into this world. Most of us at
some time or other in our lives have wondered why we were
born, and even perhaps resented being here.

Here is God's answer to Job, and also to us: "Gird up now
thy loins like a man; for I will demand of thee, and answer
thou me. Where wast thou when I laid the foundations of the
earth? Declare, if thou hast understanding—when the morning
stars sang together and ALL THE SONS OF GOD shouted for
joy." (Job 38:3-7). This is what is really being said to Job:
Stop whining and be a man. Have you forgotten how badly
you wanted to come to earth? Are you not one of my sons?
Were you not among them when I laid the foundations of the
earth? Did you not shout for joy with the others that you were
to have the privilege of being born into this world and gain a
body of flesh and bones—to learn good from evil—to learn to
handle tangible material—to choose between right and wrong
—to prove your worth? God in reality was giving Job a stern
rebuke for cursing the day of his birth. He was also reminding
him of his great eagerness to come here.

God always desires His children to "Gird up their loins
like men." His children must be self-reliant, not whining
weaklings. He led the children of Israel for forty years in one
of the most desolate spots upon this earth. Why? Because they
whined, and had to be taught self-reliance and faith in God.

In this day He again led, or perhaps drove, his noble and
great ones from the nations of the earth to this new land, to
build, to conquer, to achieve—but mostly to become "MEN"—

men of vision and courage and stamina—men who could stand united for democracy and truth and goodness and honor. On the State capitol building of California are these words: "Bring us men to match our mountains." The cry of America from the beginning of its development has gone up that invitation for the great and noble to come and partake of the greatness of a heritage of freedom, and to give of their strength to the land in which they live, be it village, hamlet, town or city.

God desires a people who can pioneer in physical, scientific and spiritual fields. He desires mankind not only to understand the purpose of their existence, but to courageously cast out all fear—to march with their faces to the light, unwaveringly and uncomplainingly. He desires that they learn to humble themselves in great and mighty prayer that they might be a great people. No man is greater than his power to humble himself. He desires a people who can exercise faith to accomplish the things beyond human power.

"And he who receiveth all things with thankfulness shall be made glorious; and the things of this earth shall be added unto him, even a hundred-fold, yea, more."

It is not sufficient that this people live just because they are alive. It isn't enough that they get up in the morning and eat breakfast, doing their morning assignments, eat lunch, finish their daily routine of tasks, eat dinner, relax and go to bed at night—not day after day—throughout a whole life no matter how busy that life. Anyone who lives a life like that is wasting it. Beyond the daily activities necessary to live comfortably, there must be a reaching, a desiring, a progress of the mind and soul, otherwise we are no better than the animals. They have as much.

Every man should live because upon his shoulders rests a divine responsibility. It has been said by many: "This old world owes me a living." That is not true. This world owes nothing to any of us. We have plundered her, robbed her, torn her jewels from her brow, bared her nakedness, feasted upon the very life of her, gouged into her very heart and at the same time continually cursed her. No man has the right to live upon this earth who does not contribute something of value in return—buildings—bridges—highways—art—melody or great understanding and kindness for every man was created to be a messenger of light and crowned with a high destiny.

Again, in Jeremiah 1:5, God informed his son Jeremiah, when he felt too young and inexperienced to take upon himself the responsibility of being a prophet to Israel: "Before I formed thee in the belly I knew thee, and before thou camest forth out of the womb I sanctified thee, and I ordained thee a prophet unto the nations."

Paul said: "In the hope of eternal life, which God, that cannot lie, promised before the world began." Here Paul is testifying that he along with all the Saints was promised eternal life before the world began. (Titus 1:2).

Also, when Paul wrote to the Hebrews he gave this enlightening revelation: "Furthermore, we have fathers of our flesh which corrected us, and we gave them reverence; shall we not much rather be in subjection unto the father of spirits and live?"

From this we understand that our earthly parents were only responsible for the physical body, but the spiritual part of us, the light and life of man, was created by God. It is even possible that before we were ever permitted to possess a body on this earth we each had to study chemistry in the school of the All-Wise Creator. It is even possible that some failed to apply themselves fully, hence we see sickly or deformed bodies. Be that as it may, physicians are learning that physical illness is not so much of the body as of the soul. They still call it "mind", but in reality they mean the governing intelligence, which is spirit.

"Howbeit that he made the greater star; as also, if there be two spirits, and one shall be more intelligent than the other, yet these two spirits, notwithstanding one is more intelligent than the other, having no beginning; they existed before, they shall have no end, they shall exist after, for they are eternal.

"And the Lord said unto me: These two facts do exist, that there are two spirits, one being more intelligent than the other; there shall be another more intelligent than they; I am the Lord thy God, I am more intelligent than they all.

"The Lord thy God sent his angel to deliver thee from the hands of the priest of Elkenah.

"I dwell in the midst of them all; I now, therefore, have come down unto thee to deliver unto thee the works which my hands have made, wherein my wisdom excelleth them all, for I rule in the heavens above, and in the earth beneath, in all wisdom and prudence, over all the intelligences thine eyes have seen from the beginning; I came down in the beginning in the midst of all the intelligences thou hast seen.

"Now the Lord has shown unto me, Abraham, the intelligences that were organized before the world was; and among all these were many of the noble and great ones;

"And God saw these souls that they were good, and he stood in the midst of them, and he said: These I will make my rulers; for he stood among those that were spirits, and he saw that they were good; and he said unto me; Abraham, thou art one of them; THOU WAST CHOSEN BEFORE THOU WAST BORN." (The above is from the record of Abraham, contained in a manuscript found in one of the ancient tombs of Egypt, entitled, "The Pearl of Great Price.")

In scripture, Christ is called the Lamb slain from the foundation of the world. All who understand the mission of Jesus Christ, the Son of the Living God, know that He was slain in symbol in the law of sacrifice for centuries before His advent into the world. And with deep research it is discovered that the promise of His sacrifice for the mistakes and transgressions of man had been understood and accepted from the very earliest records of earth, which helps to confirm that it was a promise made to those who came to earth, even before the foundations of the world.

"And they that dwell on the earth shall wonder, whose names were not written in the Lamb's Book of Life FROM THE FOUNDATION OF THE EARTH." (Rev. 17:8). If our names were written in the Lamb's Book of Life from the very foundation of the earth, or before its construction, then we surely had to exist at that time.

And since we watched the construction of the earth and may have even assisted in designing its flowers and its trees and its mountains and streams, even shouting for joy at the laying of its foundations, then surely there was a great and eternal purpose behind it. And God said, "This is my work and my glory, to bring to pass the immortality and the eternal life of man." Since that is God's work and His glory, it is also ours, for it would be impossible for Him to accomplish it without our co-operation. We must understand life and its purpose. We must comprehend our place in the great scheme of things. We must fully comprehend the great drama of the ages that has preceded our advent into this world, to take our place upon the stage of existence, and to fulfill our parts with honor. We must understand also the things that are coming on the earth, and the things that will continue to come until Righteousness is sent to rule. How can we act well our part upon the stage of life unless we understand the great plan of life? And life was meant to be eternal progress, not drab, deadly, dull, unprogressive existence.

Progress of the individual depends on the strength of the desire within. And that desire depends on his vision and his understanding, the searching power of his own soul. Some deaden this throbbing, reaching, illusive, soul-calling by drinking and dissipation. Some by spending their lives in novels or movie theatres. Some in the companionship of noisy, boisterous companions. Some in continual games of bridge. There are many ways to keep the longing urge of desire from reaching through to the consciousness, but the way of progress and achievement is to lift one's head and listen to that hungry cry from within—the cry to permit one to reach his destiny and fulfill the purpose for which he was created. Just by having the courage to listen and the strength to follow, one will soon be lifted above the common, mediocre, and find a place of honor in a world of men. In other words, he will find his calling, and his place and be able to secure it to himself, for the benefit of the whole world. No man can completely fulfill his divine destiny without lifting all the world with him to a little higher bracket of progress.

This special calling of each individual is not found through outward display. It isn't found through make-believe or bluffing or pretending. It is only found through great desire, understanding and deep humility. Sometimes it is only found through heartbreak and tears. "This is the sacrifice henceforth that I will require of thee, even a contrite spirit and a broken heart." In the deepest agony or longing of the soul one is always closest to God, if it is not brought on by great transgression. It is when one's heart is broken and his soul burdened with tears that he will most readily find God. The soil of one's soul may need to be watered with tears to make it fertile. The "broken heart" according to the New Testament Apocrypha is given as "Cleft or open heart", meaning a heart that has opened to instruction, that is prepared to receive.

Some grow bitter in trials or sorrow, and thus they seal the way of opportunity, and are left cold and unglorified by the experience that was meant to be the greatest blessing of their lives. Every sorrow opens the doorway of progress, of soul-growth, and greater power. *The deeper one's sorrows, the greater can be one's achievements.*

More is to be pitied the man who has had no sorrow or ordeal so terrifying, no misfortune so devastating that he has not needed to turn to God or be destroyed, than for those who learn the meaning of tears. There is no such thing as an insurmountable wall in anyone's life, for every obstacle can become a stepping stone along the highway of advancement. We can let a straw block our way, or we can make a mountain a stairway up.

"And he who receiveth ALL *things* with thankfulness shall be made glorious; and the things of this earth shall be added unto him, even an hundred-fold, yea, more." "All things" does not mean just the nice things. It means the tears, the sorrows, the hardships, the disappointments, if they are necessary until we learn obedience.

When Christ was betrayed by Judas he never mourned nor condemned Judas, nor his own terrifying lot. He lifted his head and said, "Now is the Son of man glorified."

Sometimes our blessings come to us wrapped in mouldy, maggot-crawling burlap, and we, screaming in protest, refuse to accept the gift. But everything that comes to us can be glorified and turned into a blessing. The gift enfolded in the mouldy burlap will contain a blessing of pearls.

No sorrow should ever make one bitter and hard—nor will it if it is used for a lever of advancement. Every disappointment can help to purify the soul, build character, stamina and strength. It is never our trials that destroy us, but our lack of understanding in meeting them. When we lose our defiance, our rebellion, our self-pity we will hold the keys of such dynamic power in our hands we will be able to lift a world, and the difficulties will melt at our glance, the touch of our fingers will be the master touch, the thoughts of our minds a singing power of utter glory—for such there is no sorrow.

"If any of you lack wisdom, let him ask of God, that giveth to all men liberally, and upbraideth not; and it shall be given him." (James 1:5). Most of us accept this as applying to those of former times, but we must remember always that no passage of scripture is of any private interpretation. In the original Greek text, it reads thus: "If any of you are destitute of wisdom, let him ask of God, that giveth to all men liberally and censures not, and it shall be given him, but let him ask in faith, not hesitating."—etc. This translation makes it clear that all the humble, those who do not pretend to know everything, can come to God and receive wisdom liberally. Wisdom is offered to all just for the asking—wisdom to fill one's destiny—wisdom to live honorably—wisdom to help make a whole world better just because that person lived in it and lived up to his highest destiny by receiving divine wisdom. "And with all thy learning, get wisdom."

There is a glorious pattern for every man's life, an individual, perfect pattern. No two people are alike, not anymore than any two plants are identical. They may be the same species, yet they are vastly different. No two leaves are alike —no two snowstorms—no two sets of fingerprints. No two lives are alike, yet each life holds a divine pattern of unfoldment, a great and holy destiny, rich in achievement and honor. When life becomes bitter and impossible, when all conditions are sordid and ugly, and living itself is a dreary burden, it is because the contact with the divine has been lost.

Criminals have lost that contact and they try to become great by stealing wealth, or by other crimes. It does not work. Greatness can never be stolen, it has to be earned, or lived. One grows into greatness. Obtaining great wealth is not sufficient, for unless the true pattern is followed life is only an empty, artificial experience without true meaning.

If there is no joy in you—if that song of ecstasy does not sing in your soul, you have lost contact with your own pattern of existence, and light vanishes and gloom and darkness will continue to enfold you. As you live true to the pattern of yourself, that deep, inner self, you will unfold as perfect, as joyous, as naturally beautiful as the tree will reach its full measure of fulfillment. No one can keep you from reaching your highest destiny if you will follow your own true pattern of life. No one can live your life for you, for only you hold the key to your own pattern of sublime glorious, complete fulfillment.

Such is the destiny written in the soul of every man who comes to earth. None are without it, that completely, individual highway of full expression and glorious achievement.

Chapter IV.

IS FAITH A WORD OR A POWER?

THE WORD "faith" held a fascination for me even in childhood. My mind used to dwell often upon it and the power it contains. I earnestly believed that I would live to see the scientists harness it as they had electricity and man would be able to press a button and use its unspeakable power—power to move mountains, heal the sick, give sight to the blind, raise the dead, cause the lame to walk, for such is the power of faith, and he who professes to have it and has not the power is a liar, and cannot possibly please God. "For without faith it is impossible to please God." And these are the signs that are to follow those who believe: "In my name they shall cast out devils; they shall speak with new tongues. They shall take up serpents, and if they drink any deadly thing it shall not hurt them; they shall lay hands on the sick and they shall recover." Yea, the blind shall see, the lame walk, the deaf hear, the dumb speak. (Mark 16:15-18; D. & C. Sec. 58:64-65; Sec. 68:8-11 and Sec. 84:65-73).

"For the kingdom of God is not in word, BUT IN POWER." (I. Cor. 4:20). Christ promised that those who even believed on His *name* should do the works that He did, even greater works. Faith has become a dead and meaningless word, though all churches claim it as one of the foundation principles of their belief, and thousands of individuals claim to be living by it—but their kingdom is only *words* not *power*. Faith is a POWER not just a *word*. If one truly has "faith" then he must have *power*.

"Wherefore, my beloved brethren, have miracles ceased because Christ hath ascended into heaven and hath sat down on the right hand of God, to claim of the Father his rights of mercy which he hath upon the children of men?

"And because he hath done this, my beloved brethren, have

24

miracles ceased? Behold, I say unto you, Nay; neither have angels ceased to minister unto the children of men.

"For behold, they are subject unto him, to minister according to the word of his command, showing themselves unto them of strong faith and a firm mind in every form of godliness.

"Or have angels ceased to appear unto the children of men? Or has he withheld the power of the Holy Ghost from them? Or will he, so long as time shall last, or the earth shall stand, or there shall be one man upon the face thereof to be saved?

"Behold, I say unto you, Nay; for it is by FAITH *that miracles are wrought; and it is by* FAITH *that angels appear and minister unto you;* WHEREFORE, IF THESE THINGS HAVE CEASED WOE BE UNTO THE CHILDREN OF MEN, FOR IT IS BECAUSE OF UNBELIEF, AND ALL IS VAIN." (Moroni 7:27, 29-30, 36-37).

All churches, all priesthoods, all forms and all works are dead and in *vain* unless there is this great power of faith in action to bring to pass the mighty works of God, for "His Kingdom is not in word, but in power."

One religious leader I knew, who claimed to be a true follower of Jesus Christ, reported on a visit to the leper colony of the South Sea Islands, at a religious conference in Eastern New York. He boasted of his great courage in stepping down from the rostrum and actually walking up the aisle of their humble chapel, and the very angels bowed their heads in shame for such a man—and my soul apologized to God for his great blindness, for truly he was more blind than the lepers as he held his Bible in his hand and quoted words he could not fulfill.

That man, who falsely claimed to be a special witness of Jesus Christ, would begin to read a passage of scripture and before he had gone beyond the third word those humble, distressed souls, with their flesh slowly rotting from their bones, would pick up the words and chant them with him. He had to read the scripture. They knew it. As he boasted of his visit, and his courage in visiting this benighted people, his very words shouted the mockery of his claim and proved that it was *vain*. If he had been an ambassador of Jesus Christ, with the power of that calling, or if he had even believed in the NAME

of Jesus Christ, he would have healed the lepers, for these
were the works that Christ did, and as all were to do who
believed on His Name. For shame to such men who boast in
their calling and have nothing but empty words, and no power,
for they are "walking in darkness at noonday."

My interest in the principle of faith matured during the depression. The untold suffering I beheld made it apparent that
the whole world was wading through deep darkness. The belief in materialism proved inadequate as securities melted
away and a world wallowed in want, fear, misery and mud.

As I beheld the want and suffering of those around me I
knew that something had to be done, but what? At first I
wished that I had money to give, an unending supply of it,
not just enough to fill the meager necessities of life, but
enough to lift the unfortunate ones entirely out of their miserable condition of want. There were homes filled with darkness
and poverty. And with the very hopelessness usually came illness and disease. These conditions seemed to gang up like
companions of evil intent. It was in these homes that were
vacuums of despair that I wanted to pour out unlimited wealth.
The desire intensified with my work of trying to alleviate the
suffering.

I saw strong men wading through the anguish of seeing their
loved-ones suffer while their spirits broke and light vanished
from their lives. I saw women break and die. I saw small children with bleak, pinched little faces and unhappy hearts. And
thus I began to feel the distress of all men, and the burden
was too heavy as my soul wept in compassion.

Then one day as I was visiting in a home of ragged, tat-
tered, sickly children, the ache grew until I felt that my heart
would break with the very burden of it as the man turned to
me with a haunted, hopeless expression saying, "What would
you do if you only had a small crust of bread to eat?" I saw
his soul laid bare before my eyes and I knew he had seen
that condition, that he had shared that crust with those helpless
little children. I tried to hide my tears as I very carefully
weighed his question before answering, then out of the very
bottom of my heart I said, "I think I would go out and share

that crust with someone' who needed it as much or more than I—and then I would no longer worry about it."

He looked at me defiantly startled for a moment; then slowly he smiled as he read my sincerity in my eyes. "Yes. I believe you would—but would that help?"

"It would at least release the strain and responsibility from my mind," I answered.

It seemed to relieve the strain from his mind too, at least for the moment. But it was not enough. I had to have more. I had to give more. "Why can't I have money?" I thought. "Why can't I? I would only use it for others. These people need so much, and there are so many who are in need!" My mind reached out in overwhelming despair to the hopelessness of trying to help them all. And in that moment of despair I heard a voice beside me. It was strong and clear and so very real I turned swiftly to see who had spoken. There was no one standing beside my chair, at least no one I could see, but my ears had heard and I needed none to bear witness of the words, "Christ never once gave money."

"That is so!" I thought. "That is so! He did not give money, yet He did more to help the human race than any other being since the world began. Just what did He do to help so much?" were the thoughts that ran through my mind.

The answer came so clear I could not possibly doubt, "He gave life and courage and hope and FAITH."

In that unforgettable moment I knew that it was not charity nor alms people needed so much as to know that they could go to God in their troubles and extremities and receive help— that no matter what their need He could supply it. It was *faith* that mankind had lost, faith to look up, faith in themselves, faith in their fellow men, but most of all, faith in the power and goodness of Almighty God—"And He could do no work in America because of their unbelief." The original said "Nazareth", but that was before America was.

In that moment my destiny and calling became a reality, clear and perfect. I had to take the word faith and make it a tangible thing in the lives of men. Yet I realized fully how brutal and cruel it would be to go into a home of gloom and depression and say, "You would not need to be in this condition if you only had faith." It would not only be brutal, it would be an insulting slap in the face, no matter how true.

Faith was what was needed, but it had to be more than just the word. It had to become a definite, tangible reality in order to be used. Ask almost any human being to go out and "*exercise great and mighty faith*," as enjoined by the scriptures, and you will meet bewilderment beyond expression. Faith is more than a word, it is a principle of existence, of progress, of achievement, even of life itself. It was more than the ghost-word of an intangible principle and I realized that I had to stand it up and give it life and meaning. I had first, to understand it myself, to hold it in my hands, to get the feel of it, and then pass it on to a fearful world. I had to teach mankind to use a principle and power greater by far than electricity. I could no longer wait for the scientists to harness it, for my soul stirred in that moment and awoke to a call that was louder than thunder or the blare of drums. The veil of eternity drew back and I was kneeling again at the feet of the Almighty, receiving an anointing of divine light. In that moment I understood the hearts of men, I felt the throbbing pulse-beat of the entire world, and comprehended the great need.

As I realized fully that I had to take that small word "FAITH" and weave it into a reality stronger than steel and place it in man's hands in tangible form, I lifted my head in complete confidence as to the result. I knew that faith had to become a definite thing of power and light. It had to be brought forth as an instrument to heal the hurts, to light the darkness, end the dismay and fulfill the desperate needs of the hungry. And that *faith* had to be given so that it could become a living part of every man's life, not something doled out as charity.

For two years thereafter the search went on. The search was an intangible thing, so intangible I cannot quite explain it, except to say that everything in my mind and soul seemed to be concentrated on a desire reaching out for understanding. I expected a word, a phrase, a thought, a sentence, perhaps, to be planted, somehow, in my rather dense mind that would make its meaning clear, so clear I could share it with a world. I did not realize that I was asking for knowledge as deep as eternity and as complete and immense as the universe. I had no idea that I was not only to be given the meaning of that precious, most powerful word, but also the system of developing it within the human heart. I did not foresee that along with this knowledge I was also asking to know the great and marvelous things that were to be accomplished by it. And now that I understand, I bow my head in breathless awe before it. And in deepest humility ask that you continue to pray as you read and study that which is to follow. He who does not approach this work with a desire to obtain all the blessings possible for man to receive, and with an open mind, will lose the light he has. He who approaches it with reverence, and with a true prayer in his heart shall receive more—even the great power of *faith*, in all its overwhelming glory, and will be given the understanding to use it.

In looking back I only marvel at my confidence as to the outcome of my quest. From the moment I shouldered the responsibility I was positive that someday I would understand *faith* and be able to place it in the hands of man.

There seemed to be a desire that rose like a flame out of the very depths of my heart, that intensified as time went on. As more and more urgent needs arose for the knowledge, my heart seemed to take hold of the desire and it became a throbbing rhythm in my soul. Toward the end of my search it seemed that a flaming petition was continually arising from the very depths of my being which found expression in this phrase, "Dear Father, I have to find this, for this is my destiny." My logical, mortal mind would gasp at the assumption of my soul, but the request, or desire became much larger than I was, at least much larger than my conscious mind.

The suffering of my fellow men drew nearer and nearer into the very fibres of my heart until I yearned with all the fire of my soul to carry their burdens that they might be free. I would gladly have become blind that the blind might have received their sight. I would have given my legs that the crippled could walk. I would have given my body to be mangled in order to have spared any fellow being pain. I would have suffered any pain to have released one human being from a moment's anguish or fear.

One day a friend who had been suddenly stricken with infantile paralysis managed to drag herself to my home and clutching my feet, sobbed in despair. I knew then that my petition had to be granted though it cost me my life—or more—my very soul. And my prayer became a burning flame ascending to the Most High, "Dear Lord, just to be able to help I will gladly give my time, my talents, my strength and energy, my body and my soul—I'll even be blind—and you can take my arms, my legs, my mind, if by the taking it can help lift mankind from this deep mud of earth and suffering into the light." Such was my prayer, and I meant every word of it. I still do. That prayer stands as long as I exist or have intelligence to think and feel.

Just the joy of giving would have blotted out the pain of any sacrifice. I could have given all that I possessed so gladly —that is, all except my soul. Even now, I tremble when I think of that. Nothing had ever mattered much to me, I guess, except my soul. I have had no talents, no great gifts, but I have had a soul, my only gift. Many, many months after the intense search of this work was ended, and it was ready to be released, I spent long winter nights kneeling alone upon the snow of a temple's steps, pleading that my soul might be spared, if possible—yet I realized that if that was the price I had to pay, I would pay it. But night after night my tears would freeze into hard little lumps in the snow as my soul cried unto the Lord—and finally peace came—and I knew that if my soul was cast out forever into outer-darkness, or upon some forlorn, derelict world, it would be worth it if only I could help others find the great and glorious light my eyes beheld. And courage came, courage to send forth light against all the powers of earth, courage to stand alone against the world—courage to hold light high above the darkness and cry aloud for earthbound men to lift their eyes unto the light— the light of God, and be healed.

And my love increased and seemed to expand unto the very ends of the earth, and then to go on to fill a world and reach on out across the universe and play a melody upon the stars. My love became so great I could only rejoice no matter what came or went, even if I dwelt forever alone in the deep darkness of eternal night, for my love would light the darkness and burn as an eternal flame of glory that could never be dimned. My love was so great for man and God that it would ring across the heavens and eventually its very melody would have to reach His ears—and I would be recalled to worship and adore at His feet and praise forever in the realms of eternal light. So grew my knowledge of light, and of love that is the foundation of it, and it reached out to enfold a world, to heal its hurts, and to forgive its sins.

The price of truth is always the very greatest price required of those who bring it, for since the very beginning of creation man has been trying to force God into an orthodox straight-jacket. To bring one ray of truth into this world had always required a price so filled with sacrifice and tears that it could never be weighed and measured by any standards on earth, for only eternity could understand. Every church and creed is cramped into small orthodox quarters of non-expansion. It has always been so. In days of old, when any truth had been assimilated by the people and finally accepted as orthodox, or final, then God would send another prophet to bear witness of more truth. And each in turn was persecuted, reviled, re-jected, and most of them were cast out and slain—then, very slowly, the truths that had cost so much would be accepted and gradually become orthodox and sealed.

At last Christ came, and He too, paid the price of bringing light into the world—and the light He brought, in time became orthodoxed according to the bleak understandings of men's minds.

Then thousands more gave their lives to break the bands of darkness, and give man the right to think, to reach—to feel and live—and their vision also turned into orthodox doctrines which glorified the past but shut out the power of God from the present, and sealed the way of light to the living, and silenced the voice of the Almighty, and sealed the minds of men.

Groups and creeds always have a tendency to become orthodox or static in their thinking, and this condition seals them
into an unpliable condition that becomes fixed, and unprogressive. Life is a living, throbbing process of advancement—not
static existence. Not dead decay.

The power of God is as great today as it was when He said,
"Let there be light, and there was light!" It is as great now
as it was in the days of Moses when dust turned to lice, ashes
to boils and the Red Sea divided at the word of a man inspired
by God. His power is as great today as it was in the days of
Christ when the lepers were healed, the blind made to see, the
lame to walk, and in the dynamic words that have rung down
the ages, "Lazarus, come forth!" The power of God did not
die with the Apostles of Jesus Christ. It is still waiting to
be brought forth in the heart of any man who will only open
his soul to receive it, and his mind to understand.

The day has come when every individual must rise from the
slumber of passivity, from the orthodox complaisancy of the
accepted rules and regulations of life, and reaching out, pioneer into new fields of spiritual progress—yea, new, unexplored realms of the spirit. The greatest mystery of life must be
explored—Life itself. The why of it—the how of it—the glory
of it—the breath-taking, unspeakable majesty and power of it.
Man must learn the dignity of living—of being. He must begin
to comprehend his purpose, and the sublime power of it.

Beside this quest, the quest for a man's soul and the power
of it, and the discovery of his own true pattern of life, locked
deep within himself, the atomic research will stand dwarfed
and insignificant. The importance of bombers, army-tanks,
battleships, submarines, ultrasonics; yea, all things on earth
will shrink in comparison. In this search man will discover
himself the sublime creation, and the pattern of his own divine
fulfillment. He will stand undismayed before a universe of
unutterable light and glory. He will know his place and walk
therein in majesty for he will learn these words given centuries
and centuries ago: "Therefore it is given to abide in you; the
record of heaven; the Comforter; the peaceable things of im-

mortal glory; the truth of all things; that which quickeneth all things, which maketh alive all things; that which knoweth all things, and hath all power, according to wisdom, mercy, truth, justice and judgment." And he will know that these great glories locked in his own soul are his to bring forth and to use.

He will "know the truth—and the truth will make him free," as he takes hold of it and lives by it. We are truly stepping into a new age—an age of light, pure and brilliant, in which we will leave all retrogressive ideas and darkness behind. Oh, man, stand with me upon the very threshold of light and view its rising splendor—and know that you, yourself are the door into it.

Chapter V.

THE POWER OF VISION

Now I shall try to unfold the great principle of "FAITH" as it was revealed to me after two full years of constant prayer and seeking. It came in such dynamic power, when I was least expecting it, and the very light of it lifted me from the floor, and my feet seemed not to touch the earth for many days. I was reading a book when my eyes fell upon these words: "There is a law irrevocably decreed in heaven before the foundation of the world, upon which all blessings are predicated:

"And when we obtain any blessing from God, it is by obedience to that law upon which it is predicated."

That sentence was like a key in my hand that opened the door to the great storehouse of eternal knowledge, and the power of creation and the law of fulfillment. I had read it many times before in my life and was already quite familiar with it, but it had never, upon previous readings, filled my soul with a living fire of divine light and knowledge.

I had always thought there were many laws; one for health, another for wealth, another for happiness, etc.

It was when the principle of faith began to unfold and the way to use it that I was shown that there is "A" law, just ONE law upon which all blessings are predicated. So in order to give a complete view of *the* law it will be necessary to start at the very foundation, in fact, where the building digs into the soil. Any building has to connect with the earth in order to have towers reaching into the sky.

"And God said, Let the earth bring forth grass, the herb yielding seed, the fruit trees yielding fruit after his kind, whose seed is in itself, upon the earth. And it was so.

"And the earth brought forth grass, the herb yielding seed after his kind, and the trees yielding fruit, whose seed was in

34

itself, after his kind. And God saw that it was good. (Genesis 1:11-12).

"So God created man in his own image, in the image of God created he him, male and female created he them.

"And God blessed them, and God said unto them, BE FRUIT- FUL, AND MULTIPLY, and replenish the earth, and subdue it; and have dominion over the fish of the sea, and over the fowl of the air, and over every living thing that moveth upon the earth."

The law of production is the seed planting, the waiting for the growth and development, and the mature and ripened harvest. This is true of the production of plants, animals or mankind.

After planting a field with grain, if the sower decides to raise something else, and plants it; then again changes his mind and plants still another crop, being unable to hold to one desire, his crop will be a hopeless jumble of nothing. "He is like a wave of the sea driven by the wind and tossed, for let not that man think that he shall receive anything of the Lord." Or if he plants his crop without cultivating it, weeding it, watering it, caring for it continually, there will be only a dwarfed, meager production.

"There is "A" law, irrevocably decreed in heaven before the foundation of the world, upon which *all* blessings are predicated." The law is: That all things *must* produce after their own kind—that this production follows the planting; the growth and harvest is also part of the law. This principle of production is the law of nature. More! It is the eternal law of God, irrevocable, unchangeable.

So much for the earthly foundation. Now we shall climb to greater heights and view the higher meaning of *the law.*

The most subtle garden is the one within each man's soul. There is fertile soil capable of producing anything, any power, any accomplishment. Man has but to desire to prepare the soil. THOUGHTS ARE SEEDS. They are living, vital things that will bring forth each after its kind—yea, many fold more than the tiny seed planted, or the thought released. Desire is the heat that generates the seed and gives it power to reach up.

"I hold it true that thoughts are things,
   They're endowed with bodies and breath and wings,
   And that we send them forth to fill
   The world with good results or ill.
   That which we call our secret thought
   Speeds forth to earth's remotest spot,
   Leaving its blessings or its woes
   Like tracks behind it as it goes.
   We build our future thought by thought,
   For good or ill, yet know it not.
   Yet, so the universe was wrought.
   Thought is another name for fate;
   Choose then thy destiny and wait,
   For love brings love and hate brings hate."

                              —Ella Wheeler Wilcox

And again:

   "You never can tell what a thought will do
      In bringing you hate or love;
      For thoughts ARE things, and their airy wings
      Are swifter than carrier dove.
      They follow the law of the universe,
      Each thing creates its kind,
      And they speed o'er the track to bring you back
      Whatever went out from your mind."

Man's great dominion, his superiority over the animals is his "imagination," his power to visualize. Man visualized a home, then set to work to build it, consequently men have homes.

Again, man saw in his mind a "horseless carriage"—he planted in his mind the seed (or thought), and after a time a harvest of reality was produced. To us now, it would be a pitifully crude thing, that first car—but then, it was a marvel and a wonder, completely fulfilling the man's expectations. Could that man, in planting that first seed possibly have fore-seen how it would produce, yea, a millionfold? Other men experimented and planted more seeds, and more and finer cars have come.

And then a man sat on a green hillside and watched the birds soaring in the air; and to his mind came the promise of the scriptures: "And ye shall have dominion over the fowl of heaven." He realized that man could not fly. Surely to have true dominion it would be necessary to fly above the birds. He planted the seed, and cultivated it, worked upon it; and man is able to outstrip the birds in the sky.

Man is continually visualizing greater things, and greater things are being produced. The radio, television, atomic energy —anything that man can possibly conceive will eventually come forth. Greater mechanical things. Greater conveniences. Greater luxuries. Yes, and greater wars if he plants them.

But the greatest seed of all has not yet been planted in man's mind, or if it has, it is promptly choked out by doubts and fears (weeds). And the greatest seed is the thought that man himself can reach any height.

No man or woman has ever lived who has not dreamed. Some have held to their dreams, and those who have held to them are the successes of this world. Many more have grown despondent or discouraged and have permitted a crop of vile, rank weeds to destroy the glory of their dreams.

"As a man thinketh, so he is." Or to be more exact: "As a man thinketh, so he will become."

When a pebble is dropped into a pond, it sends out ripples that continue in ever-widening circles until they reach the extreme edge. As far as the eye can see they end there. However, this is not so. After these ripples or vibrations have reached the edge, they rebound and, settling along the bottom, return to the starting place. In other words, they come sweeping in from every side to the little stone that started them. The same idea is true regarding the thoughts of an individual.

"He who sows the wind will reap the whirlwind;" "As ye sow so shall ye reap;" "As ye judge ye shall be judged" is a law—THE LAW—the law of production. As we plant the seeds they produce after their own kind and return unto us. It is the law given before the foundation of the world. The law is the only one given that will produce anything, whether it be grain, inventions, plenty, or perfection in an individual, it is the same.

First is the planting of the seeds. Then man's part is to keep out the weeds of fears and doubts, knowing that the law cannot fail. He must cultivate it. But otherwise he must keep his human hands out, knowing that only God can make that seed grow. He must also remember that the law is irrevocable. It cannot err. And if the seed is planted it will produce.

Mind is the greatest power in the world—greater than any locomotive in existence—"For can the thing say of him that framed it, he hath not understanding, or the thing say of him that made it, he made me not?" A locomotive turned loose without being controlled will run forth to its own destruction and perhaps to the destruction of many things. The same is true of a car, or of any powerful thing left to chance after its power is released. It is especially true of the human mind, for of all earthly things, mind is the most powerful.

We are to be judged by our idle thoughts. How else could we be judged? A powerful, runaway machine going to its own destruction—a field being sowed with weeds that will grow and produce a crop that will destroy the planter.

"Dream, dream nobly, dream manfully and your dreams will be your prophets (profits)." "Prophets" because they will foretell your future; also "profits" because by them you will receive the benefits.

Christ went to the depth of all things endeavoring to teach that the mind was the power which governed man. "Ye have heard that it was said by them of old time, Thou shalt not kill; and whosoever shall kill shall be in danger of the judgment; but I say unto you, that whosoever is angry with his brother without a cause shall be in danger of the judgment." Anger— a thought or seed sown in the mind, if permitted to grow, will ripen into discord, hate, violence.

And again: "Ye have heard it said by them of old time, Thou shalt not commit adultery; but I say unto you, that whosoever looketh on a woman to lust after her hath committed adultery with her already in his heart." He has planted the seed of transgression in his heart or mind, and the law is, that everything will produce after its kind, and after the planting comes the harvest.

"And the Lord said, if ye have faith as a grain of mustard seed, ye might say unto this sycamine tree, be thou plucked up by the root, and be thou planted in the sea; and it should obey you." Why the reference to the mustard seed? The mustard seed represents "The least among all seeds. But when it is grown, it is the greatest among herbs, and becometh a tree, so that the birds of the air come and lodge in the branches thereof." And again the planting, cultivating and growth is given.

"For verily I say unto you. That whosoever shall say unto this mountain, be thou removed and be thou cast into the sea; and shall not doubt in his heart, but shall believe that those things which he saith shall come to pass; he shall have whatsoever he saith.

"Therefore I say unto you, what things soever ye desire, when ye pray, *Believe that ye receive them, and ye shall have them.*"

The law is true and eternal. No matter what one desires, if he plants the seeds, keeps out doubts and fears (weeds), it will come forth.

If the seeds are evil they will produce nevertheless—but like the fields of poppies planted for greed, they will eventually destroy the planter.

In the early history of India the people would meet at dawn and reaching up their arms plead:

"Let no one, not even those who worship thee, delay thee far from us! Even from afar come to our feast! Or if thou art here, listen to us!

"For those who are here make prayers to thee, sit together near thy libation, like flies round the honey. The worshippers anxious for wealth, have placed their desires upon Indra, as we put our foot upon a chariot.

"Desirous of riches, I call him who holds the thunderbolt with his arm, and who is a good giver, like as a son calls on his father."

This is only part of the prayer, but it is entirely for wealth —wealth to exceed the wealth of all other nations. And the seeds sowed, grew and have been harvested. India is the wealthiest nation on the earth. Fabulous jewels are stowed there; there are caves full of them; gold and treasures hoarded in cold, underground vaults; jewels glittering in every temple and on every image. Jewels, spices, silks—riches for which Columbus was searching when he found America. With India's seeds of wealth she sowed also seeds of greed and selfishness which grew and flourished—and India with all her wealth has been one of the poorest nations on the earth, for only the few had claim to the abundance while the millions are without. There is greater poverty, more hunger, famine, destitution and want stalking through that paradise of wealth than in any other land—the crop of greed.

Columbus in planting the desire to sail around the world to reach India was not so much concerned about the wealth of the Hindoo nation as he was with the scientific belief that the world was round and it could be navigated in a circle. Columbus had that belief so strongly planted in his heart that it became a burning obsession in his soul and had to be fulfilled. It took eighteen years of cultivating through heartbreak and at times his crop must have been watered with tears, but the harvest he reaped was far greater than he ever knew—greater than India and all the wealth she possessed. Columbus discovered new worlds where freedom was to be born for all the down-trodden of every land. His burning desire constructed a highway across the sea on which the courageous of every nation might cross and learn to think new thoughts, and find new life.

"Man becomes like the thing he gazes upon." This is true even of the animals. Animals, however, have to see with their physical eyes, but man has the power to see with his mental or spiritual eyes. Jacob fulfilled this scientific law among the cattle of Laban, his father-in-law, who again and again had tried to cheat him out of his just wages. Jacob fixed spotted sticks by the water troughs and when the cattle brought forth, their offspring were ringstreaked, speckled and spotted. If Laban changed Jacob's wages, which he so often did, Jacob took the sticks away and the brown cattle which seemed to be dying out, began to multiply again.

Job, highly recommended for his patience, has been set as an example to the world to teach endurance and meekness, but let us face the truth. Job admits the planting of the seeds of his calamities in these words: "For the thing which I greatly feared is come upon me, and that which I was afraid of is come unto me." (Job 3:25).

When we can prepare our minds, without fears and without worries, for greater things, greater things will be given. The power to govern our surroundings and to build perfectly is in our hands. It is the power of thought, which is the power of Godhood.

Chapter VI.

THE PATHWAY OF GLORY

MY DAUGHTER, as a little child, had a strange disease which would recur every few weeks. It was an illness that would leave her unconscious, a lifeless little throbbing bit of humanity, burning with fever. To keep her from going into convulsions it was necessary to keep ice-packs adjusted to her head and hot-water bottles at her feet. No physician or specialist was able to help her. The over-confidence of each would, before long, turn into .a hopeless admission of defeat and I would be informed that eventually the illness would prove fatal.

Then one day, a man who knew of my search for faith, and my earnest belief in its power and the right of any man to use it, said, "If you have so much faith and believe in it why do you not heal your child?"

It was a challenge such as I had never received. I lifted my head and looking into his mocking eyes, answered with a complete confidence, "Alright! I will! You hold a high position of authority in your church, I hold none—but God will hear and answer my prayers."

From then on there was a constant prayer in my heart that my child would recover—if she were meant to live. It seemed such a tragic thing to have a life to live that would be so marred with suffering that it would not be worth the living, that I could only pray that if she were meant to live she would be given perfect health and strength—if she were meant to die, she would be taken without any unnecessary suffering. For over two years this prayer was constantly in my heart. And I knew it would be answered.

Then one night after an unusually long siege I realized she was dying. I dropped on my knees beside her bed and felt that my heart would break. I had asked the Lord to take her if it was His will, but in that moment the great tragedy of losing her blotted out everything else. In facing that great tragic moment so many have faced since the world began, I failed for an instant, and in wild, heart-broken panic I clung to her. I felt that I could never go on living without this little one with her wee, dim freckles, her tiny, turned-up nose, her reddish, golden hair tossed at random over her pillow.

A long shudder shook her tiny frame. She stiffened—then grew limp. I clasped her in my arms, holding her close against my heart. Tears streamed from my eyes and splattered upon her tiny face. The agony of my soul was too deep to express as I felt that I could not possibly let her go.

Then vaguely I sensed that I was thinking of myself, not of the little child in my arms—and a wider vision came. It was then I truly prayed, and the words washed in fire and tears ascended, "Dear God, this child is Yours first—and then she is mine. If you want her—take her—I love her so! But all that I have is Thine." I meant it. Regardless of the cost. If I died of grief then I would have to die.

I looked down for the last time, as I thought, upon that tiny, upturned face—I wanted to be alone with my child, to gaze in undisturbed solitude before I called anyone to mar our last silent communion together. It was a desperate struggle to clear the tears from my eyes enough to see through them, but when I finally did, I was speechless with gratitude and awe. My child slept in peace, all fever gone. Such a thing had never happened before, and when she began to recover it was always so slow and gradual that the days almost ran into weeks, and by that time the illness would be on its way back again.

When I fully realized that she had been restored to perfect health, I felt as Abraham must have felt when Isaac was restored to his bosom. My tears of sorrow were turned to tears of gratitude as I placed her gently in her crib. The room seemed filled with a warmer glow than shone from my dim, muffled light. And looking up in wonder, I seemed to see no ceiling to the room—the open dome of heaven shone above.

And then, so near that I was startled, I saw the veil of heaven drawn back as the curtains of a stage—and He stood there—with all the glory, majesty and power of eternity stamped upon His brow—the Savior of the World.

He smiled a smile that must have warmed the universe—a smile which is impossible to describe. It was so filled with love I wondered why the hard stones did not melt before it—love that drifted into the darkest corners of the earth—lighting the World—bringing peace, and calm and rest.

As my soul worshipped, He spoke. Love and tenderness dripped from lips majestic and divine—and yet it was His eyes I watched—eyes that knew all things, that penetrated into the very marrow of one's soul and left it throbbing with a devotion that seemed to melt the very bones.

"I am so eager, and so anxious to pour out my choice gifts upon my children here, as they are prepared to receive them." He said it with such longing earnestness.

For a moment I caught a glimpse of those choice gifts, health, strength, vitality, wisdom, understanding, majesty, eternal life, power to rule not only this earth, but power to reach out into eternity. These things, yea, greater, He holds within His hands, and with infinite patience and love waits to grant them unto us. There need be no poverty, no pain, no tears.

I could not fully grasp the magnitude of what I saw—I, who through the years of heartache, had believed that mankind was meant to suffer and endure—that misery was the heritage of man within "this vale of tears."

"We are not meant to suffer?" The question rushed from my lips in wonderment and unbelieving awe.

He smiled gently and as He drew back, these words reached me as the curtain closed, "Even I learned obedience by the things that I suffered—after one has learned obedience there is no need for suffering."

I sat trying to comprehend the full meaning of blessings so great, and happiness and power so complete, but my mind was unable to fully understand—then before me stood a little child to whom was handed a string of priceless pearls—so priceless they seemed like glorified dew that would vanish at the touch. The child grasped these precious gems in a grimy, dirty little hand, and dangling them unheeding by his side, dragged them through the dust. I watched in horror and dismay—and then I groaned, for there he stood before a bead-counter of ten-cent, shoddy trash and, casting the pearls beneath his feet, cried for red glass beads.

Then only did I faintly grasp the magnitude of what I'd seen. Joy, peace, glory could be ours, wisdom and knowledge, majesty and might—these things like priceless pearls were ours for the asking and appreciation of such gifts—but we cast them aside in search of red glass beads; or in search of the meaningless empty things of the world. We chose the grime of earth in preference to the light of God with all its unspeakable glory.

My child was healed permanently and completely. About two weeks later she came in radiantly happy and said, "Remember that night those beautiful women came to take me to the heavenly Father . . ."

I turned to her in startled surprise as I realized how very earnest she was, and knew that she expected me to understand.

All I could say was, "What women?"

Impatiently she answered, "Those women who came that night I was so sick."

"But—what were they like?" I persisted.

"Oh, they were so beautiful!"

"But what were they dressed like?" I asked.

For a moment a puzzled look spread over her face, then she answered slowly, "I guess they had on white nightgowns." She had never seen a nightgown, so was not too sure.

"What happened then?" I probed, holding my breath as I looked into her earnest little face that was a trifle impatient with me because she felt I already knew all about it.

"They started to take me up into the light. It was so bright —and they were going to take me to the heavenly Father— then you started to pray—and they brought me back."

Always that is the first thing we talk about after we have been separated for a long while, my daughter and I. I never saw what she saw. She never beheld what I was shown, but to both of us those experiences are more real than anything else in our lives.

My daughter is married now, and has two children. They were born almost without pain. Last year she took a thorough physical examination. The doctors asked her about the T. B. she had had. Very much surprised she answered, "Why, I've never had T. B." Then she did remember that as a child she did cough lots, that at night she had to be rubbed with hot-camphorated oil in order to sleep. But the X-rays showed her lungs to be filled with scars, showing the disease had had a real hold, though there had been no more cough after that memorable night, and there is no living trace of the disease at the present time. It was a strange thing that none of the experts or specialists had ever suspected that she had T. B. too, along with whatever other strange illness it was that nearly took her life.

Today, and from that night years ago her health has been perfect. She is a living testimony to the power of God, and of His great love and goodness and willingness to answer the petitions of His children. And I know that nothing is impossible, and that God lives—that "He is a God of miracles," if we will only permit Him to be. It is mankind who restricts His power.

The power to reach for higher things than just ordinary living calls for, is within each man. His thoughts are the seeds he plants. His thoughts and desires will be the crop he reaps. There is truly nothing that is impossible to those who will develop vision and live by that vision, without wavering. Back of every achievement, every act, every accomplishment is desire—or thought that has reached the point of its fertility, or unfoldment—and thoughts are seeds.

The greatest gift God has given to man—the law of production, has been the one most trampled and abused—pearls trampled ignorantly, sometimes defiantly, underfoot, while cheapness has been desired. What law has been more defiled than the glorious law of planting human seeds—the gift of co-creation with God—that God-given heritage to produce after our own kind, or the humble, glorious gift of being parents to sons and daughters of Almighty God?

This perfect and heavenly law in the power of evil souls has brought the greatest crimes, misery and destruction to the human race, and the greatest suffering. For destruction always comes to nations when they have become morally impossible. Just as this great and holy responsibility has not been understood, so the planting of pure and perfect seeds within our own hearts and minds has been trampled and ignored. We have failed to see that we are the sons and daughters of God, with all the attributes of God, and that we have to cultivate and develop these glorious qualities by planting the seeds of glory and success within our fertile souls.

Visualize the thing you desire to become, hold it in your mind continually. Never let doubts and fears come like vile, noxious weeds to crowd out and kill your crop. Cultivate it. Believe it, and you shall receive it. This is THE LAW—the unchanging, eternal law of God. There are not many laws— just the one—the law that everything shall produce after its kind. The fulfilling of the law is the planting—the cultivating —the waiting—and the harvest. It is the same whether it be grain, stock, or thoughts sowed within one's soul. It is the *one eternal law.*

Knowing this, we realize that it is not only weak to permit doubts and fears to take possession of us—it is wicked. Understanding this, and knowing the law is eternal and cannot err, we plant with our crop, whatever it be, that glorious seed of faith, and we know that it, too, will produce—yea, an hundred-fold. New glories will appear and heaven draw near.

Man creates according to the power of his visualization. The higher the civilization the more developed is the power to visualize. The imagination is a God-given gift. It is the power of the mind to "image in" to the spiritual realm the seeds of desire. Modern man has visualized great things—he has brought them forth into reality. While the African of the jungle has not developed his power of visualization, consequently he is an unprogressive being. And, indeed, an African from his primitive hut would be more astonished and over-

whelmed at the wonders and magnificence of one of the great
cities of Europe or America than we will be at the glories of
worlds farther advanced than our own—and yet, the difference
may still be as extreme. Only our power to visualize can possibly prepare us even for heaven.

"Heaven," the word, is from the Greek "Oranus," which
means, "expansion." "The kingdom of heaven is within you,"
means that the power to reach up, to expand or to develop
and grow is within us.

When man begins to visualize the immensity and grandeur
of the things in store for him, *in this life*, and the law of production, nothing will be impossible. When he fully realizes
that he is, indeed, a son of God—a literal son—when he holds
to the vision without doubt, or fear, he will become like God.
The words of the Saviour will be fulfilled in all their majesty
and power: "Verily, verily, I say unto you. He that believeth
on me, the works that I do shall he do also; and greater works
than these shall he do; because I go unto my Father. And
whatsoever ye shall ask in my name, that will I do." (John
14:12-13). All things will be subdued unto him—he will come
into his kingdom, his heritage. Power and dominion will be
given to such a one. But it will be a dominion of love and not
of hate, or greed, or destruction.

Get the vision of the thing you desire to be, hold it in your
mind and in your heart—cultivate it—work for it—for that is
the law upon which all things are produced. If you desire any
blessing you will have to fulfill that law. "Unto him that hath
shall be given, and unto him that hath not shall be taken away
even that which he hath." Naturally! One planted and produced—the other held what little he had to him, afraid to
plant lest he lose it, and it perished in his grasp.

Picture yourself perfect in body, in mind, and in soul.
Pray the Father to help in the growth of your perfect crop.
Then wait—or believe—and holding to it, keeping out the
weeds, will give it the power to come forth. It is *the law*, and
it is irrevocable. Even God himself cannot revoke it for it was
made before the foundation of the earth, by a God who can-

not lie, and the promise was given that it would be the law upon which all things should be produced.

"Without vision the people perish." Could anything be more true? A nation will perish if its leaders have not foresight or vision. A church will become a thing of dead and lifeless dogmas if the leaders or head has not vision or continued revelation or direct contact with God. But it means even more. Any individual without vision will perish. Weeds will automatically grow from his useless, idle thoughts and the strength of the soil will gradually weaken and eventually fail to produce in feeble, old age—and man becomes senile, and finally dies.

We may fool our friends, we may almost fool ourselves about our secret, hidden, undesirable thoughts—but the crop will come forth as sure as God lives, for within us is planted the seeds of our thoughts, and within us is written the record —we, ourselves, are the book of life—our life—and in time that record will be read.

"Without vision the people perish"—vision of higher things.

Even sickness in time will prove to be only a crop of weeds planted in the mind—sickness, poverty, sorrow, yea, even death. When we have learned the law and work with it, growing daily more like God, it will be like the flower growing in the green bud that suddenly bursts the sepal and the perfect flower is revealed. Man will then live in harmony with his own soul—sorrow and sickness will be no more, and when he has lived to be the age of a tree, the great perfection will come upon him in all its resurrected glory—and "He will be changed in the twinkling of an eye, from mortality to immortality."

Marden, in "Every Man a King," says: "The coming man will be so much master of his thoughts that he will make himself one great magnet for attracting only those things which will add to his prosperity and enhance his happiness. He will be able to keep his body in perfect harmony by harboring only the health thought, and knowing how to exclude the disease thought, the sickly thought. The coming man will always be cheerful, because he will entertain only the thoughts which will produce happiness; he will not allow clouds of worry or anxiety, or the darkness of melancholy, the blackness of jealousy and envy to enter his mind. He will never mourn but will always rejoice."

"We have all sinned, and come short of the glory of God." None of us have seen the reality of the law and we have fallen short. Nevertheless, mankind has been told, oh, many times, to be perfect even as the Father in Heaven is perfect; and God never gave His children a commandment that was impossible to keep, if one but desires to keep it. "I will go and do the things which the Lord hath commanded, for I know that he giveth no commandment unto the children of men, save he shall prepare the way for them that they may accomplish the things which he commanded them." No commandment, however, looks easy. In fact, they are all impossible until we are willing to live by them, then, putting our hand to the plow, we will find that he will prepare a way for us to accomplish anything which He has commanded or requested of us. The desire or vision must first come to us, and as we follow it with all the power we possess our ability to complete the task will be perfected by the help of the Almighty.

We have all failed to catch the vision. We have even cultivated our little weeds and humored them. We have not only tolerated our weaknesses but at times have even tried to glorify them. The first criminal tendency is always, "self-justification." Every criminal in prison can justify himself in his own mind for his crimes. He is always in the right. It is the world that is in the wrong. It takes strong men to live this higher law—men who are willing to face the contemptible qualities within themselves and then begin to eliminate them.

We should endeavor to catch the glorious vision of perfection and nothing less would ever satisfy us—only perfection. Seek the vision. Hold it in mind. Have faith in it and it will come forth because that is *the law* irrevocable, for He said, "If you do what I say, then am I bound; but if ye do not what I say then ye have no promise."

No person would think of letting his hand reach out and slap the other pedestrians as he walked along the street, or permit his feet to strike out viciously, kicking those with whom he came in contact, then try to justify it by this weak "lame-brained" remark, "I just cannot control my hand" or, "I'm sorry, but my feet just won't behave." Such a man would be a complete imbecile. Yet we make no pretense of controlling our minds. We let them drift hither and yon with every fluttering fancy. They are just as much ours to control as our hands or our feet.

Have you ever found yourself sitting, lost in abstract meditation, and had someone break in with: "A penny for your thoughts?" And you rather foolishly answered, "Why . . . I wasn't thinking of anything." Which, of course, is a speech to cover up, for it is impossible to hold the mind blank for more than a moment or two at a time; and the truth of the matter is that if you gave them your line of thought, you would probably be locked up for a lunatic. Next time this happens to you, follow your thoughts back through the maze of bewildering links and you will know exactly what I mean. Your train of thought may have started by observing a bird light on the shrub by your window, and you will recall a bird you followed as a child, trying to throw salt on its tail. That will bring to your mind that you finally fell down in your disappointing attempt and soiled your clothes. Your mother scolded you right in front of a neighbor, who was an old "meanie" anyway who wouldn't let you play in his grove of trees. The trees remind you of a vacation in the mountains, years later—that vacation may lead your thought to the President's most recent vacation—and from there your mind may go wool-gathering in modern politics. So from the bird in the shrub by your window, your thoughts have wandered to either the good or bad of the political situation of the moment. But could you tell your friend, who had offered you a penny for your thoughts, the weird road your mind had been drifting along? After all the tiny threads that connected one thought with the next were so finely spun, it would be ridiculous to try to put them together again for anyone else—but do it for yourself. Do it every time you find yourself day dreaming. Before long you will admit that your thoughts were wasted and rambling, and surely not worth even a penny. When you can do that, then you will begin to realize that you are wasting the energies of the mind and soul.

Such mind relaxation may not be altogether a crime occasionally, but those who never hold their thoughts in control, who never *think* constructively, who never plant, consequently never harvest beyond the weeds that grow automatically from their useless, idle thought, are being cheated. Unless life pays us back in richness and value for every day spent we are permitting the golden coins of time, allotted to us, to be squandered—and at the end our lives will be spent, and there will be nothing to show for it.

Thinking is planting, cultivating, achieving. We will have to work diligently, and how long it will take for the perfect thing to mature will, perhaps, depend on the condition of the soil, and the care we give, but the controlling factor will be the intensity of the desire to achieve. This also must always be understood, no crop will ever come forth until the seed has been planted, cultivated, followed by the waiting in patience. But as we work with understanding, wait in faith, our powers will be increased an hundred-fold, the elements will obey our voice—the sick be made well—the blind see—the lame walk— the poisonous reptiles and the wild beasts will lose their enmity. All things have been given into man's hands—man, who can rise to Godhood or sink below the level of the beasts.

In the first chapter of James, we find that ancient apostle was trying to teach this marvelous law:

"James, a servant of God and of the Lord Jesus Christ, to the twelve tribes which are scattered abroad, greetings.

"My brethren, count it all joy when ye fall into diverse temptations; knowing this, that the trying of your faith worketh patience. But let patience have her perfect work, *that ye may be perfect and entire, wanting nothing.*" (Surely then, after we have planted the seeds of righteousness and perfection, if we wait in patience, or let patience have her perfect work, our harvest shall produce and we shall want for nothing.)

"If any of you lack wisdom, let him ask of God, that giveth

to all men liberally, and upbraideth not, and it shall be given him. But let him ask in faith, nothing wavering (no changing). For he that wavereth is like a wave of the sea driven by the wind and tossed. Let not that man think that he shall receive anything of the Lord." (Naturally, for he has broken the law rather than fulfilled it, and has planted so many things that none of them can come forth, and he will receive nothing).

And again, starting with the thirteenth verse:

"Let no man say when he is tempted, I am tempted of God; for God cannot be tempted with evil, neither tempteth he any man; *But every man is tempted, when he is drawn away of his own lusts* (or thoughts), *and enticed. Then when lust hath* CONCEIVED, *It bringeth forth sin, and sin, when it is finished* (or produced) *bringeth forth death.*"

The following quotations are from James Allen's little book, *As A Man Thinketh*:

"He who has conquered doubt and fear has conquered failure. His every thought is allied with power, and all difficulties are bravely met and wisely overcome. His purposes are seasonably *planted*, and they bloom and bring forth fruit which does not fall prematurely to the ground."

"To put away aimlessness and weakness, and to begin to think with purpose, is to enter the ranks of those strong ones who only recognize failure as one of the pathways to attainment; who make all conditions serve them and who think strongly, attempt fearlessly and accomplish masterfully."

"Man is buffeted by circumstances so long as he believes himself to be the creature of outside conditions, but when he realizes that he is a creative power, and that he may command *the hidden soil and seed of his being out of which circumstances grow*, he then becomes the rightful master of himself."

The great failure of mankind at the present time is its failure to *think*. The human race has ceased to think. Two or three minds are doing all the thinking for all mankind. The greatest bondage in the world is mental bondage. It is better to be a beaten slave, and serve with bloody stripes than to become a mental slave, without power to think beyond the loud shouting of one's associates, or leaders.

Oh, men of earth, lift your minds to think, for your minds are the connection between your physical beings and your souls—it is the connection between your life and God—it is the power that can glorify you. It is the power of creation—the power of Godhood.

Each individual holds his destiny within his own hands. He plants his seeds, and harvests the crop. His life is joy and happiness, progress and satisfaction, purpose and plenty, or it is a lack of the worthwhile things, according to the thoughts he holds. "Figs do not grow on thistles." "By their fruits shall ye know them." No wonder! Everything produces after its kind, and their fruits are the harvest they have planted. One man will be a fertile garden of glory, another an unclean stench of filth and barrenness. Each man has been his own builder, for destiny has no favorites, for any man who cometh to God shall be strengthened and acknowledged no matter how humble he is, or how meager his abilities, for God is no respecter of persons. One's parentage may be the lowliest of the earth, one's opportunities as bleak and few as were Abraham Lincoln's, but with the power of thinking comes the power to think oneself out of any condition in life. Some may be even deficient in vision and wisdom, but that too, will be bestowed on any child who will only ask and believe.

Sometimes people try to lie themselves out of a difficult situation, but lies will produce their own harvest and the refuge they have built of lies will destroy them.

Some children are so immersed with negatives and fear thoughts by their parents that their lives and minds hold nothing but the seeds of failure from infancy. For them the task is more difficult—but not impossible. If they will only open their hearts and minds to understand, then follow the vision as it unfolds, their lives will become a glory of divine achievement. The broad glorious path of light is wide open for every child of life to plant their feet upon if they will only "see".

No speck of man's thinking power should be blurred or befuddled by dissipation. One's brain should grow sharper and keener with use, therefore anything that would tend to rob one of his greatest gift, *the power to think clearly, should be shunned above all things.*

The noxious weeds which were to grow henceforth upon the earth, through Adam's transgression, were also the weeds of doubts and fears within man's mind. These are the most noxious of all weeds. They were to grow until the earth was redeemed—that redemption is near at hand—and as the noxious weeds in our minds are rooted out and overcome, so shall the earth yield in her abundance.

Tomorrow there will be a race of thinkers on the earth—men who know and understand the power of thought and use it constructively and gloriously. Those who refuse to make the effort to develop and control their minds will be left behind —or like those of the present day, will be destroyed and annihilated because they refuse to use the great powers God gave them.

The power to control one's mind is within each individual who has a mind. Those who let others' ideas and thoughts fill their minds may be progressing, but the greatest work of all is to harness one's own mind. Original thinking alone reaps the full harvest or reward. Those who use their minds to control for greedy purposes shall perish with their gains, for their very greed and selfishness shall grow as a jungle and they will become lost in it and perish without vision.

This world in the near future is to be trod by holy men and wise—you of the present day, who can grasp the glory of your possibilities, will be among the leaders of a new dispensation on the earth. You will know that the power of love is greater than the power of hate and that glory and achievement is meant for every human soul. You will become great in power and majesty, helping to redeem a broken-down world of fearful men who have groveled in blindness and despair. You great ones of the future, power and dominion and glory will be yours forever and ever. You will first learn to rule yourselves, then by the power of God, you will be able to go forth in wisdom and love to counsel cities and nations and men. You will walk as no others have walked on this humble, tear-stained earth, except *The One*, for you will become like Him, Sons of God.

CHAPTER VII.

THE ATOMIC POWER OF THE SOUL

CHILDREN on this earth are required in the progress and growth of development to mature physically to the stature of their parents. This is one of the chief purposes of life. It is most necessary in this realm of mortal advancement. Yet parents sometimes remark that they wish their children would just stay small and never grow up, which is an unthinking, selfish thing to say. No parent would be happy in seeing his children unprogressive and standing still just for the mere pleasure of keeping them always under the parent's control. We were put here to grow up, to become adults, to be free to live our own lives, to think our own thoughts.

However we still remain children mentally. Education is not mental maturity. Learning is not mental maturity; nor is sophistication, nor pride, nor even worldly accomplishments. Mental maturity is the full developed power of being able to control and use the yet unfathomed power of the mind—and the soul. It is true that inventors, artists, musicians, builders and some others have learned to concentrate to a certain extent and to tap the greater supply of power, but definite thought control has never been understood as the soul maturity necessary to prepare for Godhood—for the full power of achievement.

Educational processes of the present day take one farther from the true process of thinking than anything else. One gets his credits in the schools of modern training on how well he can memorize other men's thoughts, books, courses of study. Knowledge is poured into him which he is required to remember—knowledge or facts that will probably be obsolete within a few short years. He may even become an encyclopaedia of facts, and as dead and lifeless in using them as a dull book upon a shelf. Intelligence is living, feeling, reaching, an alertness of enthusiasm that must be forever pliable. Real thinking will never permit one to become a fossiled container of stagnant knowledge, but a continual miracle of advancement. Mental maturity is the finding of the path that leads to the deep and hidden possibilities of the human mind, and gives a glimpse of their full value, and opens the way for the complete development.

Up until this day there has been a period of preparation between death and the resurrection in which to attain to this state of maturity. Now, however, we are facing a new day—a day when man will "be changed in the twinkling of an eye from mortal to immortal beings," and this law of thought control will have to begin to work on this plane in order to prepare for the Millennium, for there will be no period of death and waiting in which to complete this maturity. It shall have to be done here on this earth.

This law of thought control may seem difficult at first, perhaps at a few casual tries, impossible in the ordinary stress of living. Yet in observing more closely it seems to be the most practical thing that we could possibly undertake and the most worthwhile.

It is quite easy to discover that the greatest part of our lives is spent aimlessly wandering up and down in the halls of the past, plucking a memory here, another there, as flowers from the garden of dreams. These flowers, however, have very little value unless we need them for some special occasion to make the present a richer glory by some experience gleaned in the past. But memories that we gather at random, as we wander aimlessly along, wither at our touch and we cast them thoughtlessly away, to pass on to gather other memories, and in turn leave them behind. So on and on in our minds we wander back down the pages of the past. The past is gone forever—we cannot truly bring it back. By continually abiding in it we lose the glory and the value of the present and we may even lose the future. It is true that the future is the Lord's. We cannot reach out and claim one moment of it before it arrives. Only the present is ours, to glorify, to bless, to send on into the tomorrows, crowned with the touch of our hands upon it. If we lose the present, if we fail to value it, to glorify it with every breath and thought, then we will also lose the future. Live each moment as you desire the future to be, and the future will fulfill your desires. Leave the memories and enrich each moment of the present with intense desire, far vision and deep worship.

Worse than memory gathering, we sometimes inhabit only the halls of fantasy. We are children, mentally immature. As a race it is time for us to grow up, to open the hallways of the future by glorifying each moment of the present. So, with our heads held high, our faces to the light and with courageous understanding in our souls, we are to meet this great destiny. It is the future destiny of all mankind. Our every thought must become a purpose—and that one great purpose should be to become like our Heavenly Father, for no parent ever existed who did not plan on his children achieving as much as he had, or more, if he is not a jealous, wicked parent. To watch one's children mature is a continual joy in the life of a true parent.

When worry is permitted to take hold of one's mind it is like an old, broken-down phonograph record that goes round and round in the mind, whirling into the same squeaking grooves, the same worn-out notches, bringing nothing but discord, confusion—dismay—terror—fear—ill health, and sometimes insanity. Around and around it whirls, through dreary days and sleepless nights—unanswered—unsolved. When one learns to control thought it becomes a simple thing to weigh carefully every angle of the problem confronting one, seeing its difficulties, its hopeless aspects, even its utter impossibilities, its unsolved conditions. Then it will be possible to turn off the record, to relax the mind and to go to sleep in peace, knowing with confidence that it will be solved. As one commands one's mind to relax, after giving the subject very careful thought upon every angle, it is possible to turn the difficulty over to the subconscious part of the mind for the solving, which in turn has the power to reach out into the realms of Divine Light and receive answers. The most glorious thing is the amazing thoroughness of such a process, the ease with which the difficulty is completely taken care of, the impossible situation ironed out. When this becomes a habit one soon learns to cast out all fear—all fear is darkness. Darkness eventually is eliminated—and "there will be no darkness in him—and he will be filled with light and comprehend all things."

This is a new day, a day of glory, of mental and spiritual progress. This is the time of preparation for God's day on earth. It is also our day—a day in which we are to leave the dark shadows of the past and light the future by the spiritual desires of the present.

The very purpose of controlled thinking is to bring power and glory to every individual who has been created as a child of the Most High God.

As one goes more deeply into the study of thought control, he realizes that it is the key of progress and happiness. Existence, even in Celestial glory, would not be worth having if we were forever to be slaves to our rambling, wandering thoughts that chase each other around our brains like squirrels in a cage, our spells of temper, our moods, our idle thoughts which waste ninety percent of our brain power. We have been slaves as surely as we have lived. We have been lashed along, or dragged about by our noses with thoughts of fear, doubts, gloom, worry or just purposeless wandering. If joy has ruled for a short time, our happiness has been snatched in half-hearted degree, for always there would be the knowledge that it probably would not last—there would be tomorrow—and tomorrow. Even a few hours might bring a state of mind bordering on despair. Almost every moment has been unpredictable.

If this condition were to continue forever in our minds, thoughts ruling us instead of our ruling our thoughts, then life and existence would be a dreary, sordid, meaningless thing, not worth the living.

As one learns to become a musician by so many hours of concentrated practice, so it is possible to control one's thoughts by so many hours of definite work. Just the desire and the will to practice brings the most astonishing results.

At first it seems almost impossible to control every rambling, runaway thought. Every thought seems to turn into a laughing, shouting, screaming, boisterous, mischievous child that will keep just beyond reach. To control the mind in this manner, in chasing down every stray, rambling thought one has to work many, many months. This is not necessary. There is indeed, the hard way, the way in which one learns to turn his brain inside out to understand just what thoughts are, how they work, what they accomplish and how to control them. If one works in this manner he will find, at first, that it is necessary to chase each thought around in his mind until it is cornered and then it is necessary to almost hurl it bodily from the brain. This process takes sometimes an hour or more—an hour just to corner one elusive, defiant little thought that will sneak in again the moment your back is turned.

There is the easy way in which one can fill his mind so full of the vision desired, so full of prayer and hope and love that there is no room for anything else. This will be explained more thoroughly later on.

Thoughts can be such harmless, inoffensive, mild little things as they trip to and fro through one's mind. But just try to send them out and they turn into fighting little demons struggling for existence. There is no such thing as a single thought, for each miserable little entity holds hands with friends, and they in turn with friends and relatives. There is never an end to them. They cling together and fight equally hard to hold their place, like roots cling to the soil. There is never just one that needs to be conquered. They are legion. But however harmless they may seem they turn into battling armies the minute one tries to banish them. They will kick, and struggle and clutch and scream, fighting to hold their own. It becomes necessary at first, to almost pick up each one bodily and hurl it out, then bolt the door of consciousness against it. Then in unlocking the door for even a small crack to evict its playmate, or friend, who follows, it will edge its way back in.

This method demands great patience, but it is a marvelous training. It is an interesting method of procedure if one has the time and energy to spare. It is an education in itself and reveals the startling fact that thoughts are living, vital little entities, each with a distinct personality, even as people. On completing this method one has to spend hours, days, weeks and months on constant awareness of his own thinking process and after awhile the sub-conscious mind is trained to assist, and when a little wandering thought slyly edges its way in there is a warning from that deeper consciousness. Then before there is time to turn the attention upon the intruder it flees, slamming the door behind it. If one is curious enough to open the door a tiny crack to see what little thought had entered, it considers that an invitation in and rushes forth with its relatives and friends and then one finds that he has to only turn with stern command and they flee, and are gone.

The value of the super-conscious or spiritual part of the brain becomes a priceless help in this work. It is the part of us that never sleeps or relaxes. It is the part of the mind that when once it has learned to type, can manipulate the key-board without any help whatsoever from the conscious mind—or the part of us that finally learns to drive a car without having to think, or to play a musical instrument without having to search desperately for each key. It is the mind that gives us mastery in any field of achievement. It is quite necessary to get this super-mind trained to help in the controlling of thoughts. It always takes rigid, concentrated training to prepare this sub-conscious or the super-conscious to co-operate, and change one from being a mediocre person into a master.

The result of such training in the mind is most amazing. The brain instead of feeling clogged, tired and stupid seems to be alert to almost everything, yet worried about nothing. There is a calmness and control that is majestic, and a joy and glory that is beyond anything that has ever been imagined. There are no longer discordant thoughts, but only confidence that the glory of this work will continue forever and ever, and that our thinking can control our destinies, for by proper thinking there is no room for dislikes, hates, discords or confusion. Minds trained like this will in time become so pure that Christ will be able to reveal His mind and will to the children of men by direct contact.

"Be still, and know that I am God."

Only a few have ever done this, yet it is as practical as breathing or eating. Some have come to this point from dire necessity when deep sorrows have left a bleak confusion of terror and fear too great to be endured; or when worry and worldly problems have almost submerged them. Then for a moment they have kneeled down and with the power of their intelligence, demanded the screaming elements or thoughts and nerves to "BE STILL!" They have felt the peace and glory of having every warring atom and cell of their bodies instantly grow calm. They have felt their jangling nerves become perfectly in tune with the universe—and they have known for a few minutes, at least, that God is God. That He is very near. That it is possible to speak and He will hear.

This is a glorious experience, and every human being is invited by God to try it. There will be another chapter later explaining how this achievement may be accomplished.

Not only is it a beautiful experience to bring occasional calm out of chaos, but it is possible to attain this point of power all the time—to abide in it continually—or to abide in Him and in His love and peace, in which the screeching problems of the outside confusion melt into the peace and joy of achievement. Then it is that we find it easy to fulfill the command, "Look unto me in every thought; doubt not, fear not." (D. & C. 6:36).

"Verily, thus saith the Lord; it shall come to pass that every soul who forsaketh his sins and cometh unto me, and calleth on my name, and obeyeth my voice, and keepeth my commandments, shall see my face and know that I am." (D. & C. 93:1).

"But the day soon cometh that ye shall see me, and know that I am; for the veil of darkness shall soon be rent, and he that is not purified shall not abide the day." (*Ibid.*, 38:8).

This promise to know God is God, is therefore, not just a promise of the mind. It will become a literal reality as we prepare ourselves to receive the promises He has given.

"Draw near unto me and I will draw near unto you; seek me diligently and ye shall find me; ask, and ye shall receive, knock, and it shall be opened unto you." (*Ibid.*, 88:63).

"Seek me early and ye shall find me."

"And this is life eternal, to know thee, the only true and living God and Jesus Christ, whom thou hast sent."

Desire is the flame that will fulfill anything. Intensify your desires—intensify them until they burn as a fire within you, until the very flame reaches into eternity to gather from the universe the material necessary to fulfill them. Intense desire cuts the pattern from the spiritual realms and gathers the material substance to fulfill the complete pattern, to make it a reality, tangible and true. Mere "likes" and "wants" are seldom realized. Wishing is not sufficient. But intense desire always carries with it the power of its own fulfillment, as the seed or life-germ carries with it the power to fulfill and bring forth the mature, perfect product of its existence. The time of the achieving of a desire will be based primarily upon the intensity put into it. When it fills the soul, when the desire is so intense that other things do not matter, when it has thoroughly tested the patience, endurance and earnestness of the individual, then it will be granted. That desire will be fulfilled when it has been so intense that it is imbedded into every cell and fibre of the being. If you can desire anything that badly, and it is a righteous desire, then you may have it.

The time of the achieving of a desire will be always an individual consideration. No two radishes mature at the same time, though planted at the same hour. No two flowers bloom at the same moment of precision. No two people desire with the same intensity. No two desires have the same value. Some can be answered almost instantly—others take time to mature into perfection—but for those who can contact the Spirit, time is not.

When one desires to control his thoughts more than he desires life, knowing that by controlling them he can control his own destiny, then only does it become easy, and then only is life worth the living.

The hard, black shell of the walnut, those heavy, black

shells of the hardest nuts known, is easily broken and cast aside as the soft substance within, as a dynamic force of living energy, lightened by desire, begins to grow, desires to expand. So everything that holds us back, every impossible, insurmountable barrier, every wall will crumble before the intensified desires of the soul.

The atomic energy of the soul can be released through sincere, intense desire and *continued* prayer. NOTHING IS IMPOSSIBLE! All that is needed to accomplish anything is the knowledge of God's laws, the understanding of the power of faith and the law of exercising it, plus vision that leads to desire. "EXERCISE" means to "train by use; exert; practice; employ actively; make anxious; harass; to undergo training; bodily exertion or mental or physical development; labor; work." With this definition of the word "exercise" as given in the dictionary we can readily understand why exercising great and mighty faith has been neglected. Or rather not understood.

This atomic energy of the soul is generated in the mind of man. It includes the key of progress and eternal power. If a grain of sand, a speck of soil, a drop of water, holds such unspeakable power when released back into its original source of energy, then consider the great power that is stored in the mind or soul of man. Think of its incomprehensible achievements when used in full understanding, in comparison with the strides of the past few years without its full power being even tapped.

Faith includes the knowledge and the power to use the spiritual energy of creation to fulfill the desires of righteousness —and to perform the works of God. All spirit or energy is matter in a more refined degree than is registered on mortal senses. And all matter is spirit or energy, or light.

Matter, as we understand it, is congealed or condensed in its vibrations into tangible form so that mortals are aware of it. The birth of an atom is the gathering of this energy, or spirit into mass. The death of an atom is the releasing of the mass back into energy, or spirit.

The work of the present-day scientists is to take the mass, or the atom and return it speedily and swiftly back into the source from which it came. This is a marvelous thing to be able to release the spiritual energy in matter. The very power of this releasing bears witness of the dynamic energy contained in even the inanimate materials of the earth.

If this power is so great even in the lower, mineral kingdom, which is the lowest form of existence, then try and comprehend what it is like in the highest form of life—man.

The work of the future is a much greater work than the work of the present-day scientists. The work of the future is to take the spiritual energy, through the great principles of Faith, and bring it into tangible form—"For faith is the substance of things hoped for," etc. "Substance" means the material, which in this case is the "evidence of things unseen," therefore is spiritual energy. By believing, or understanding this great spiritual force, it is possible to bring things "hoped for" into tangible form or manifestation. THIS IS FAITH. Anything short of this power is not acceptable to God. It is the power of God in the lives of men. It is really the work of the scientists in reverse. Or rather, their work is in reverse as they are working the laws of God backwards, or contrary to God's great plan of creation. It is His will that men should take hold of this dynamic energy and light of God and create with it— not destroy with it.

Faith is this great, dynamic spiritual energy as it is directed or set in motion by the intelligence and desires of the mind of man. It is the mind, or thoughts of man that has the power to reach out and take hold of this force of creation as his understanding opens. And the opening of his understanding is the "believing" that always is given along with the principle of faith in the scriptures. The "belief" mentioned, is the believing that this great Spiritual power or force does exist, and faith is the actual using of it. It is to be understood in all its mighty field of glory in order to be used freely by man. And then it can only be used with great love and deep humility, for it is the power of God in action—a power so much greater than any power known that even the power of the "hydrogen bomb" would be insignificant in comparison, if it were used in its fullness. For all power is based on the *one* great power

of Almighty God—the power of *faith*. For it was by faith
that the atom bomb, the hydrogen bomb and everything else
that has been produced has been brought forth.

As man opens his understanding to comprehend this dynamic principle he will understand that the word "FAITH" has
been a forgotten word and its meaning lost in the individual
lives of men. It is only being used for mechanical productions.
It is being used to complete a machine age of complete frustration, for man is being belittled by the very works of his
own hands instead of finding his own power and taking his
place in a higher realm of divine achievement. Yea, man himself stands more weak and trembling than ever before. There
are more and more hospitals, more and more mental cases,
more and more unhappiness and insecurity—more and more
disasters—more deaths—more suicides—more misery—more
fear.

When man becomes fully conscious, or fully comprehensive
of the dynamic principle of "FAITH", knowing what it is, and
how to use it, it will be a simple thing to restore the flesh of
the leper, the eyes of the blind, the hearing of the deaf, the
limbs of the lame, or any of the other works of God, in the
name of His Beloved Son, Jesus Christ, as given continuously
in the scripture. Yes, it will be a simple thing to do the works
that Christ did—*and do even the* GREATER WORKS that were
promised—for all power is contained in the living, active principle of *faith*.

As man uses this powerful force or principle to gather into
tangible form the unseen substance of eternal elements to
glorify God and to fulfill his own personal needs, he will not
require miles upon miles of land, acres and acres of buildings,
nor millions upon millions of dollars worth of machinery. He
will need only a pure heart aflame with inspiration and a love
that is deep and perfect, plus vision to see and *know*. And the
positive *knowing* can only come through earnest, humble
prayer—not lip prayers, but prayers deep from the very heart
of man. As one learns to comprehend this great power—or
spirit energy that composes all substance, it will be the most
natural thing in the world for him to take hold of his divine

heritage and begin to work the works of God, "For all that the Father has is yours" including *power.* "And the kingdom is not in word, but in power."

The scientist has discovered that the atom is composed of pure energy. As they continue in their search they will learn that energy is light, and light is spirit. They will know that this spirit energy is set in motion by the mind of man, and is *"faith"*, the great dynamic gift of God. It is the power of God through which the worlds were made. It is a principle of everlasting creation and glory that God desires man to use—not in reverse, but in all its creative glory. As man begins to use this glorious, powerful force of creation nothing will be impossible to him. And without it, it is impossible to please God. Neither can man be saved without it, as given in the scripture, for our lives are wasted and in vain. The faith to raise the dead, to move mountains, to overcome all evil and misery still slumbers in the seed of the plan waiting for man to bring it forth for the eternal glory of God and the benefit of man.

As one begins to understand the power of controlled thought —thought that has cast out fear, overcome hates and discords and confusion, he will as naturally find his way into these greater things as the flower lifts its face to the sun, as the tree ascends from the seed, or as the harvest follows the planting.

Thoughts are to the mind what food is to the body. A starved, underfed body cannot thrive. Neither can an underfed, neglected mind. A body fed on an unbalanced or insufficient diet becomes ill. Sagging muscles, pimples, skin blemishes, scurvy, over-weight, rheumatism and many other ailments can be traced directly to wrong diets. Too much dieting on the other hand, can also be detrimental. A body fed on garbage becomes a soggy, pitiful thing. A mind fed on evil or wrong thoughts can become even more so. If a mind is fed only upon sensual thoughts the body also is affected and becomes an instrument of shame and darkness instead of a temple of light. A diet of pure food is necessary to health, but if the mind is not also given pure food the body will still suffer. Any mind that is fed only on unkind thoughts, criticizing thoughts, condemning, hateful, morbid, jealous or dishonest thoughts will drag the body down—and will eventually destroy it. Souls are glorified or destroyed by thoughts, "For as a man thinketh, so he is." You are your thoughts. They are you. You are noble, mediocre or evil, according to your thinking. A man is made or unmade by himself. He alone is the builder or the destroyer.

Only glory and light and joy can possibly come to the man who has ceased "sowing the dragon's teeth," and instead cultivates the power of his own possibilities. He who plants only love and peace can reap only the fulfillment of the perfect life in all its unfolding light of glorious, happy achievement. And as he follows the highway of divine thinking he will as surely ascend beyond his present conditions as the airplane has surpassed the ox-team.

In this great work of thought control one soon learns that it is not necessary to watch every individual thought, but rather the caliber of one's thinking. When every unkind·thought, fear thought, or evil thought is replaced with thoughts of beauty, love, joy, perfection and that inner ecstasy one will have completely conquered darkness and will be filled with Light, and comprehend all things.

CHAPTER VIII.

HOW THOUGHTS ARE PLANTED, AND HOW THEY PRODUCE

IT IS TRUE that thoughts are seeds. Each is a living entity of vibrating life, but every thought is not planted, or will not grow any more than every grain of wheat that comes forth will produce. No seed will grow unless it is planted.

Grain comes forth only after it has been planted in the earth. There it germinates, breaking its outer shell, and gathering from the elements the strength and power of fulfillment, which it holds locked in the vision within itself, it comes forth multiplied.

In the same way thoughts will only produce after they have been planted. This planting is done by holding to the thoughts with deep intensity until they are dropped into the realm of the emotions. This is conception. You have heard the expression, "he conceived the idea." This is an absolute fact. When thought and emotion mingle the thought is conceived and will come forth. When they connect with the feeling, or emotions they become living, vibrations, generated into growth and power, expanding into life and will as surely grow into their full stature of fulfillment as a kernel of wheat will grow if planted and given the necessary conditions to produce.

A thought must be harbored as an emotion, such as a fear, or a deep desire, which find lodgment in the vibrating essence of life, then only is it liberated into the forces of creation. This point where thought and emotion meet is also the place where vibration is released, AND VIBRATION IS LIFE. Thus the life force is generated in the thought or seed and it reaches out to gather to itself its own, be it good or bad.

The place of vibration is the center of life in each human being—when that life center and the conscious mind become united, with complete understanding, the body and the spirit

69

blend in the power of the "at-one-meant," and-the mortal and the spiritual become completely united—the material seed, or thought, is released into the emotions, or source of life, to produce and grow. The word "father" in its earliest meaning was known as "first cause" or "first mover." Thus the mind is the first mover, or the cause, and has the power to plant the seeds of thought into the emotions, which is the female counterpart and contains all that is necessary to bring the seed forth to complete fulfillment. Thus the great creative-principle of Almighty God is complete in every child of earth. Yea, "all that the Father has, is yours." This is the complete power of the imagination—the power to "image in" to the spiritual realm the living seed of thought that it might generate and come forth multiplied into tangible reality.

The great magic switch that I had hoped the scientists would develop for us is already ours. It is the point where thought contacts the emotions. At the center point, where intelligence contacts that inner point of feeling, is where the eternal source of power is released. This is that magic switch or contac: of unlimited Faith. It is the contact with ALL power—the very keys of creation. And each man already has that magical switch or power of contact right within himself. No scientist could possibly perfect it for us. It has always been ours to use. It always will be.

Yea, all that the Father has is ours—the power to create and to bring forth—each thought after its kind, each seed after its kind—such is the law. Unlimited power lies within the soul of man, and God is no respecter of persons.

That is why the First and great commandment was given in the following words of power, "Thou shalt love the Lord thy God, with all thy heart, with all thy soul, and with all thy mind." If that was fulfilled in the being of every man, with this background of pure, unselfish, understanding, devoted love released to the very Highest of all, nothing would be impossible in the life of the individual. That is truly the greatest law, the most perfect of all commandments, and the most beneficial to man. It contains all power, and all fulfillment right within itself.

Since the powers of creation, the power to bring forth any condition of happiness, misery, glory, or death is in the being of man, it is quite necessary to understand just what this power and privilege contains, and what man's responsibility is. This very power makes apparent the reason why depressing thoughts must be "overcome," for they are instantly connected with the emotions, hence they grow like weeds, speedily and swift—a crop of destruction, or at least ills, woes and earthly miseries.

Any negative thought instantly sprouts into growth. Why? Because our emotions have been trained to harbor fears, hates, jealousies, discords and confusion. These are weeds, and they grow as swiftly, as rank and as destructive. They destroy completely any crop of hope, wasting the power of the soil, contaminating the body and the mind, even as weeds can destroy the true fertility of the soil. On the wings of the wind these weeds rush forth to multiply their burdens, the varied ills and miseries of mortal life.

These are not just words. They are truths as eternal as unchanging and positive as the laws of sunrise and sunset, seed time and harvest, life and growth.

This perfect law of production will produce just as readily all the glorious gifts of joy, peace, happiness, abundance, health and vitality as the negative crops of sickness, poverty, distress and death. "There is a law irrevocably decreed in heaven, before the foundations of the earth, upon which all blessings are predicated; and if we obtain any blessing from God, it is by obedience to that law." Many fulfill this perfect law unknowingly, hence they receive the blessings of life. Many more break it, unknowingly, and they suffer the consequences. The law is exact, unfailing, eternal.

Understanding this glorious law and working with it is power unspeakable. It is a law that belongs to the children of Almighty God, for we are heirs of the kingdom of godhood.

We ourselves create every condition on earth. To cultivate the habit of cheer will prepare the soil for any harvest. To keep out all despair, or fear, fulfills the law of faith and gives one the power to take hold of that intangible substance out of which all things are formed. To send out only love and kindness from the thoughts and emotions will bring a harvest of utter glory. Even if one has no intense ambitions, but only desires to live a peaceful life with mental and temporal security, it can only be guaranteed by watching that every vibration that is released is in tune with the great laws of the universe, which are always peace. Any contrary vibration is against the highest laws of creation and will bring discord and confusion into one's life. To have a life that is at all worth living, it is quite necessary to understand these great powers, and this law of production—this law that reaches into the intangible elements and brings forth into tangible form the desires of our hearts glorified, or our fears and worries multiplied.

God's promises to us will never fail—the law is irrevocable. It is eternal. It cannot err. It is power beyond the full comprehension of man—it is truly the very power of creation, and the law of it. Therefore we *can* thank Him for the things which we desire when we pray, and believing, they will be fulfilled unto us. Thus we learn "to walk with Him" in the power and majesty of creatorship, glorifying light, overcoming darkness, despair, fear, confusion and eventually death.

"And it shall come to pass that he that asketh in Spirit shall receive in Spirit.

"He that asketh in Spirit asketh according to the will of God, *wherefore it is done even as he asketh.*

"And again, I say unto you, all things must be done in the name of Christ, whatsoever you do in the Spirit (in order to give them perfect light and pure conception).

"And ye must give thanks unto God in the Spirit for whatsoever blessings ye are blessed with."

True gratitude is the song of the soul. It is the true sunlight of perfect production. It gives light and energy to the soil of the soul.

"Then, having done all stand!" (Eph. 6:13).

The present holds the future enfolded in its embrace as surely as the acorn holds the oak or the seed holds the flower. The thoughts and desires of today are the realities of tomorrow. So is given the command: "Take no thought of tomorrow." Today is the planting time. Live today perfectly in every thought, with true gratitude singing in the soul, and tomorrow will unfold as beautifully perfect as today is.

Cultivate the joy of ecstasy and your life will become filled with light. Live each moment to its fullest glory, filled with divine anticipation, vibrating with an inner song of high devotion and gladness, and the world will lay its choice treasures at your feet—and heaven will unfold its glory. These higher realms of light are man's true heritage.

The rule of the "Alcoholics Anonymous" is that each day is to be lived with this thought, "I will keep sober for *this day*." They claim that any person can refrain from drinking for one whole day—so they concentrate on the one day—the day at hand. And that day "at hand" is always present—and thus it can grow into weeks, and into months, and into ultimate achievement and happiness.

The law of perfection is much the same, only it requires a little more careful living. It is: "This moment I shall give out only love and light and joy for the glory of God, and the benefit of man." Any individual can fulfill that law for an hour no matter how impossible his life may seem. Then if he can fulfill it for one complete hour he can for another hour —and another—and soon the hours reach into days—the days into weeks—the weeks into months—and the months into a life of glorious fulfillment.

Root up the weeds that have been planted within you— either by your parents, ancestors, associates or by yourself. Never again let disgruntled, fearsome thoughts feed on the strength of your soul. But even more important, never again as long as you exist, use your power of creation to plant seeds that will destroy your life, your happiness and joy, and the lives of others.

Here it will be necessary to handle briefly the topic of hypnotism in order to reveal the great, hidden powers of the mind. For many years the subject was ridiculed and considered more or less of a fraud. Now, however, under the extensive research of psychology and science it has been proved a

very real and often dangerous power, for it is being used upon
men to destroy their moral fibre, to change their characters
and to overcome their wills.

In a recent current magazine appeared an article entitled
"Hypnosis," written by Doctor G. H. Estabrooks, who is chair-
man of the department of psychology at Colgate University.
He has pioneered in developing hypnotism for wartime uses in
this country, and has written several books on the subject.

Modern psychology has completely shattered the old beliefs about hypnotism. It has proved it to be a definite reality
—and a very deadly weapon.

The old belief of no one being able to hypnotize another
against his will has been disproved. A person need only be
taken when he is completely relaxed and off guard, or when
he is too weary to realize what is happening, to be placed
under an hypnotic spell. Also the idea that no one can be
forced to do anything while in an hypnotic state which he
would not do when he is awake is entirely false. It is a known
fact now, that he can not only be compelled to do things in an
hypnotic state that his former morals would not permit, but
he can be compelled to fulfill such suggestions even after he
is awakened and in a complete state of consciousness. This can
be accomplished by working on the emotions, by changing
thought-reactions.

It takes time to break down those "taboos" of the mind and
character that have been embedded into one's being through
a lifetime of living, but it can be done. Sometimes many treat-
ments must be given, in which the hypnotist reaches into those
productive realms of the subconscious, those unfathomable
realms where the record of all past experiences are archived,
where all the reactions to those happenings are stored—in fact,
he must delve into the very source of the emotions. By planting new thoughts and new reactions, the subject will slowly
respond to the treatment of the hypnotist and after he is fully
awakened will obey and fulfill those hypnotic suggestions—
even to the point of turning traitor to his country or murdering
his best friend.

Thoughts planted deep into the subconscious mind of a

child are as much a part of him, as his hands or his feet. It is
an eternal reality that if one can be given a child until it is
eight years old, and use those eight years to plant ideas into
the fibre of its very being it is almost impossible to ever up-
root them, be they good or bad. If they are good they are
almost never uprooted. If they are bad the only way they can
be uprooted is by a slow, patient teaching process of proved
logic that gradually takes the place of error. This is a slow,
painful process unless the individual has learned to think. To
an adult mind that has been sealed since childhood into a certain way of thinking it is almost necessary for the individual
himself to "jack up" his skull to permit more truth to enter.
While an elderly person will find the changing of the mind
an almost impossible task. That is why Christ said, "New wine
must be put in new bottles." If new wine is put into old bottles,
or elderly people, with hard, set minds the great truths cannot
be absorbed and thus the bottles and the wine will be lost.

The only possible way to grow into *all truth* is to be willing
to unseal the mind—to open wide the doors of the heart and
soul and let eternal truth come forth and gradually fill the
conscious mind. Truth belongs to every individual—it is every
man's heritage. It was born with him—only the conscious
mind has blocked the way to it by having been sealed by ideas
that were only partial truth. All humanity has been partially
hypnotized by the negative, or vague, shadowy, half-truths
planted in the mind, often in childhood. We carry a race consciousness of "taboos" while our great latent powers are left
completely undeveloped. We live entirely on the surface while
within each man is the power to move mountains. We have
been hypnotized from infancy into a mediocre condition with
inferior abilities. We have gone on in our shadowy march,
groveling, crawling through sordid conditions of life with inferior achievements. We have continued to heap more self-
hypnotism upon ourselves, and our lives have become completely orthodox, stinted and unworthy as we have continued
to plod down the darkened, misguided highway of ills, sorrows, disappointments and endless strivings. The very mechanical achievements have put to shame our own lack of advance-

ment. With heads crammed with knowledge, yet with no personal powers developed beyond our predecessors of many generations, we stand personally impotent, relying wholly upon
the mechanical inventions for our strength and power. Until
man himself gets the full vision of his own possibilities he
will continue to plod slowly down the dark road of decay—
to the grave.

This is not the way Christ brought. "I came that you might
have life—and have it more abundantly!" "He who believes
on me need never die!"

It is time we arise from our grave clothes and unhypnotize
ourselves, jack up our skulls, unseal our minds, and step out
into life—life that is ever-present, unending, glorious, eternal.
And there is only one possible way for this new light to find
place in the hearts and minds of men and that is for them to
humble themselves so completely to the Divine Spirit of Almighty God, that they might become new—or as Christ gave it
—"be renewed." Then only can they accept it.

Nothing is impossible to the mind that will open wide to
His Spirit. And to the mind that has put on the humble, pliable, teachable condition of a child's all Truth can and will
come. It is the minds sealed with the importance of their own
position and learning that will fail to grasp truth or any part
of it.

Insanity, morbid mindedness, inferiority complexes and innumerable other tragic mental ailments have been inflicted
entirely by self-hypnotism, or by our own thoughts of fear,
injustice, hates, distrusts, discords, jealousies and confusion.
It is much easier to hypnotize one's self than to be hypnotized
by another. Most of us are self-hypnotized at least on one or
more points of our make-up, eccentricities and even our characters. When we understand this power of self-hypnotism it will
be a simple thing to eradicate all our foibles and follies, our
weaknesses and sins. We will then need no psychiatrists, but
will use freely and intelligently our own God-given power of
correct thinking.

From the Science Digest, September 1948, is an article entitled "Time Slowed by Hypnotism."

"Time can be slowed so that incredible tasks can be accomplished in the mind, in the course of only a few seconds.

"This is done by suggestion during the hypnotic trance, Dr. Linn F. Cooper, Georgetown University physician reported in the *Bulletin* of the University's Medical Center at Washington."

A young lady of the Georgetown University was hypnotized by Dr. Cooper, and told to count the cotton bolls in a patch near her home. She counted for what she declared afterward, was about eighty minutes. She told of doing it very carefully looking under the leaves so that she would not miss any. She took her time, without hurry. When finished she snapped into consciousness and reported that there were 862 bolls. Later this was verified. In actual time, the young woman had only been hypnotized for just three seconds. It is utterly impossible for a conscious person to even count to 862, let alone walk along cotton rows checking cotton bolls, in three seconds of time.

This experience may be interesting to show that there is a part of our inner minds that is surely in direct contact with the realm where time and space do not exist.

This information on hypnotism has been included in this work for a very definite purpose. If there is such power stored within us then it is our right to use it. It belongs to us to make use of. And if it is possible for a soldier or an officer to be seized by an enemy country and have thoughts planted in his sub-conscious mind that will bring forth whatever is planted, even after he is completely awakened from the hypnotic trance, then it is possible for us to do that planting within ourselves. This divine right belongs to us, and to us alone, each individual who has a mind. Hypnotism is a wicked thing, no matter how it is used. No one has the right to use his conscious mind to plant the seeds of thought into the emotions of another. This system could be classified under no other name than mental rape.

If each human being understood the power of his own mind, the strength of his own creative powers and of his soul, and the great loving power of God, to the extent that he would learn to use the powers within his own being for the good and the glory of a world, for progress, for understanding, for perfection, letting in the power and light of God, no one would ever be able to touch his mind, or his emotions, nor to trespass upon his divine rights. Understanding his own power and using it man can always be master of himself and every condition.

As we begin to comprehend the great powers stored within our minds and to use that power for the happiness and advancement of not only ourselves, but the human race, no one will be able to turn us into stool-pigeons or traitors, for we will be walking completely in the light, and in perfect control of every corner and recess of our minds, and every faculty and attribute of our beings. Our inner minds will be opened wide, those subterranean caverns, to the sunlight of the Holy Spirit of God, to its love and its light, and none will have the power to trespass nor destroy. Those sacred realms within us will be ours to rule—and the things we plant in harmony with the law, will come forth a hundred-fold to glorify our lives.

The mind is like an iceberg, nine-tenths of its strength and bulk is submerged—only one-tenth of our mental capacities is contained in the conscious mind, yet it is all ours to understand, to use and to rejoice in.

Below is given a passage from the New Testament Apocrypha, II. Clement V:1. Clement was a disciple of Peter, and afterwards Bishop of Rome. Clemens Alexandrius called him an apostle, as did many of the ancient historians.

A Fragment

L. ". . . For the Lord himself, being asked by a certain person, when his kingdom should come? answered, When two shall be one, and that which is without as that which is within; and the male with the female, neither male nor female."

There is a verification of this passage from the Orient, bearing witness that Christ testified that His Kingdom would come when the outside of man became like the inside, with the spiritual taking over—thus is the kingdom brought forth. When the conscious mind and the inner-mind of emotional and spiritual power of creation become united with complete understanding the "at-one-meant" will have been accomplished —and all things will be possible.

Chapter IX.

"SEEK AND YE SHALL FIND"

ONE of the most beautiful records of the development of faith is given in the Apocryphal New Testament writings of Hermas. Just who this Hermas was cannot be positively ascertained, although he was a Greek convert. He lived in the early days of the Christian Church, and may have been the one mentioned in Romans 16:14 by Paul. If it is this same Hermas he was a bishop of Phillippi.

"When I had prayed at home, and was sat down upon the bed; a certain man came in to me with a reverent look, in the habit of a shepherd clothed in a white cloak." (Hermas 1:1).

"The Shepherd, the angel of repentance—commanded me to write." (II Hermas 1:10).

"Again he said unto me: remove from thee all doubting and question nothing at all, when thou asketh anything of the Lord, saying within thyself; how shall I be able to ask anything of the Lord and receive it, seeing I have so greatly sinned against Him?

"Do not think thus, but turn unto the Lord with all thy heart, and ask of Him without doubting, and thou shalt know the mercy of the Lord; how that He will not forsake thee, but will fulfill the request of thy soul.

"For God is not as men, mindful of the injuries he has received; but he forgets injuries, and has compassion upon his creatures.

"Wherefore purify thy heart from all the views of this present world; and observe the commands I have before delivered unto thee from God; and thou shalt receive whatsoever good things thou shalt ask, and nothing shall be wanting unto thee of thy petitions; if thou shalt ask the Lord without doubting.

"But they that are not such, shall obtain none of these things which they ask. For they that are full of faith ask all things with confidence, and receive from the Lord, because they ask without doubting—but he that doubts will hardly live unto God, except he repents.

"Wherefore purify thy heart from doubting, and put on faith; and trust in God; and thou shalt receive all that thou shalt ask. But and if thou shouldst chance to ask somewhat and not (immediately) receive it, yet do not therefore doubt, because thou hast not presently (immediately) received the petition of thy soul.

"For it may be thou shalt not presently (immediately) receive it for thy trial, or else for some sin which thou knowest not. But do not thou leave off to ask, *and then thou shalt receive. Else if thou shalt cease to ask, thou must complain of thyself, and not of God,* that he has not given unto thee what thou didst desire.

"Consider therefore this doubting, how cruel and pernicious it is; and how it utterly roots out many from the faith, who were very faithful and firm. For this doubting is the daughter of the Devil; and deals very wickedly with the servants of God.

"Despise it therefore, and thou shalt rule over it on every occasion. Put on a firm and powerful faith, FOR FAITH PROMISES ALL THINGS, AND PERFECTS ALL THINGS. But doubting will not believe, that it shall obtain anything, by all that it can do.

"Thou seest therefore, says he, how faith cometh from above, from God, and has great power. But doubting is an earthly spirit, and proceedeth from the Devil, and has not strength.

"Do thou therefore keep the virtue of faith, and depart from doubting, in which is no virtue, and thou shalt live unto God. And all shall live unto God, as many as shall do these things." (II Hermas, chapter 9).

This record of Hermas agrees perfectly with the teachings of the Savior of the world wherein he taught by parable that continued asking is necessary—not just once, not for a week, not for a year—but if the thing is worth having, then one must continue to petition God until by the development of faith the gift can be completed. Even God cannot perform any great works except through the faith of man. Christ could do no great works in Nazareth because of the unbelief of the people. Continued asking, in itself, develops faith. Faith grows with the petition.

"Behold I say unto you that whoso believeth in Christ. *Doubting nothing, whatsoever he shall ask the Father in the name of Christ it shall be granted unto him; and these promises are unto all, even unto the ends of the earth. And whosoever shall believe in my name, doubting nothing, unto him will I confirm all my words, even unto the ends of the earth.*"

Faith is a petition of the soul knocking at the throne of God, or the gates of heaven. "Ask and ye shall receive, seek and ye shall find, knock and it shall be opened unto you. *For everyone who asks receives, and he who seeks finds. And to him that knocketh it shall be opened.*" No promise of the scripture is greater. No one will be turned away. This very asking, seeking, knocking is planting the desire into the realms that have to bring it forth again, for this is *the Law.*

"And he spake a parable unto them to this end, that men ought always to pray, and not to faint (grow discouraged, or give up). Saying, there was in a city a judge, which feared not God, neither regarded man; And there was a widow in that city; and she came unto him, saying, avenge me of mine adversary. And he would not for awhile; but afterward he said within himself, though I fear not God, nor regard man; yet because this widow troubleth me, I will avenge her, lest by her continual coming she weary me." (Luke 18:1-5).

"And he said unto them, which of you shall have a friend and shall go unto him at midnight, and say unto him, friend, lend me three loaves; for a friend of mine in his journey is come to me, and I have nothing to set before him; And he from within shall answer, and say trouble me not; the door is now shut, and my children are with me in bed; I cannot rise and give thee. I say unto you, though he will not rise and give him, because he is his friend, yet because of his importunity he will rise and give him as many as he needeth." (Luke 11:5-8).

It is quite necessary to begin to exercise great and mighty

faith to be able to escape the things that are coming upon the earth.

The scriptures repeatedly testify that Christ will come the second time in "A day of wickedness and vengeance"—or in a day when nations and people are seeking revenge. When hate fills the hearts of mankind. We have seen a day of vengeance and retaliation wreaked upon the leaders of almost every country who helped to lead the nations into World War II. We are now able to see this same vengeance begin to lift its head in war atrocities and wickedness.

However along with the wickedness of this day was to be a people purified and prepared to meet the Redeemer of the world. An angel, informing Daniel of the things that would happen at the end of time said: "Many shall be purified and made white, and tried; but the wicked shall do wickedly and none of the wicked shall understand." (Dan. 12:10).

And again, in speaking of the elect in the last days: "For they shall hear my voice, and *shall see me,* and shall not be asleep, and shall abide the day of my coming; for they shall be purified, even as I am pure." This mentions expressly a people who shall abide the day of His coming because they are already purified.

There is a very important record I would like to quote here that explains the work and ministry of the first Comforter, as promised by Christ to the Saints in the fourteenth chapter of St. John. There is also a promise of a second Comforter, or the Lord Jesus Christ Himself to visit those who would be purified. "The other Comforter spoken of is a subject of great interest, and perhaps understood by few of this generation. After a person has faith in Christ, repents of his sins, and is baptized for the remission of his sins and receives the Holy Ghost, (by the laying on of hands), which is the first Comforter, then let him continue to humble himself before God, hungering and thirsting after righteousness, and living by every word of God and the Lord will soon say unto him, son thou shalt be exalted. When the Lord has thoroughly proved him and finds that man is determined to serve Him at all hazards then the man will find his calling and his election made sure, then it will be his privilege to receive the other Comforter, which the Lord hath promised the Saints, as is recorded in the testimony of St. John, in the 14th chapter, from the 12th to the 27th verses.

"Now what is this other Comforter? It is no more or less than the Lord Jesus Christ Himself: and this is the sum and substance of the whole matter; that when any man obtains the last Comforter, he will have the personage of Jesus Christ to attend him, or appear unto him from time to time, and even He will manifest the Father unto him, and they will take up their abode with him, and the visions of the heavens will be opened unto him, and the Lord will teach him face to face, and he may have a perfect knowledge of the mysteries of the Kingdom of God; and this is the state and place the ancient Saints arrived at when they had such glorious visions— Isaiah, Ezekiel, John upon the Isle of Patmos, St. Paul in the three heavens, and all the Saints who held communion with the general assembly and Church of the First Born." (Joseph Smith's Teachings; pp. 149-151).

And again, "If your eye be single to my glory, your whole bodies shall be filled with light, and there shall be no darkness in you; and that body which is filled with light comprehendeth all things.

"Therefore, sanctify yourselves that your minds become single to God, and *the days will come that you shall see Him*: for He will unveil His face unto you, and it will be in His own time, and in His own way, and according to His own will.

"Remember the great and *last* promise that I have made unto you; cast away your idle thoughts and your excess of laughter far from you." (D. & C. 88:67-69).

"But the day soon cometh that you shall see me, and know that I am; for the veil of darkness shall soon be rent, and he that is not *purified* shall not abide the day." (*Ibid.*, 38:8).

"Charity is the pure love of Christ and it endureth forever; and whoso is found possessed of it at the last day, it shall be well with him.

"Wherefore, my beloved brethren, pray unto the Father with all the energy of heart, that ye may be filled with this love,

which he hath bestowed upon all who are true followers of his
Son, Jesus Christ; that ye may become the sons of God; that
when he shall appear we shall be like him, for we shall see
him as he is; that we may have this hope; that we may be purified even as he is pure." (Moroni 7:47-48).

"Behold, when ye shall rend the veil of unbelief which doth
cause you to remain in your awful state of wickedness, and
hardness of heart, and blindness of mind, then shall the
*great and marvelous things that have been hid up from the
foundation of the world from you*—Yea, when ye shall call
upon the Father in my name, with a broken heart and a contrite spirit, then shall ye know that the Father hath remembered
the covenant which he made unto your Fathers, O house of
Israel." (Ether 4:15).

There are many who pin their hope on the erroneous idea
that we need do nothing but sit down, inactive, and *believe*,
and we will "be saved by grace." We will be saved by grace,
but only after we have done everything in our power to perfect
ourselves and to glorify God in every thought and word and
act of our lives. Thus it is possible for us to grow from grace
to grace, or advance from one point to a higher point, until
we are enfolded in the complete love and light of our Maker.

"Even so faith, if it hath not works, is dead, being alone.

"Yea, a man may say, Thou hast faith, and I have works;
shew me thy faith without thy works, and I will shew thee my
faith by my works.

"Thou believest there is one God; thou doest well; the devils
also believe, and tremble.

*"But wilt thou know, O vain man, that faith without works
is dead?"* (James 2:17:20).

The proceeding scripture should be burned into the heart
and mind of every human being, for just to believe is doing
not one whit better than the devils are doing. Grace only
comes after one has hungered and thirsted after knowledge,
then with all his soul sought, with an open mind, to appease
that hunger and thirst by continued study, opening his mind
and soul to the divine direction of the Almighty, toward truth,
not just one passage, not one narrowed, bigoted belief, but ALL

truth—which is the growing from grace to grace, then having done all he may be sure that the grace of God will not fail him, and he will be led into all truth.

This advancing, or growing from grace to grace, or purification is never an instantaneous achievement. It has to be reached by preparation.

"We consider that God has created man with a mind capable of instruction, and a faculty which may be enlarged in proportion to the heed and diligence given to the light communicated from heaven to the intellect; and that the nearer man approaches perfection the clearer are his views, and the greater his enjoyments, till he has overcome the evils of his life and lost every desire for sin; and like the ancients, arrives at the point of faith where he is wrapped in the power and glory of his Maker and is caught up to dwell with Him. But we consider that this is a station at which no man ever arrived in a moment; he must have been instructed in the laws and government of that kingdom by proper degrees, until his mind is capable in some measure of comprehending the propriety, justice, equality, and consistency of the same." (Joseph Smith, the American Prophet).

"For in many things we offend all. If any man offend not in word, the same is a perfect man, and able also to bridle the whole body." (James 3:2).

"Whoso offereth praise glorifieth me: and to him that ordereth his conversation aright will I show the salvation of God." (Psalms 50:23).

This bridling of the tongue has to come about by a control of the mind, by a righteous desire of the heart, and by the exercise of the will. Gradually as one walks along this path of high attainment he grows from grace to grace, and thus he is truly saved by the grace, or truth of God—but only as he lives up to each truth that penetrates into his understanding.

"Look unto me in *every thought*; doubt not, fear not."

Christ repeatedly informed his followers that they "Would be *judged by every idle thought*." It isn't the thoughts that are used in our work and our service that will condemn us. It will be those rambling thoughts that steal into our minds in our unoccupied moments and rob us of our power—these are the thoughts that steal from us the energy to pray always, to hold our minds to the achieving of our righteous aims, to complete our assignments on the earth in honor.

There are many more passages of scripture filled with promise and instruction on this subject, but I shall not quote them here. You who are seeking will find the others—and God will enlighten your souls.

"Therefore, woe be unto him that is at ease in Zion!

"Woe be unto him that crieth; All is well!

"Yea, woe be unto him that harkeneth unto the precepts of men, and denieth the power of God, and the gift of the Holy Ghost!

"Yea, woe be unto him that saith; We have received, and we need no more!

"And in fine, woe unto all those who tremble, and are angry because of the truth of God! For behold, he that is built upon the rock receiveth it with gladness; and he that is built upon a sandy foundation trembleth lest he shall fall.

"Woe be unto him that shall say: We have received the word of God, and we need no more of the word of God, for we have enough!

"For behold, thus saith the Lord God; I will give unto the children of men line upon line, precept upon precept, here a little and.there a little; and blessed are those who harken unto my precepts and lend an ear unto my counsel, for they shall learn wisdom; for unto him that receiveth I will give more; and from them that shall say, We have enough, from them shall be taken away even that which they have." (2 Nephi 29:24-30).

"And now, behold this is wisdom; whoso readeth, let him understand and receive also;

"For unto him that receiveth it shall be given more abundantly, *even power*." (D. & C. 71:5-6).

"For my kingdom cometh not in word, but in Power." If one desires to have the power to do the works that Christ did in order to prove his belief in Christ—yea, even the power to do the *greater works*, then he must have the ability to open up his heart and soul to receive more and more truth until he is filled with light, and comprehendeth all things. This is the "Grace" of Almighty God that is promised.

There is always the promise of continued light and knowledge to be given: "We believe all that God has revealed. We believe all that He does now reveal. *We believe that He will yet reveal many great and important things pertaining to the kingdom of God.*" This book has only been written to point the finger of light to the things that have already been revealed. There is no new revelation in this work. If the things that have already been revealed are rejected, or not understood, then how can more possibly be given?

In the precious record known as the "Word of Wisdom" is given the following promises: "And ALL *Saints* who remember to keep and do these sayings, walking in obedience to the commandments—shall find wisdom and great treasures of knowledge, even hidden treasures." Here is the promise that any individual who is seeking for righteousness shall find wisdom and great treasures of knowledge, even knowledge that has been hidden from the world. No one is restricted from this command of God to ask, seek and knock.

"The Spirit of Revelation is in connection with these blessings. A person may profit by noticing the first intimation of the Spirit of Revelation; for instance, when you feel pure intelligence flowing into you, it may give you sudden strokes of ideas, so that by noticing it, you find it fulfilled the same day or soon; (i.e.) those things that were presented unto your minds by the Spirit of God, *will come to pass*: and thus by learning the Spirit of God and understanding it, you may grow into the principle of revelation, until you become perfect in Christ Jesus." (Joseph Smith).

In order to separate truth from error, it is necessary to live humbly, to live prayerfully, to have the Holy Ghost for a constant companion, for it is as great a wickedness to reject truth and light as it is to follow the dark teachings of the apostates. The Spirit of Christ enlightens every man that cometh into the world, and if one will judge truth by that Spirit of Christ which is within him he need never err in judgment.

"Verily, thus saith the Lord unto you concerning the Apocrypha—There are many things contained therein that are true, and it is mostly translated correctly; There are many things contained therein that are not true, which are interpolations by the hands of men. Verily, I say unto you, that it is not needful that the Apocrypha should be translated. Therefore, whoso readeth it, let him understand, for the *Spirit manifesteth truth;* and whoso is enlightened by the Spirit shall obtain benefit therefrom; and whoso receiveth not by the Spirit, cannot be benefited." (D. & C. 91).

"Without revelation direct from heaven, it is impossible for any person to understand fully the plan of salvation. We often hear it said that the living oracles must be in the Church, in order that the Kingdom of God may be established and prosper on the earth. I will give another version of this sentiment. I say that the living oracles of God, or the Spirit of revelation must be in each and every individual, to know the plan of salvation and keep in the path that leads them to the presence of God." (Brigham Young, the great Western Colonizer).

"I am so far from believing that any government upon this earth has constitutions and laws that are perfect, that I do not even believe that there is a single revelation among the many God has given to the Church, that is perfect in its fulness. The revelations of God contain correct doctrine and principles, so far as they go; but it is impossible for the poor, weak, low, groveling, sinful inhabitants of the earth to receive a revelation from the Almighty in all its perfection. He has to speak to us in a manner to meet the extent of our capacities." (*Ibid*).

"And no man receiveth a fulness unless he keepeth his commandments. He that keepeth his commandments receiveth truth and light, until he is glorified in truth and knoweth all things." (D. & C. 93-27-28).

God, indeed, gave more in revelations than the mind of man has been able to grasp or comprehend. It is only by humbling oneself before the Almighty in great and mighty prayer that the power and glory of His great teachings are able to find a place in our souls and understandings—and only by deep, true living can we make them a part of our lives.

"And who shall say that Jesus Christ did not do many mighty miracles? And there were many mighty miracles wrought by the hands of the apostles.

"And if there were miracles wrought then, why has God ceased to be a God of miracles and yet be an unchangeable Being? And, behold, I say unto you he changeth not; if so he would cease to be God; and he ceaseth not to be God, and *is a God of miracles*.

"And the reason why he ceaseth to do miracles among the children of men is because that they dwindle in unbelief, and depart from the right way, and know not the God in whom they should trust.

"Behold, I say unto you that whoso believeth in Christ, doubting nothing, whatsoever he shall ask the Father in the name of Christ it shall be granted him; *and the promise is unto all, even unto the ends of the earth.*"

There is no restriction upon the power of God. No human being, or angel has a monopoly upon righteousness, no human being, no matter how poor, how meek, or humble, or weak is restricted. God is not just the God of the mighty, the powerful, the rich, and those in high places. He is the God of the rich or poor, bond or free, great or humble, wise or weak—all who will only turn to Him and received the glorified pattern of their individual lives.

"Seek me early and ye shall find me," this is the invitation to every human being and none will be restricted, from the darkest corner of Africa to the most benighted spot of Russia. Seek Him diligently, at any time, at all times, and you will find Him. And when you find Him there will be no reproach for your past mistakes, no belittling, just the music of the universe rejoicing that another has found his way "home".

Damnation can only come to the one who thinks he possesses all the light and knowledge God has to offer and seals his mind against more truth. For that individual progress is stopped and he is damned; and it is the same whether it is spelled "damned" or "dammed." A dam across a river builds a restraining wall to hold back the tide, the free flow of the waters. Damnation is the same thing—a wall has been constructed by believing too little and sealing the way to more truth and more knowledge. Man's true heritage is to "know *all* truth."

The gift of the Holy Ghost will lead to *All* truth, but when one has reached that point he will also have all power, all love, all goodness and kindness, and will go forth in such humble devotion to do the greater works that none can ever doubt his authority—for it will not be in the words, but in power—and he will become the servant of all, with such compassionate tenderness as he seeks only to lift his fellow men to his level of progress.

If one man can have that contact and that power, any man can have it, for God is no respecter of persons. "He that cometh to me will be accepted." The only way any individual can possibly have a greater claim on the approval of God is by special righteousness, not special "self-righteousness." All that is required of any to make that divine contact is "A contrite Spirit and a broken (or cleft or open) heart," according to the New Testament Apocrypha. This cleft, or open heart makes the meaning much more clear. It means that one needs only unseal himself, cast out his pride, his bigotry, and a super-superior attitude of being God's specially anointed. "Ask and ye shall receive; seek and ye shall find; knock and it shall be opened unto you. For *everyone* that asketh receives; And he who seeks finds; and to him who knocks it shall be opened." "Seek me early and ye shall find me." These promises are for every child of earth. "How often would I have gathered you as a hen gathers her chickens under her wings, but you would not."

Gracious, glorious race of men, know this, "That no prophecy (or promise) is of private interpretation." There is nothing too great for you to ask, or desire, that is for the glory of God and the benefit of man. "Seek ye the best gifts." You can ask anything in His name if you only *believe*, and it will be granted unto you. Then is given the test to see if you believe and if you love Him. "He that loveth me will keep my commandments." Not one of them, *but all of them*—not living by one or two passages of scripture, excluding the others, but "living by EVERY WORD that proceedeth forth from the mouth of God." And His words never end, to those who are in tune to hear His voice. To live the Sermon on the Mount as well as the law of repentance—to love one's neighbors as himself—to love God with all one's heart, soul, mind and strength as well as to attend church, fulfilling all the *spiritual* obligations as well as the secular. The outside of men has conformed to the rites and rituals of the Christian creed, but the inside of man is as unclean today as it was in the days of Christ. Only the pure, perfect, divine Christ-like love and deep humility can possibly fulfill all the laws. In this way only will man become worthy of the greater power—and become so in tune with the infinite that new knowledge will continually unfold until he is led by the Holy Spirit of God into ALL TRUTH—and will be filled with light and comprehend all things. But this condition is every man's right who will fulfill the laws—who will continue to hunger and thirst after righteousness, not high positions,—who will seek diligently—and who will learn to love greatly.

Oh glorious race of men, I thank the great eternal Creator, the Father of us all, my Father, and your Father, that He has let me come to this beautiful world and be a humble traveler with you along the road of light. I rejoice that the humble street-cleaner, or ragged house-keeper, can be as important in His sight as the proudest monarch, yea, even more so, if he is more worthy. I glory in His love that is so perfect and so all enfolding that none can be excluded by the whims of the self-righteous. None are ever excluded from this great and mighty love, except those who exclude themselves and refuse to "cleanse the inside of the cup," remaining in their unclean condition of worldly pride and blindness. For it is truly the inside of man that needs to be cleansed, his way of thinking, his way of feeling, and his way of being. He who will cleanse the inside of himself will as surely find the outside cleansed and made perfect as he will behold the glorious lily unfold from the drab, green bud.

To him who will only seek for this inner purification nothing will be impossible. My soul rejoices continually that there are none so humble that they have been forgotten. None so lost in insignificance they cannot be heard. None so miserable, so destitute, so burdened that they cannot find help and power to surmount any difficulty if they will only ask.

Oh, Lord God, Almighty, I glory in You with every fibre of my being, with every ounce of strength and intelligence I possess. My heart melts in gratitude before Thy great and boundless love—a love that notes the sparrow's fall—a love that reaches into the hearts of men, to heal and bless and forgive—and enfold—a love so great it can cleanse the soul from darkness if it will only discard its pride and open to Your tenderness and compassion. Yea, let thy "Spirit cover the earth even as the waters cover the sea." Let thy most humble ones, from the highways and the byways of earth, be brought to rejoice forever before Thee and partake of the marriage feast. Let the halt and the lame, the poor and the blind, the meek and the lowly come into Thy presence and praise thy Holy Name forever more. Let those who have drunk of the dregs of bitterness find sweetness in Thy forgiving mercy. Yea, let all the earth rejoice! Let the proud and the haughty be humbled that they might learn to find Thee, and to know Thee in their hour of great humiliation and distress. Gather them close and blot out their evil and their proud self-righteousness. Forgive, oh Lord, though they have sealed the doors of light to those who trusted in their strength and followed their vanities, and forgive all who flattered them in their worldly power. Yea, let thy arms be opened wide to all who will only turn to you in their distress, who will only "ask, seek and knock." Yea, let the meek and the humble and those who have truly loved Thee, be exalted forever in Thy sight—and let the reign of all unrighteousness, whether in institutions, businesses, nations or churches be brought to a speedy end. Let unrighteous dominion end forever—and let thy Beloved Son, Jesus Christ be brought to reign, He whose right it is to reign—so be it—Amen.

Chapter X.

THE STOREHOUSE OF ETERNAL KNOWLEDGE

THE MIND of man is a greater power than any machine or instrument conceived by man, for it was the mind of man that conceived the machine or instrument, then brought it forth. When idle thoughts are conquered, or at least all discordant, evil thoughts, when we can turn our attention at will, without wavering, upon any subject and hold it there, we will be able to open the great storehouse of eternal Truth.

Every successful inventor, every scientist who has discovered new facts, every inspired religious leader, every musician who has brought to earth new melodies has tapped this limitless source of eternal knowledge.

One man with a vague, intangible idea in his mind holds to it until it becomes a burning desire that is released into his emotions, and is there conceived. If he permits no doubts to destroy it, it will presently come forth into manifest form, for his life will be concentrated to bring forth his conception from the spiritual realm into tangible reality. After it has been conceived he may work for months, even years, to perfect it and give it a material body to glorify its soul. As he continues with his work his confidence increases, or at least his desire is intensified. His invention may not work, at first, but he has that *inward knowing* that it should—then finally that feeling that it HAS TO WORK! It becomes an obsession pounding continually in his mind. "What is lacking?" "Would this work?" "Would that work?" "How is it to be completed?" "How?" "*How?*" "HOW?" Questions forever seeking answers. Questions knocking, demanding the complete fulfillment of the birth of the mental child within. "Ask and ye shall receive. Seek and ye shall find. Knock and it shall be opened unto you." The last little gadget of perfection is often so elusive—the final touch that gives life and breath to the mental child and stands it upon its feet and makes it live.

If the inventor grows discouraged and gives up, another man will have the honor of fathering his brain child. But if he continues, no matter what the odds, he will receive the answer. It will come, perhaps at a time when he is least expecting it. But it always comes—and when it does, it is usually in a sudden flash of revelation. Through his great patience and greater persistence he has *opened* the storehouse of eternal *knowledge* to benefit a whole world. These brain children that have been born of great thinkers become the property of the human race.

Every invention comes to earth in this manner, every melody, every great truth, every new bit of knowledge. No information has ever been revealed to man without the intense searching of someone who had a mind that could not be silenced. Each truth has been given through the mind of *one* man who was willing to spend days in seeking, years in reaching and months in knocking. With hundreds of minds reaching through to get the keys of atomic power, all searching, all working, all reaching, the spiritual power of earth was placed in the hands of man more speedily by far than if only one man had been reaching—but when it came—the final key of controlling it—it came through the mind of one man—one man who was reaching harder and more earnestly than others.

These men with restless minds, searching for knowledge, who have refused and are refusing to be content with the meager bit of revealed knowledge, are the great benefactors of the human race, and as a rule they have been required to pay the price. First they had to visualize the thing they desired. They had, by the effort of *thinking*, to create the desire. They had to rise above the stupid contentment of passivity to obtain a level of achievement beyond their predecessors. They had to be willing, to some extent, to give up the pleasures of the world, that they might benefit a world; for by separating themselves from the multitudes they were able to pioneer into uncharted fields—alone.

The truth that the world does not seem to possess is the knowledge that EVERY MAN has the power and the right to tap this great source of eternal information—these archives of eternity. "Ask and it shall be given to you; seek and ye shall find; knock and it shall be opened unto you. For *everyone* that asketh receives; and he that seeketh finds; and to him that knocketh it shall be opened." This bit of scripture is not just words. It has been given more times than any other truth revealed to man. It contains more promises than books could possibly reveal. To be understood it must be used. It is a promise without any "IFS". It is a definite promise regardless of goodness, badness, race, color or creed. It stands alone, with only the integrity of God backing it up.

Within each man is stored the energy, if he will use it, to seek, to search, to desire and to reach, until the very heavens open and bestow upon him his requests, for the law of God is that true prayer has to be answered.

If, within the grain of sand, the drop of water, a few drab particles of earth, is stored atomic or spiritual energy—then know that within the soul of man is stored a spiritual power far transcending that of any inanimate, earthly substance.

The mind has three realms, which in a way, could be compared to the three degrees of glory. (I. Cor. 15:39 and II. Cor. 12:2). The lowest, "Telestial," is comparable to the dim light of the stars in glory. It is also the lowest realm of human thought. It is where the failures, the criminals, the outcasts, and degenerates, and the filthy of heart and mind reside. Their thoughts cling to the grubby ashes of existence while they abide in the slums, the prisons, and the dingy places of darkness, for in this kingdom there is not the slightest ray of hope, faith, or light—just accepted failure in all its ugliness.

The next realm is the "Terrestrial," or the one comparable in brilliance to the moon. This is where the honest, the honorable and those who have hope reside. This is the part of one's mind also where worldly achievements are accomplished. Men who are successful in business abide here. This is the realm of all the financial successes, all those who can capably handle worldly materials and affairs. Sometimes this realm is invaded by the greedy and selfish, who are like gangsters, but these will eventually be evicted in shame and disgrace, for this kingdom belongs to those who can live the Golden Rule, who can do to others as they wish to be done by.

The next realm is the "Celestial," comparable to the sun in its glory. It is the spiritual part of one's mind, situated in the very top. It can never be invaded by robbers, for thieves cannot break through or steal. It can only be reached by loving devotion to the Most High God. It belongs to those who truly "love the Lord their God with all their hearts, with all their souls, with all their mind and with all their strength." This love must be genuine, so spontaneous, so beautiful and understanding that it links hands with eternal light and all darkness flees from it.

When we are dwelling on the lower level of our minds, we are receiving all the thoughts of that lower group. In fact, we are associating with them, abiding with them, conversing with them—being one with them. And as we receive their thoughts we also broadcast them on to dull the minds and burden the hearts of all who are already on that failure plane; hence, the great judgment against our idle thoughts if they are of low caliber. Lucifer is continually broadcasting into this realm, for it is his kingdom.

The kingdom we abide in mentally is also influenced by the contributions of our thoughts, and the realm we habitually inhabit in life will be the one we will inherit in eternity. Which is another great reason for the necessity of thoughts belonging to the individual, instead of the individual being the slave of his thoughts. "For that which is filthy shall be filthy still and that which is righteous shall be righteous still," according to the Book of Revelations. This is speaking of the "Hereafter" which means "Here after they are brought forth from their graves." The most perfect translation has this added: "Those who are happy shall be happy still and those who are unhappy shall be unhappy still."

Most people are subject to the "blues" occasionally—but those who take a slump into the lower regions, to wallow in depression, self-pity, self-justification, fear, or cling too long and too hard to sorrows will often find the stairway back up to the higher regions greased and almost insurmountable. They may even have to "pull themselves out by their own boot straps." If they should reside too long in the basements of their minds they might even lose the knowledge of the higher realms. Here again is the necessity of understanding the higher laws and powers of thinking. It might be well also to mention here that self-pity is one of the greatest dissipations of the human race, and one of the most detrimental. It seals the way of progress. Anyone indulging in self-pity has, at least momentarily, lost his place in the regions of light.

The positive promise is: "He who is thankful in all things shall be made glorious, and the things of this earth shall be added unto him a hundred-fold, yea, more." Gratitude is the song of the soul that will lift any individual into joy, and light no matter what his condition is.

Few people in this day and age ever enter the upper story of their beings and view the great spiritual realm of eternal power. It is the kingdom of high devotion, of deep humility, of eternal peace, of perfect poise, boundless love and majesty. To be able to abide in this realm permanently is the ultimate achievement of all success, all power, all joy and all light.

To the worldly-wise it may seem, at a casual glance, most impractical—but since we have already shown the temporary existence of practical things, let's venture into this realm and view the eternal values from this higher vantage point. This is the realm where one locks fingers with the divine. It is the realm where all power, and all knowledge is obtained—this is connected with the super-conscious, which is the divine mind, where one thinks with true thinking, knows with real knowing, and gradually becomes immune from all the ills and distresses of mortal living—where all doubts and fears are conquered— where light increases until one enters the great light of divine thinking—loves with the divine love of pure understanding— and receives the power to accomplish anything to which he sets his hand.

As one learns to hold his place in this kingdom of perfect peace and majesty, he understands fully the Sermon on the Mount. He knows that by seeking first the "Kingdom of God and its righteousness" all other things will be added, as also expressed by Christ in these words: "Labor not for the meat which perisheth, but for that meat which endureth unto everlasting life, which the Son of man shall give unto you." (John 6:27). His love becomes perfected, and thus he has fulfilled all the laws and receives all the blessings. His very ability to love brings the greatest happiness of all. Every man's happiness is measured by his capacity to love. The greater a man's love, the greater his happiness. A man who does not love, or who has not developed the capacity to love, has no real happiness, or capacity for happiness.

If one loves God with all his mind, then EVERY thought, EVERY desire, EVERY aim must be consecrated to God. It is necessary to make one's mind *all* prayer—every breath a melody of devotion—one's heart all love—and one's soul a glorified song of compassion, mercy, understanding, and humility.

It is quite possible that, without thinking too deeply, there will be those who will say, "Why, to keep one's mind *all* prayer would be fanatical." But would it? Christ's mind was all prayer and love and devotion; "Then answered Jesus and said unto them, "Verily, verily, I say unto you, the Son can do nothing of himself, but what he seeth the Father do: for what things soever He doeth, these also doeth the Son likewise. For the Father loveth the Son, and sheweth him all things that himself doeth; and he will show him greater works that ye may marvel." (John 5:19-20). "For I have not spoken of myself; but the Father which sent me, He gave me a commandment, what I should say, and what I should speak. And I know that His commandment is life everlasting; whatsoever I speak therefore, even as the Father said unto me, so I speak." (John 12:49-50). From this, Christ tells that the Father was even going to show him greater works. In that case he would have to be ever alert and ready to receive. He also informs us that every thought he had, and every word he spoke was given him from his Father. And yet, there is no one, either friend or enemy of Christ who would say that he was a fanatic. He was the one perfect man, living the one perfect life. And if we claim to be children of God, then of us it is required to live life even as Christ lived it. "For what things soever He doeth, these also doeth the son likewise."

"I will tell you who the real fanatics are: they are they who adopt false principles and ideas as fact, and try to establish a superstructure upon a false foundation. They are the fanatics; and however ardent and zealous they may be, they may reason or argue on false premises till doomsday, and the result will be false." (Brigham Young, the great American colonizer). This is the best definition of fanaticism that is possible to obtain. A fanatic is also one who glories in his own special passport into heaven and gloats over the fact that all others are to be excluded. Fanatics may also be detected by their spirit and methods. Any breath of intolerance is the vibrating thought of the fanatic. They either endeavor to force their ideas upon others, regardless of the free-will of man or condemn them into eternal damnation. Fanaticism is always cruel, bigoted and condemning without the vestment of compassionate love to cloak its harshness.

As one learns to love truth and light, and goodness, and glory—and God, his love begins to reach out to the race of men with a desire to serve, to bless and to help. He has compassion for the weak and erring sons of men and not condemnation. He wishes, through the great love and devotion of his heart, to lift them to a higher level of progress and existence, even at the sacrifice of himself, if necessary. He learns, also as the great teachers of truth have ever taught: "His mind and lips must lose the power to hurt and wound before his voice can be heard among the Gods."

When one has reached the stage where he can keep his mind a song of glory and devotion and his heart all love, he has the privilege to "ask anything and have it granted." By this time his thoughts are so purified there are no selfish desires left, no selfish motives, no desire for self-aggrandizement, no hate, no discord, no darkness. His whole desire is to magnify God's name upon the earth and to help lift His sons and daughters out of the mud into the light, and he will hold towards all the love "That passeth understanding." This is also the point one reaches where there shall be "no darkness in him—and he shall be filled with light—and *comprehend all things.*"

Thus the great eternal storehouse of knowledge opens its portals and one may gather of all its truths and treasures— not just a final gadget to some invention—not just a phrase of melody—not just one scientific fact—"But all truth!" Of course it would be impossible to use all truth at once—but whatever is necessary for his work and progress in lifting him- self and the world to a higher level will be there for his con- stant satisfaction and glory. It is then that he can step out of the realm of the physical, or revealed knowledge, into, shall we say, fourth dimension? That is, mentally—and he can have whatsoever he asks.

Pioneering is done as far as new lands on earth are con- cerned. There are no new seas to cross, no new continents to explore, no new hemispheres to conquer, but the spiritual pioneering is only starting. This book contains the record of realms beyond the comprehension of man. There are new fields, new, unexplored possibilities for every earnest seeker after true freedom. None are exempt. One needs no emigration quota, no passport. He needs only a strong heart and a soul on which the finger of inspiration has lighted the power of vision. With this equipment he can carve out his future in the realms of the spiritual powers of eternity, hitherto untouched by man, where every great effort is a joy and every achieve- ment an endless glory.

Chapter XI.

"ABIDE IN ME AND I WILL ABIDE IN YOU"

THE FOLLOWING is a chapter of love and mercy and light. If you believe in God the Father and in His Son, Jesus Christ, and in the Holy Ghost, then of necessity you also must believe in the promises of the scripture, for Christ said, "The scripture cannot be broken," and they shall all be fulfilled even to the last "jot" and "tittle," or even to the dot on the "i" and the cross on the "t". When Christ said "The Scripture" in this instance, he was referring to the 82nd Psalm. If the book of the Hebrew songs was so inspired that they were considered scripture, and so sacred that they would stand before God until completely fulfilled, then the words that Christ Himself spoke would be doubly sacred and important.

We understand His teachings of faith, repentance and baptism, and most Christians accept them with all their hearts, thinking they have accepted all his words and instructions, yet the Sermon on the Mount is so often ignored. So very few think that it applies to mortal living, yet that is just where it does apply.

"Then answered Jesus and said unto them, Verily, verily, I say unto you, the son can do nothing of himself, but what he seeth the Father do; for what things soever he doeth, these also doeth the son likewise." (John 5:19).

"I can of mine own self do nothing; as I hear, I judge; and my judgment is just; because I seek not mine own will, but the will of the Father which hath sent me." (John 5:30).

"For I have not spoken of myself; but the Father which sent me, He gave me commandment what I should say, and what I should speak.

"And I know that his commandment is life everlasting; Whatsoever I speak therefore, even as the Father said unto me, so I speak." (John 12:49-50).

The foregoing teachings had been given at various times during Christ's ministry, undoubtedly to prepare them to receive the greatest and last sermon of his mortal life. The following was given after the *Last Supper*, in the remaining minutes he had with his beloved disciples who had stood by him in his ministry. Judas had departed and the eleven were given the most precious, endearing teachings he could impart to them. John, it seems, was the only one who fully grasped these teachings and applied them in his life, and wrote them in his record.

"Believest thou not that I am in the Father, and the Father in me? The words that I speak unto you I speak not of myself; But the Father that dwelleth in me, he doeth the works.

"Believe me that I am in the Father and the Father in me; or else believe me for the very work's sake.

"Verily, verily, I say unto you, He that believeth in me (or believes these things I am now teaching) the works that I do shall he do also; and greater works than these shall he do because I go unto my Father (that if you believe, I will be able to direct you even as my Father has directed me).

"And whatsoever ye shall ask in my name, that will I do, that the Father may be glorified in the Son.

"If ye shall ask anything in my name, I will do it.

"If ye love me and keep my commandments," (or these sayings). (John 14:10-15).

"At THAT *day* ye shall *know* that I am in my Father, and ye in me, and I in you. (At *That* day when you understand and believe these words and apply them literally ye shall *know* the full meaning of these highest teachings).

"He that hath my commandments (teachings) and keepeth them, He it is that loveth me; and he that loveth me shall be loved of my Father, and I will love him, and will manifest myself to him."

"If a man love me he will keep my words: and my Father will love him, and *we will come unto him and make our abode with him."* (John 14:20-21, 23).

These teachings are also verified in Revelations, chapter three, verse twenty: "Behold, I stand at the door and knock;

if any man hear my voice, and open the door, I will come in to him, and will sup with him, and he with me." He stands at the door of every man's soul and knocks, and any man who will only listen, and open the door shall have the privilege of a heavenly guest.

In the undefiled, unmutilated record of Moses, is given an account of this closeness of contact between God and man. It is beautiful and clear. Enoch, the outcast, hated and despised, and of slow, stammering tongue is instructed in the majesty of God and His power: "Behold, my spirit is upon you, where-fore all thy words will I justify; and the mountains shall flee before you, and the rivers turn from their course; and thou shalt abide in me, and I in you, *therefore walk with me.*" The great works which followed in the life of Enoch testify to the truth of Christ's teachings: "And so great was the faith of Enoch, that he led the people of God, and their enemies came to battle against them; and he spake the word of the Lord, and the earth trembled, and the mountains fled, even according to his command; and the rivers of water were turned out of their course; and the roar of the lions was heard out of the wilderness; and all nations feared greatly, so powerful was the word of Enoch, and so great was the power of the language which God had given him." (Moses 6:34 and chapter 7).

"I am the true vine, and my Father is the husbandman.

"Every branch in me that beareth not fruit he taketh away: and every branch that bearest fruit, he purgeth it that it may bring forth more fruit.

"Abide in me, and I in you. As the branch cannot bear fruit of itself, except it abide in the vine, no more can ye, except ye abide in me.

"I am the vine, ye are the branches; He that abideth in me, and I in him, the same bringeth forth much fruit; for without me ye can do nothing.

"If ye abide in me and my words abide in you, ye shall ask what ye will, and it shall be done unto you.

"Herein is my Father glorified, that ye bear much fruit, so shall ye be my disciples." (John 15:1-2, 4-5, 7-8).

Though these are the most important sayings of Christ's

life few have ever given them a thought, or if they have it is with the idea that they are not to be taken literally any more than the Sermon on the Mount is to be taken at its full value. Thousands insist that they believe the Bible, that they believe the teachings of Jesus Christ, yet they deny the true fact of these teachings, or worse still, ignore them completely. These teachings can no more be explained away and ignored than can the Life of the Master. And the command is, "Thou shalt *live by every word* that proceedeth forth from the mouth of God!" "If you love me, you will keep my words." To keep His words means to live by them—or at least to keep them alive in the chambers of "inner knowing" until they are perfectly comprehended. "If any of you lack wisdom, let him ask of God, who giveth to all men liberally, and it shall be given him. But let him ask in faith, nothing wavering . . ." etc.

It is time that those who profess to be Christians, and followers of the Son of God stop running away from issues which they do not comprehend. Every word spoken by Jesus Christ is a direct guide to true living, and no one is living true to the pattern He set unless he lives by every word that proceedeth forth from His mouth. Of course faith is necessary because He taught it, and because without it a life is a vain and useless thing. Of course repentance is necessary—and repentance means a "right-about-face", or a complete changing of one's life. This can only come as one learns to understand the true teachings and turns from the old, dead way of living to the *way of Life*. Repentance does not belong just to the sinner. It belongs just as much to those who have only lived on half-truths and ignored, or denied the full Gospel of Jesus Christ. Of course Christ taught that authority was necessary, but authority in the hands of a man who denies the power thereof, or who cannot use that power is vain. How can anyone claim to believe in Christ and to be a follower of Him, yet deny or ignore anything He taught as a part of the way of life? No wonder the works of Christ are dead—no wonder there are none who have ever done the *greater works* that were promised to those who *believe*. Modern Christianity is a shivering skeleton of dead works clothed with the glorious word "Christianity."

"Or have angels ceased to appear unto the children of men? Or has he withheld the power of the Holy Ghost from them? Or will he, so long as time shall last, or the earth shall stand, or there shall be one man upon the face thereof to be saved?"

"Behold I say unto you, Nay; for it is by faith that miracles are wrought; and it is by faith that angels appear and minister unto men; wherefore, if these things have ceased woe be unto the children of men, for *it is because of unbelief*, AND ALL IS VAIN." (Moroni 6:36-37).

Christ never wasted words. Certainly on the last eve of His mortal existence He was not going to start chattering just to hear himself talk, or to fill in the time. In the last hour of his mortal ministry He was giving the deepest, most loving message of all his teachings—words that hold the glory of majesty and the keys of power to do even *"greater works"* than He had done—the keys to *ask anything and have it granted*—the power to receive the Second Comforter, or the personage of Jesus Christ and the Father to attend one.

After Christ had spent as much time as there was left, trying to give the true understanding of His words, "Abide in me and I will abide in you," he gave this saying, "I have yet many things to tell you, but you cannot hear them now." (John 16:12).

If Christ, of Himself, could do nothing, except the Father which abode in Him, did the works, how can any mere mortal think that any authority will give him the power to do the works of Christ, unless he abides in the vine? Or lives life as Christ lived it? Yea, He must live in direct contact with that "Still small" voice of God centered in his own soul. He must develop his ears to hear, for this source of all-knowing is the "vine".

One thinks with the mind. One feels with the heart. But the center of the soul is situated just a little below the heart, in the center of the body. That is why it is given that we should love God with all our hearts, minds, and souls. When the intelligent desire of the physical mind can unite with the love of the heart and the great power of the soul then can the words of Christ be completely fulfilled; "If you love me you shall have whatsoever ye ask." We are to love with ALL *our hearts,* ALL *our minds, and* ALL *our souls.*

As these forces blend and unite we find that at the center of the soul is a fountain of light. This can only be contacted through that great INNER STILLNESS—"BE STILL *and know that I Am God."*

With this great stillness comes such glory and peace as the outside world can never comprehend. As one learns to abide near this fountain of light, he finds that he will never again thirst or hunger. It is at this source of light, or where the life force of the vine contacts the branch that life and true knowledge comes flowing in. It is here where the seed of faith is planted, and eventually grows into *knowing.* It is from here that all great power is manifest, all works are done—not from the human intellect, but where the vine contacts the branch. This is the point where one comes to the great faith where he knows that nothing is impossible for God is working through him. Gradually, oh, so gradually, it is possible to learn to abide always in this source of joy, majesty, glory and divine light—AND CHRIST IS ITS SOURCE. Thus He abides in us, and we learn to abide in Him, or His eternal source of light until we are filled with light and comprehend all things.

This fountain of light is the fountain of living waters mentioned in John 7 and verse 37: "If any one thirst let him come to me and drink. He who believes in me as the scriptures has said, out of his heart shall flow rivers of living water." Many have interpreted this to mean, "Out of their *mouths* will flow rivers of living waters, or words." With the words must be the power to back up the words—"For my kingdom is not in word, BUT IN POWER." (I Cor. 4:20-21).

As one learns to turn to this source of light and stops depending on his own intelligence and power, the work becomes an everlasting joy of achievement. Quite suddenly the point of high attainment is reached and there are no fears nor darkness left. They are gone completely, banished as the darkness of a room is banished when the lights are turned on. Or as the darkness of the night dissolves when the sun comes forth. "For it is not by measure that God gives the Spirit," but in all its complete power and glory to those who are prepared to receive it. The confusion of a wrangling, dismal world cannot reach him, for confusion and fear are only a lack of light even as darkness is a lack of light. When the soul is filled with light there can be no darkness. He who has learned to *Be still and knows that God is God* has opened the door and Christ no longer needs to stand without knocking, but enters and sups with him, and his inner being becomes a temple and he needs go no more out into darkness and confusion.

When one learns to turn to the great source of divine light within, where the power of God and Christ can contact him, there is nothing that can hurt him, for truly that person is abiding in Christ. "And in THAT day you shall know that I abide in you and you abide in me."

It may take days, weeks, even months of constant work and practice to attain this perpetual state of Celestial light. In quiet moments—in the dusk of evening or the dawn of light learn to become still. It is the point one reaches when he takes his burdens or problems with which he has been heavy laden, to the Lord. "Come unto me, all you who labour and are heavy laden, and I will give you rest. Take my yoke upon you, for my yoke is easy (for it is love) and my burden is LIGHT." This "light" does not mean light in weight, but it is the great light that completely disperses darkness.

Gradually one learns to retire into this stillness of dynamic power in moments during the day—any moment—every moment—then eventually the fountain of light enfolds him and he becomes filled with light and comprehends all things. Then only he is born of the Spirit. He truly becomes one with Christ, seeking only to express the words of Christ, when one no longer speaks his own words, but the words of the Redeemer of man. It is then that life finds its full expression of meaning and it is as though the Christ were living the life of the individual and the individual were living the life of the Messiah, because they have become one in purpose—and that purpose is to diffuse light.

That is the point where we truly become one with Him—then it is that we truly "love Him and keep His words." (John 14:23).

Then it is that we realize that He is the vine and we the branches—that of ourselves we can do nothing, but He does His great and mighty works in and through us. This is the power by which miracles are wrought, and no man can perform any miracle unless he is cleansed from *all* sin, all bigotry, all pride, all self-seeking, and as a humble believer in the power of God, acknowledges that God does the works.

It is when we have contacted this great source of light and power that we appreciate more fully the great glory of God being manifest in every seed, bulb, flower and tree—the power of life, growth and perfect•expression. Within the seed is all the desire and fulfilling reach of perfection to draw upon the eternal forces of light and energy to bring forth and express the gorgeous blossom that is enfolded within the seed. The seed conceals the satin petal, the vivid colors and the perfume of the flower. The dark bulb holds eternal secrets—the acorn majesty. Such is the expression of God moving in eternal power and everlasting life. If within the seed, the bulb, the acorn, the breath of God whispers and lights the flame of desire and fulfillment, then surely within the soul of man lies potential powers to complete the march of godhood and fulfill the perfection of the Celestial children of God our Father—not just the power of completing our drab mortality—but the sublime power of glory and light and perfect achievement.

It is then that we *know* that "FAITH PROMISES ALL THINGS, AND THAT IT PERFECTS ALL THINGS." We know that within the branches (which are us) are the tiny buds of divine aspirations. We cannot produce them nor bring them forth, for of ourselves we can do nothing, but as we reach into the Divine source of light centered in our souls, or the vine, which is Christ, the buds of our desires, which are always God's desires, will blossom and ripen into a glorious harvest of fulfillment. We then shall do even the *"greater works"* because He went to His Father, from whence He can direct this great source of power into our souls whenever we are open to receive.

"Ye have heard how I said unto you, I go away and come again unto you. If ye loved me, ye would rejoice because I said, I go unto my Father." (John 14:28).

When a branch of a peach tree produces an especially large, luscious peach, no one ever goes to that branch and brags on it, saying, "My, how marvelous you are. What a wonderful bit of work you did in producing such a magnificent peach." Not a bit of it. Nor does the branch expect such praise. Behind the branch is the tree, and behind the tree is the husbandman, the soil, the elements—besides men glory in the fruit rather than in the branch. Yet every man who achieves anything wants all the praise and all the glory. When we learn to walk in true humility then we will find the door to His Holy Spirit wide open.

Exercising faith means contacting that divine power of light. Faith is not just dead, inactive believing. It is divine energy set in action by the mind. Faith *is* Spirit. "It is the substance of things hoped for—the evidence of things not seen." It is the life-giving seed out of which all tangible things materialize.

From the Autobiography of Parley P. Pratt, page 294, is given the following: "Brother Joseph, while in the spirit, rebuked the Elders who would continue to lay hands on the sick from day to day without the power to heal. Said he: 'It is time that such things end. LET THE ELDERS EITHER OBTAIN THE POWER OF GOD TO HEAL THE SICK, OR LET THEM CEASE TO MINISTER THE FORMS WITHOUT THE POWER.'

Yea, let all men cease to administer the forms of Christianity without the power to do the works that Christ did— "For these signs are to follow those who believe: in *my* NAME they shall cast out devils: they shall speak with new tongues, (or the divine tongues of angels).

"They shall take up serpents, and if they drink any deadly thing it shall not hurt them; they shall lay hands on the sick and they shall recover." . . .Etc. (Mark 16:15-18). They shall have the power to move mountains and do even greater works if they will learn to believe in the NAME OF JESUS CHRIST, and understand and fulfill the meaning of that name.

CHAPTER XII.

THE POWER AND MAJESTY OF ALMIGHTY GOD

Everything on earth is moving forward at such a rapid pace man himself has been left far behind. New ideas, new facts, new power, new knowledge is flooding upon the world faster than man can use it—and unless he begins to grow, in some degree, to measure up to his surroundings he will be annihilated.

Of all things on the earth Christianity alone has stood still. Oh, it may be true that each church is making a few more converts, that there are children reaching an age in which they may become members—but what are the creeds and doctrines of the Master doing for these millions of individuals? "Have they become free?" Have they lost their burdens, their fears, their prejudices, their darkness and confusion? Have they found that contact whereby they can prove that they believe in Jesus Christ, by being able to do the works that He did, even the *greater works*? If they do not have this power, if they are not free from all earthly miseries, if they cannot heal the sick, the blind, the lame, the halt, then Christianity is a dead and useless thing in the lives of its followers. At best it is only a rather impotent sedative.

True Christianity, and by that, I mean the applied teachings of the Son of the Living God, in every phase, in every "jot" and in every "tittle," is the most dynamic power ever placed in man's hands. It is the perfect way of life. It contains power unspeakable. It is life in its complete fullness. It is joy and glory and happiness complete. It is an obedience that is not a burden, but a devotion of sublime glory leading one to the highest exaltation of existence—a life right here on this earth of supreme peace and abiding power. It is majesty that will lead to divinity, and give man the power to move mountains, not figuratively, but literally. It alone can save the world—

not as it is being taught and lived today—but as Christ lived it.

It is time that His teachings came out of the musty covers of the past and become a living, vital reality of the present. Mankind is worn out with listening to what the prophets of old said and did—or even what the Apostles of Christ did, or the Saints, or their own forefathers, though these accounts are of value in giving one a view of his own possibilities. Man must be shown just what this same force and power can do for him —how it can change his life—solve his problems—speak through his lips—burn in his heart—work through his hands. Man must know that what has been done once can be done again—that he is as much a child of God as any other human being who has ever lived upon this earth. He must begin to visualize what he can do, for man's ears are truly dull of hearing the word of the Lord, without seeing its powers made manifest. "For the kingdom of God is not in word, but in power." "Let the elders either obtain the power of God to heal the sick, or let them cease to minister the forms without the power."

This power does not come from man, no matter what his calling or authority. The power to work the works of God comes only through the power of God, or when man has become so humble he has completely submerged himself and permits the power of God to operate through him. If Christ, who was the Son of God, could do nothing of himself, then surely man cannot take upon himself any authority or power. He can only use that power, which belongs to God, as he is humble enough to contact God, thus letting God work through him.

In order to even begin to get the vision of this dynamic power of the Almighty it will be necessary to view briefly some of the evidence at hand concerning the Almighty Creator of heaven and earth—and all things that in them are. To place all the available scripture on the subject into this work would be impossible. Therefore I shall only make a list of the most important passages at the end of this chapter—and to him who truly desires to know All Truth—to know the only true and living God, and Jesus Christ whom he has sent, I would advise a thorough study of the references given—to pray earnestly to understand them with an open and unsealed mind. Truth and understanding can never penetrate a sealed mind. Neither can light penetrate it—and only earnest prayer, prayer that is an acknowledgement of not knowing, like the mind of a little child, can have power to unseal a mind that is already set.

There are verses upon verses which declare God to be omni-present, omnipotent and omniscient, or filling all time and space, being all-powerful, all-knowing, all-glorious and so breathtakingly dynamic in His power and scope that the mind of man must continually expand to even begin to comprehend Him. The divine records of scripture give a vision of such majesty, such breathtaking glory, such supreme, incomprehensible, all-existing power that man stands lost in contemplation, and completely overwhelmed by His *awe-full-ness.*

The word "fear" which has been handed down from the old English was more closely related to the word "awe" than the word "afraid." In the old Anglo-Saxon, from which the word fear came, meant "awe-inspiring," "breathtaking," "over-whelming." Thus, the command to *fear* the Lord did not mean to be afraid of Him, but rather to seek to begin to comprehend His unspeakable majesty and to share in his power—or in other words, "seek to know God."

In the record of the creation of the world we get a glimpse of this power—there is vision, knowing, the confidence of the true architect, the talents of the artist, and the tender love of the Creator. These gifts and powers blend with the master words of, "Let there be!" "And it was so!"

We can see Him upon Mount Sinai as the whole mountain quakes with the flaming majesty of His nearness, bursting into burning glory at His presence. We can stand silently awed as we view the Red Sea divided. We can hold our breath as we walk between its walls of water. Yea, we can walk down the hallways of the ages and know that His very fingers engraved the archives of the universe—that His plans, or thoughts, became a world—that His breath brought life—that His love fulfilled all existence.

We can hear His voice demand, "Am I a God at hand, saith

the Lord, and not a God afar off? Can any hide himself in secret places that I shall not see? Saith the Lord. Do not I fill heaven and earth? Saith the Lord." (Jer. 23:23-24).

With David we can sing:

"Oh Lord, thou hast searched me, and known me.

"Thou knowest my downsitting and mine uprising, thou understandest my thought afar off.

"Thou compassest my path and my lying down, and art acquainted with all my ways.

"For there is not a word in my tongue, but, lo, O Lord, thou knowest it altogether.

"Thou hast beset me behind and before, and laid thine hand upon me.

"Such knowledge is too wonderful for me; it is high, I cannot attain unto it.

"Whither shall I go from thy spirit? or whither shall I flee from thy presence?

"If I ascend up into heaven, thou art there: if I make my bed in hell, behold, thou art there.

"If I take the wings of the morning, and dwell in the uttermost parts of the sea;

"Even there shall thy hand lead me, and thy right hand shall hold me.

"If I say, Surely the darkness shall cover me; even the night shall be light about me.

"Yea, the darkness hideth not from thee; but the night shineth as the day: the darkness and the light are both alike to thee.

"For thou hast possessed my reins: thou hast covered me in my mother's womb.

"I will praise thee; for I am fearfully and wonderfully made: marvellous are thy works; and that my soul knoweth right well.

"My substance was not hid from thee, when I was made in secret, and curiously wrought in the lowest parts of the earth.

"Thine eyes did see my substance, yet being unperfect; and in thy book all my members were. written, which in continuance were fashioned, when as yet there was none of them.

"How precious also are thy thoughts unto me, O God! how great is the sum of them!

"If I should count them, they are more in number than the sand: when I awake, I am still with thee." (Psalms 139:1-18).

We can lend our listening ear of attention and hear Him say, "One Lord, one faith, one baptism, one God and Father of us all, WHO IS ABOVE ALL AND THROUGH ALL AND IN ALL." (Eph. 4:6).

We can hear the challenge: "And what agreement hath the temple of God with idols? For ye are the temples of the Living God; and God hath said, *I will dwell in them, and walk in them; and I will be their God, and they shall be my people.*" (I. Cor. 3:16-17 and II. Cor. 6:16).

We hear the unmistakable invitation ringing down the years: "Seek me early and ye shall find me." Or "Seek me diligently and ye shall find me." "For in him we live and move and have our being." (Acts 17:28).

We hear the tender words of promise, "Draw near unto me and I will draw near unto you." "If you will abide in me, I will abide in you."

Then we contemplate the very name "Jehovah" and again stand awed by the marvel and the wonder of it. Many times before God appeared unto Moses, He had announced Himself to the various patriarchs of old in such words as: "I am God." "I am the Almighty." "Behold, I am the Lord Thy God." etc. Then to Moses He gave the greatest, most dynamic, superb introduction of all.

"And the angel of the Lord appeared unto him in a flame of fire out of the midst of a bush; and he looked, and behold, the bush burned with fire and was not consumed.

"And Moses said, I will now turn aside and see this great sight, why the bush is not burnt.

"And when the Lord saw that he turned to see, God called unto him out of the midst of the bush, and said, Moses, Moses, and he said, Here am I.

"And He said, draw not nigh hither: put off thy shoes from off thy feet, for the place whereon thou standest is holy ground.

"Moreover he said, I am the God of thy father, the God of

Abraham, the God of Isaac, and the God of Jacob. *And Moses hid His face; for he was afraid to* LOOK *upon God.*" (Ex. 3:2-6).

"And Moses said unto God, who am I, that I should go unto Pharaoh, and that I should bring forth the children of Israel out of Egypt.

"And he said, Certainly I will be with thee; and this shall be a token unto thee, that I have sent thee: When thou hast brought forth the people out of Egypt, ye shall serve GOD UPON THIS MOUNTAIN.

"And Moses said unto God, Behold when I come unto the children of Israel, and shall say unto them, the God of your fathers hath sent me unto you; and they shall say to me, what is his name? What shall I say unto them?

"And God said unto Moses, I AM THAT I AM: and he said, thus shalt thou say unto the children of Israel, I AM hath sent me unto you.

"And God said moreover unto Moses, thus shalt thou say unto the children of Israel, the Lord God of your fathers, the God of Abraham, the God of Isaac, and the God of Jacob, hath sent me unto you: *this is my name forever, and this is my memorial unto all generations.*" (Ex. 3:11-15).

"And God spoke unto Moses and said unto him, I AM THE LORD; and I appeared unto Abraham and unto Isaac, and unto Jacob, by the name of God Almighty, but by my name *Jehovah* was I not known to them." (Ex. 6:2-3).

"Jehovah" is the Greek rendition of the Hebrew word "Yehveh" or "Ehyeh" which signifies "I AM."

This name "*I Am*" the Israelites regarded as an ineffable name, not to be spoken; they substituted for it the sacred, though to them the not forbidden name, Adonai, signifying the Lord.

Yet when God spoke to Moses out of the burning bush, proclaiming himself to be "I AM THAT I AM" he said "This is my name for ever, and this is my memorial unto all generations."

In other words, any one from then on throughout all generations of time who used the simple phrase, "I am" would be bearing witness of God, for no man could possibly exist unless God existed. If any man should humbly declare, "I am a street-cleaner," "I am a farmer," "I am a doctor," "I am a king" he would be bearing witness to his own existence and being, hence to the existence of the Creator also. These words *"I am"* bear witness to the very fact of life, which is of God. It is the very testimony of being, or existing. And as man proclaims "I am . . ." he is also bearing testimony of his own relationship to God, and God's relationship to him.

Such is the testimony of God in every man's being—the testimony of life.

There are many passages of scripture that identify God as being all power, all light, all existence, filling heaven and earth. There are many more that make Him into a personal Being who can appear and talk with His children face to face. These seemingly conflicting descriptions need not be upsetting. The mind of man is far superior to anything he has ever invented. Man is so much greater than any of the mechanical marvels of this atomic age that there is no way to compare his supreme superiority—only man doesn't realize it. God does. God knows what He is. He uses His powers with complete and perfect understanding and full knowledge. Thus we see a God of mighty, unspeakable power—a God who is truly omnipresent, omnipotent, and omniscient— a God who knows and comprehends all things, who is everywhere present, and who is all power, operating through His Holy Spirit, touching all things, filled with wisdom and love unspeakable. If then, in direct contrast, according to man's way of thinking, we see a God who sits upon a throne, surrounded by myriads of angels, far away, and very much occupied by heavenly matters, not having time to be concerned with the affairs of men, then it is because man has lost the vision of God—not God of man. And there is no conflict in these descriptions except in man's power to comprehend. Because man is restricted and does not in any way understand what vast powers he has within himself—he tries to judge God according to his own restricted powers. Man is truly traveling in almost the "worm consciousness" of his potential powers. This restriction is not something that God has placed upon man, but something that man has placed upon himself—and accordingly has also placed upon God. If we would cease trying to judge everything by the standards of our own mortal concept, and turn to the Spirit within, we could begin to *comprehend* even God, "For the Spirit itself beareth witness with our spirit that we are the children of God."

It is utterly impossible for one person to reveal God to another. Only God can do that. No books can reveal Him. They can only bear witness of His existence. But it is up to each individual to find Him through his own efforts, his own searching, his own seeking and knocking. When God said, "Seek me diligently and ye shall find me," He did not mean that we would have to travel out to some far distant sphere, and some far-off time, to reach out into the immensity of space. No. God meant for us to begin to search for Him from the very point in which we are standing, and right now. Therefore it is a search of the spirit and has to be carried on in our own hearts and souls, lighted by an ever increasing flame of desire, that we might "Know Thee, the only true and living God, and Jesus Christ whom Thou hast sent—for this is life eternal."

Then in John is given the information that the Spirit will lead us to Christ, and that Christ will reveal the Father to us. Therefore the first step necessary in the search is to begin to prepare ourselves to be worthy to be directed by the Spirit of God, to understand its functions and its power. This search for God cannot begin out in space, but must begin right within man.

"The earth rolls upon her wings, and the sun giveth his light by day, and the moon giveth her light by night, and the stars also give their light, as they roll upon their wings in their glory, in the midst of the power of God.

"Unto what shall I liken these kingdoms, that ye may understand?

"Behold, all these are kingdoms, and any man who hath seen any of the least of these *hath seen God moving in his majesty and power.*

"I say unto you, he hath seen *him*: nevertheless, he who came unto his own was not comprehended.

"The light shineth in darkness, and the darkness comprehendeth it not; *Nevertheless, the day shall come when you shall* COMPREHEND EVEN GOD, being quickened in him and by him.

"Then shall ye know that ye have seen me, that I am, and that I am the true light that is in you, and that you are in me, otherwise ye could not abound." So we must seek to know Him through that light that is within our own selves.

The above scripture also informs us that if we have beheld any of the wonders of heaven, the planets, the stars, the marvels of creation, earth, and nature, we HAVE seen God moving in His majesty and power—but in order to KNOW we will have to "COMPREHEND" Him. Therefore it will have to be our Spiritual understandings that will have to expand, and our spiritual vision begin to contemplate and comprehend, rather than just our mere physical eyes and minds beholding.

This is verified in the following: ". . . That inasmuch as you strip yourselves from jealousies and fears, and humble yourselves before me, for ye are not sufficiently humble, the veil shall be rent and you shall see me and know that I am—not with the carnal neither natural *mind*, but with the spiritual.

"For no man has seen God at any time in the flesh, except quickened by the Spirit of God.

"Neither can any natural man abide the *presence* of God, neither after the carnal mind.

"Ye are not able to abide the presence of God now, neither the ministering of Angels, wherefore, continue in patience until ye are perfected." (D. & C. 67:11-13).

From this we learn that it is only possible to "comprehend" God after we have completely purified ourselves with a perfect cleansing that casts out fears, jealousies and all pride, along with all human weaknesses, for the natural man means one with all his human traits of blindness and bigotry, pride and confusion, worries and darkness still upon him. "Carnal mind" means one who thinks entirely upon the earthly plane or the physical, material realm. Therefore it is quite necessary that one lift his vision to begin to embrace the spiritual conception of existence. After this complete purification the promise is given that the veil will be rent and then man, being "quick-ened" or "spiritualized" by his higher concept of thought, in tune with the Holy Spirit, will be able to see God, but not with his physical or natural mind and eyes, but with the full *knowing* of his whole being, with his whole soul, and with every little ounce of his intelligence. It will be a complete, all-inclusive comprehension of positive KNOWING God—and *"In that day* you shall *know* that *I am* in my Father, and you in me, and I in you."

The complete purification is necessary before one can receive the "fullness of the Father" else he would be utterly consumed by the profound glory filling his being, for no natural, or unpurified man could possibly abide the presence of God, or comprehend Him.

And the light which is the force back of all creation and all existing things "is the same light which shineth, which giveth you light. It is the same light that enlighteneth your eyes, which is the same light that quickeneth your understandings:

"Which light proceedeth forth *from the presence of God* to fill the immensity of space.

"The light which is IN all things, which giveth Life to all things, which is the law by which all things are governed, EVEN THE POWER OF GOD, WHO SITTETH UPON HIS THRONE, WHO IS IN THE BOSOM OF ETERNITY, WHO IS IN THE MIDST OF ALL THINGS." (D. & C. 88:6-13). This great light mentioned above is explained in these words: "He that ascendeth up on high, as also he descended below all things, in that he *comprehended* all things, that he might be IN AND THROUGH ALL THINGS, THE LIGHT OF TRUTH. Which truth shineth. THIS IS THE LIGHT OF CHRIST. As also he is in the sun, and the light of the sun, and the power thereof by which it was made"—and the stars, and the earth upon which you stand—etc.

"*He comprehendeth all things, and all things are before him, and all things are round about him: and he is above all things and in all things, and through all things, and is round about all things: and all things are by him, and OF HIM, even God, forever and ever.*" (Ibid., verse 41).

Now, to even begin to comprehend this great force of light,

which is called the Spirit of Christ, or the power of God, who sitteth upon his throne in the bosom of eternity, it will be necessary to consider the cosmic ray, which is known as "Nature's Mightiest Force."

"As long as the world has existed, the tiny charged particles called cosmic rays from outer space have been hurtling through its atmosphere and driving deep into its rocky crust. As long as there have been men on the earth their bodies have been pierced 20 times a second by these infinitely minute bits of matter." Yet it has only been within the last forty years that scientists have been aware of this force. It has become the most arduous branch of modern physics. It has led scientists to the equator and to the poles, to the highest mountains, and into the deep caverns of the earth. Scientists stand overwhelmed before this endless source of power and boundless energy—but none know its source, nor its purpose. Some have even designated it as the "death cry of the universe."

Calling the boundless energy of the cosmic rays "The death cry of the universe" is the most untrue statement that could be made about it. It is the very pulse-beat of the universe. It is the force of light and life, sent out, shall we say, from the throne of God, who is in the very bosom of eternity. This force is life eternal, renewing the soil, giving growth to plants, vigor to a world and is the quickening force in the soul of man. It is boundless, everlasting energy. It is activity in its unceasing release of breathing, living, majestic power.

This great cosmic energy is light—"And light is Spirit—even the Spirit of Jesus Christ." From some great central sun, in the very bosom or center of eternity, far above our little sun, this power pours out over the entire universe. It might be called the life force of all existence, of worlds and plants and men.

These little charged particles of cosmic rays are more or less broken up as they hit the atmosphere of the earth. For this reason we do not receive the full force of the bombardment of this gigantic force, or "The Mightiest Force of the Universe." If this great power was withheld for one second only, there would be instantaneous death and disintegration of all composed things. Or, in other words, there would be one grand atomic explosion of the entire earth that would probably rock our whole galaxy, for as the light or power of this cosmic force would be withdrawn, every particle of this earth and everything on it would be drawn instantly back into that great source of power from which it was originally composed.

These cosmic rays are broken up in their shattering collision with the atoms of the earth's atmosphere, creating secondary particles in much the same way as a ledge can be shattered and broken up by a heavy bombardment of shells. This bombardment of the cosmic rays against the atmosphere is known as nature's most gigantic cyclotron, or atom smasher.

At the present time scientists are interested in cosmic rays only for the purpose of studying the component parts of an atom and what holds it together. In searching from this angle they are putting the cart before the horse, yet it will lead them onward to new truth. They will soon know that the cohesive power of the entire universe is an intangible element, called LOVE—and that all things are composed, fundamentally, of energy, which is light—and light is *Spirit*.

It is the earth's atmosphere which is the great retarder of the full force of the cosmic ray. If it were not for the thick, almost impenetrable veil of atmosphere which stands as a wall of innumerable atoms, the force and power of these rays would be stupendous. Perhaps the removal of this veil of atmosphere can best be described by John the Beloved, in Revelations 6:14: "And the heaven departed as a scroll when it is rolled together; and every mountain and island were moved out of their place." This is a most interesting bit of scripture, telling of the time when the earth's atmosphere, that holds back the cosmic rays from reaching us in their full power, will probably be rolled back. Then the great force of these rays will come full and direct from the throne of God, without any withholding veil. In other words, "The veil will be rent." The very shock of this complete bombardment of life and light will be death to the wicked. It will be so great that every mountain and every island will be moved out of their place. It will reveal fully, and completely the knowledge and power of God, and the following scripture will be fulfilled, "For the earth shall be full of the knowledge of the Lord, as the waters cover the sea."

The results of this removal of the veil when it is rolled together as a scroll will bring the following results: "Behold the day of the Lord cometh, cruel both with wrath and fierce anger, to lay the land desolate: and he shall destroy the sinners thereof out of it.

"For the stars of heaven and the constellations thereof shall not give their light: the sun shall be darkened in his going forth, and the moon shall not cause her light to shine. (The above is verified in Isa. 24:23; Joel 2:10; and 3:15; Matt. 24:29; Mark 13:24; Luke 23:45; Rev. 6:12 and D. & C. Sec. 29:14; 34:9; 45:42; 88:87 and 133:49).

"And I will punish the world for their evil, and the wicked for their iniquity; and I will cause the arrogance of the proud to cease, and will lay low the haughtiness of the terrible.

"I will make a man more precious than fine gold; even a man than the golden wedge of Ophir.

"Therefore I will shake the heavens, and the earth shall remove out of her place, in the wrath of the Lord of hosts, and in the day of his fierce anger." (Isa. 13:9-13).

The next reaction will be not a period of darkness, but one of blinding light described as follows: "And there shall be upon every high mountain, and upon every high hill, rivers and streams of water in the day of the great slaughter, when the towers fall.

"Moreover the light of the moon shall be as the light of the sun, and the light of the sun shall be sevenfold, as the light of seven days, in the day that the Lord bindeth up the breach of his people and healeth the stroke of their wound." (Isa. 30:25-26).

From the foregoing it is easy to understand what will cause the great earthquake that has been predicted by the prophets of the Lord—an earthquake so great that every mountain will be lowered, every wall fall, the islands and the continents thrown back together as "they were in the beginning." It is also easy to comprehend how great cities shall sink into the sea. Always the moon has a tremendous pull upon the sea, and during full moon tides surge up as though the ocean itself were being pulled out of its bed. This same pull is felt upon the land, except it is not so apparent because of the density of the hemispheres. But if the moon became as bright as the sun, then no land could remain unshaken, no sea undisturbed, no wall stand. The very continents would be shaken as a piece of cloth, and the sea would be hurled or pulled up over the edges of the land in waves so high all the great cities would be submerged, for all great cities are built upon rivers, lakes or seas. Then if the sun is to be sevenfold brighter than seven days that would make it forty-nine times brighter than an ordinary day. No wonder the wicked shall lift up their voices and curse God and die—and five out of every six of all the Heathens that gather down to Jerusalem with the Russians to battle will die on the battlefield—for it will take God to conquer the Russians.

The foregoing contains an account of the things that are to come when the Lord shall arise to make bare His holy arm— and to show forth His power to save a world from utter destruction. The great shock to the earth when the full impact of the dynamic force of the cosmic ray, and cosmic means great, when the great light is released in its fullness over the earth the wicked will die. To those who learn to know God and to understand His righteousness will be given the power to escape such utter destruction as shall be poured out without measure upon a world that is bent on destruction—either self-destruction, or destruction by the wrath of the Almighty because of their great wickedness.

If this gives a picture of a terrifying, unjust God that is not intended. He will have to intervene in this manner to save the world, for it will be the very exploding of men's bombs that will cause the earth to be flung out of its course and to rend its atmosphere. At the time when all men would be utterly destroyed, if God did not intervene, He will step in to save the world He created with such infinite love. He will have to step in to save those who have not failed in seeking, in some measure to fulfill at least the laws of the Golden Rule. But for those who have fulfilled the higher laws of loving the Lord their God with all their hearts, souls, and minds, the experience need hold no dismay.

"And ye shall eat in plenty, and be satisfied, and praise the name of the Lord your God, that hath dealt wondrously with you and my people shall never be ashamed.

"And ye shall know that I am in the midst of Israel, and that I am the Lord your God, and none else: and my people shall never be ashamed.

"And it shall come to pass afterward, that I will pour out my spirit upon all flesh; and your sons and your daughters shall prophesy, your old men shall dream dreams, and your young men shall see visions:

"And also upon the servants and upon the handmaidens in those days will I pour out my spirit.

"And I will shew wonders in the heavens and in the earth, blood, and fire, and pillars of smoke. (The bombings).

"The sun shall be turned into darkness, and the moon into blood, before the great and the terrible day of the Lord come.

"*And it shall come to pass, that whosoever shall call on the name of the Lord shall be delivered.*" (Joel 2:26-32).

This promise of any individual who is upon the earth during this great destruction, who will only call upon the name of God, will be saved. This is verified in Acts 2:21 and Romans 10:13.

Afterward will come the great peace that men have been giving their lives for, for over two generations. "And many nations shall come, and say, Come, and let us go up to the mountain of the Lord, and to the house of the God of Jacob; and he will teach us of his ways, and we will walk in his paths—and he will judge among many people, and rebuke strong nations afar off; and they shall beat their swords into plowshares, and their spears into pruninghooks; and nation shall not lift up sword against nation, neither shall they learn war any more." (Micah 4:2-3). This scripture is also verified in Isaiah chapter 11, and in the last three chapters of Revelations.

This great day is at our doors—the great day of God

Almighty—when the armies of Russia move down toward Iran and into the valley just north of Jerusalem, the valley of Jehoshaphat know that the rest will soon follow. Know that soon the great and mighty Spirit of God shall cover the earth in its complete fullness of power, with no restraining barrier of outer atmosphere to hold out its full power and force.

This boundless flow of released energy of cosmic rays would indeed be the "death cry of the universe," if it were only being poured out upon the universe without any returning of the energy or power dispersed. But the process of breathing is drawing in the breath of life and then again dispelling it. This is also the process of the cosmic rays. It is a circulating, inhaling, exhaling process of the eternal energy of life. It might also be compared to the circulatory system of the human body—the eternal gathering of the blood back to its source to be purified, and then the pumping of it through the body again. This is life, never ending, eternal. So is the life-giving energy flowing back continually to the great central source from which it comes. It sends out, but it gathers back. Every prayer offered—every ounce of effort spent in achieving some worthy accomplishment—every melody released—every vibration of love from a human heart—every sacrifice—every spark of courage ever exerted—every thunder storm, every howling wind, every wrung-out tear—every anguished pain is gathering energy and releasing it back again into the eternal source of life. Yes, from the suffering altars of mankind energy is being returned. The price of every birth is paid in released anguish and pain. Scientists have not yet become aware of this returning, ever flowing, unceasing circulation of eternal energy, nor of the great powers contained in the righteous desires of a human heart.

In the beginning, this whole glorious force of light, life and energy, through which and by which the worlds are, and were created, was called "Christ," which means "anointed with light." It was *the Word*. And that WORD was the light and life of worlds, and of men—it became flesh—and is the essence of true light—the light of God. Thus it is definitely true, "That in Him we live and move and have our being." And "That by

Him, and through Him we consist" or "abound", or in other
words, exist. And thus it is, that we are not only made by Him,
but we are made OF HIM, as the scriptures testify, for we are
made, fundamentally, or, are composed of this very light force
—this eternal energy—this source of all life. We are immersed in it. We are composed of it, but are without comprehension of it. It is "The light that shineth in darkness and the
darkness comprehendeth it not." We do not any more comprehend it than the fish comprehends the water.

This light is also known by the title of the Holy Spirit of
God. And as we become aware of it, knowing that it not only
surrounds, but is also in and through us, we can draw it to
us with increased power and intelligence. When we cease to
ignore it as a rejected factor in our lives, it will become a
source of divine power within us. We can bathe in its light
and be refreshed, not just the outside of our bodies, but every
little cell and particle of our beings can be renewed by it.
When we begin to contact it with our consciousness we can be
in instant connection with the mind and will of the Almighty
God. We will feel His power flowing through us. When we
learn to love and reverence this Holy Spirit its love will enfold
us completely and no evil will be able to touch us.

"And to know the love of Christ, which passeth knowledge,
that ye might be filled with the fullness of God." (Eph.
3:19).

There is a record from India that describes the Holy Spirit
of God as the "Whole I Spirit of God." As we receive of this
complete gift of glory and light we no longer absorb or use
just enough of this cosmic light to barely sustain life and
keep us going; we can, through opening our understandings,
contact it in its fullness, this "Whole I Spirit" which fills all
space, contacts all knowledge, and is perfect, divine Christ-
like love, and light, for in its realms time and space do not
exist. "It is everywhere present." Through this glorious me-
dium of Spirit man can keep in direct contact with God—and
the very light and power and intelligence of God can abide in
him. He can become one with it. And gradually as he purifies
himself and gathers this source of loving, enfolding light to

him, he will be able to fully comprehend even God, "Being quickened in Him and by Him."

The Holy Spirit of God is the most sacred gift that can be fully bestowed upon man, for in its fullness is contained all light—"And if your eye be single to my glory, your whole bodies shall be filled with light, and there shall be no darkness in you; and that body which is filled with light comprehendeth all things (even God).

"Therefore, sanctify yourselves, that your minds become single to God, and the days will come that you shall see him; for he will unveil his face unto you, and it shall be in his own time, and in his own way, and according to his own will.

"Remember the great and last promise which I have made unto you; cast away your idle thoughts and your excess of laughter far from you." (D. & C. 88:67-69).

The Holy Spirit of God contains all that the soul of man could possibly desire—wisdom, light, life abundant and eternal, understanding, peace, joy, happiness and plenty—for all things will be added to the one who is fully possessed of it. It is love so gentle and enfolding there can be no discord, fears or confusion. It is the full perfection of life and power. It has always been with us, surrounding us, knocking on the door of our intellects, seeking admission, but we have never opened our minds to receive it. "Behold, I stand at the door and knock, and if any hear my voice, and open the door, I will come in and feast with him, and he with me." "It is the Spirit that enlighteneth every man that cometh into the world." It enlightens each man according to the heed and diligence and reverence he gives to it. It is known as the great and glorious gift of the Holy Ghost only when one has opened his mind and heart, through deep desire and perfect love, and true obedience, to receive it in its fullness. Then he receives all that it can bestow.

Most people are inspired occasionally. Some reach at times, a high pinnacle of inspiration—and then again they are left to themselves, in darkness. This is caused because of lack of understanding of the laws of the Spirit. This Holy Spirit is pure beyond any substance that man can possibly conceive. It is pure light—it is the very essence of perfect love—it is the divine power of Almighty God—it is tenderness, compassion and mercy, therefore any discord, any selfishness or greed, any bigotry or pride, any boasting or boisterousness, any uncontrolled thought or word of jealousy or anger will shut it out from our consciousness—and thus the benefits are eliminated from our bodies and they begin to sag, to wither and grow old—and die—and we drag through life, groping blindly along wondering what is wrong.

With full and complete understanding this need never be, this lack of the Spirit of God in our lives. This great and Holy Spirit is always around us, filling all space, enfolding us in its divine love, seeking to find admission into our consciousness—for that is truly the only place from which it is excluded. "Draw near unto me, and I will draw near unto you." It is a condition of awareness. As we become more conscious or aware of it we gradually begin to feel the force of this great spiritual power, and to comprehend the glory of it. This is done by keeping every thought high, every breath a song of glorious praise and devotion, every thought a melody. This will banish darkness and we will be able to bask continually in the blessings of the Holy Spirit of God and to rejoice in Its power and light. It will prepare our hearts and minds to receive the full revelation of Jesus Christ—and eventually He will reveal the Father to us, and we will comprehend even God. Thus our progress to divinity is an orderly procedure based entirely upon our desires to know and comprehend. All power, both in heaven and on earth can become ours to use, if we will only believe, then follow that belief to its complete fulfillment.

It should no longer be an incomprehensible thing to "comprehend" even God. In fact, it should not be difficult at all to begin to understand, since man has invented the radio and television. One person can broadcast, and the thunder of his words go out instantly to encompass the earth. Any instrument that is tuned in can pick up his words, share in his song, feel the very vibrations of his thoughts. And now it is possible to behold his face. If man can bring forth these wonders, under the inspiration of God, these wonders we are already beginning to take "for granted," surely God, who comprehends all things, who is so much mightier than man, and so divinely perfect in the full awareness of ALL His powers can accomplish as much.

It is assuredly possible that God can guide the universe and yet be aware of the sparrow's fall. It has been said that all things belong to Him. I think it could best be expressed that He belongs to all things—to the sparrow, for he created it and gave it life—to the world he formed—to man made in His own image and likeness, with all His attributes. He belongs to all things with such tender, infinite love, such longing and patience that all suffering could be instantly healed if only proud man would permit it, and stop trying to rule all things in his human blindness. God, through the Spirit of His power can instantly contact all space. He can hear the whisper of a child, the cry of the widow, the prayer of the righteous and help to guide the destinies of men, for Spirit fills all space— and in it there is no space, nor time—it is everywhere present, in complete, instantaneous contact with itself, from the throne of God to the very farthest realm of the universe. No World has ever been created by Him and forgotten—no man can ever completely withdraw from Him. Yet with all this boundless, unending love and power, God never tries to force himself upon any man. It is always, "Draw near unto me, and I will draw near unto you." "Seek me early and ye shall find me."

God never forces Himself upon any child of His. Nevertheless there is a standing invitation to, "Come unto me and I will give you rest." And the words, "How often would I have gathered you as a hen gathers her chickens under her wings, and ye would not." "Seek me and ye shall find me, for every one who seeks finds." "Ask and ye shall receive knowledge and wisdom, and love and truth and power, or anything that becomes a burning desire in your heart." "Knock and the doors of the kingdom of heaven shall be opened unto you." "For everyone that asks receives, and he who seeks finds, and to him who knocks it shall be opened. Or what man is there of you, whom if his son ask bread, will he give him a stone? Or if he ask a fish, will he give him a serpent? If ye then, being evil, know how to give good gifts unto your children, how much more shall your Father which is in heaven give good things to them that ask him?" Added to this is, "If any of you lack wisdom, let him ask of God, who giveth to *all* men liberally, and up-braideth not, and it shall be given him. But let him ask in faith, nothing wavering, for he that wavereth is like a wave of the sea, driven by the wind and tossed."

"Yea, he yearns Jealously over the Spirit which He made to dwell in us." (James 4:5-6 Original Greek).

Thus as we learn to "ask in the Spirit," or release our desires into this great Spirit substance, we are fulfilling the law and the desire of God, and are asking according to His will, and the law is that it will have to be fulfilled.

Each individual who has learned to love God, will also *know* and feel that divine love of the Father enfold him. He will know of a protection, a security, a peace and a power that nothing else on earth can give. And for each individual who seeks God diligently there will come the time of great *knowing*—for the eternal law of God is that earnest, continued prayer *has to be answered*. The continued asking will purify the soul and prepare it to receive whatsoever it asks. Yea, anyone who knocks, and continues to knock, at the door or veil of God's inner sanctuary, or Celestial kingdom, shall have that door or veil opened. This is the promise of the Almighty to every child of earth—"FOR EVERYONE WHO ASKS RECEIVES." Then when God has at last been found, and one *knows* Him, he finds to his unspeakable, breathtaking wonder that man him-self is a part of the very glory and power of the Almighty. He then steps forth to fill his place in the power of God, and nothing is impossible.

God cannot be monopolized. He belongs equally to every child of earth. No man, or group can possibly have a monopoly upon God. He belongs to every man who will seek diligently to find Him. He will answer the cry of any man who will ask for help, for wisdom, knowledge and understanding—yea, He will continue to pour out knowledge upon any seeker after Truth until the very storehouse of knowledge is opened wide and that man will be filled with light and comprehend all things—that man who will only believe, who will ask, who will knock and who will seek.

And the time has arrived when mankind will no longer accept teachers who teach only with words, who try to fill the road that leads to God with their own personalities. These men will be shoved aside, for they are neither entering in themselves, or permitting others to enter. Every man has the right and the power to find God, to be directed by Him, to walk with Him, to know His mind and will—for God belongs to every man. He cannot be monopolized, though down the ages thousands and thousands of souls have been sacrificed by those who have professed to have such a sacred monopoly.

The whole works of man have been backwards, each trying to convert, instruct, and purify or perfect everyone else—without first purifying himself. The work of God must first be perfected within each man before he can have the power or vision to assist in saving his brother. After he has removed the beam of imperfection from his own being then truly he will see clearly and have the full power to remove the moat from his brother's vision so that he too can see the light. And light and direct contact with God is the direct heritage of every man—and no man has the right to try to lead others, who does not have the power of that contact—"For the kingdom of God is not in word, *but in power*"—power to do the works of God, to heal the sick, open the eyes of the blind, cause the deaf to hear, the lame to walk—to do all the works that Christ did— even *greater works*. Seek for God—and *find Him* and that power will be yours. He stands waiting to bestow it upon you, when your soul is humble, when your heart and mind is completely purified, "for no man can perform a miracle in the name of Jesus Christ until he is purified and cleansed from all sin." To such nothing is impossible.

God Himself is *all* power, *all* love and *all* light. When you find Him you too will share in these great gifts for you too will be like Him, "For all that the Father has is yours." You already have access to all this unspeakable power. Everything that the Father has is already yours—use it. "Know the Truth and the Truth will make you free" from every darkness and every lack.

Thus God stands in His great and mighty majesty, in His humble, tender love, in His infinite compassion and patience waiting for you to turn to Him so that you can receive literally all that He has and become like Him, compassionate, loving, humble, merciful and at last be clothed in the full light of knowing and majestic power. These great blessings can only be glory to you as you ask for them, as you seek for them and as you desire them. Any gift that is not desired is not appreciated, brings no joy and is considered as a thing of naught. In order to use His gifts they must be understood, appreciated and desired with a great and holy reverence.

Stand for a moment above the tumult of the day and feel the great, all-knowing love of God enfold you. It is not necessary to try to reach Him by long-distance cablegram, or through some saint or symbol. Man has lost the contact because of such methods. They have placed God out somewhere in infinity, on some far distant, unreachable sphere some x-rillion miles away, then try to reach Him. Cease trying to send your prayers across eternity through the strength of your intellect. Instead, "Be still" and whisper softly into the little microphone right within your own heart. Speak your words softly, firmly as you speak to your own subconscious mind when wishing to impress something upon it that must be remembered —then *believe*. Open your soul to feel His great love pour into your being, every fibre and tissue of it. Bask in that love, and in His all-knowing as His power and forces are permitted to become active in your life—then watch your own desires be fulfilled as you continue to praise and give thanks, glorifying Him with every breath and every thought. Christ tried so hard to teach that God belonged to all—to you—to His own followers, to everyone, showing plainly that even He did not have a monopoly upon the favors or power of the Father, for He so often said, "To my God and your God"—"To my Father and to your Father." This is as true today as it was then, for no matter how battered and beaten you are, how terrible your mistakes have been, how blundering your way, how rebellious your mind, how dull your understanding—He is still your Father—and the moment you turn to Him, He will turn to you—to gather you close—and the heavens will rejoice and the very angels sing.

Thus this great and mighty God, this heavenly Father of ours, whose power reaches to the endless boundaries of space, Who loves with a love beyond the understanding of men, Who is all-powerful, all-knowing becomes a very personal God to every man who diligently seeks Him—even as He was the personal God of Abraham, and the God of Isaac, and the God of Jacob—so is He my God, and your God. The very reverence and diligence exerted in learning softly to use one's own little broadcasting and receiving set, the very developing of the tenderness of the heart in fulfilling its true function, will automatically purify anyone who begins to use it. "And Christ commanded the multitude that they should cease to pray, and also his disciples. And he commanded them that *they should not cease to pray in their hearts.*"

Yea, "seek me diligently and ye shall find me." "Diligently" according to the dictionary means, "steady application, industrious, persevering; prosecuted with care and constant effort." "Seek me early and ye shall find me," means to seek Him always upon arising, before your day is started—"Be still" then whisper gently into your little "speaker" your needs for the day, give thanks always to Him for having heard you, for He does always hear you when you speak thus—and soon you will *know* "That *I am*, God." As you pray thus you will soon learn to let go, with your physical mind, of the worries and the fears, and will let Him work out a day of glory for you—thus you learn to walk with Him.

In Acts 17:26-28, Paul gives us this information: "And hath made of one blood all nations of men to dwell on the face of the earth, and hath determined the times before appointed, and the bounds of their habitation.

"That they should seek the Lord, if haply they might *feel* after him, and find him though HE BE NOT FAR FROM ANY ONE OF US:

"FOR IN HIM WE LIVE, AND MOVE AND HAVE OUR BEING."

In the original Greek it does not say "feel after him," but definitely "FEEL HIM." Thus the knowledge of God comes first as a "feeling", which can be expanded into positive knowledge and "You shall *know* God." Yea, "Be still and know that I am, God."

"Him that cometh to me, I will in no wise cast out," said Christ, no matter how lowly, how sinful, how poor or miserable. There are none who will ever be rebuked who turn with all their hearts to Him. None will be condemned. "If any of you lack wisdom, let him ask of God, who giveth to all men liberally and upbraideth not." Here is the perfect pattern. First must be the *"asking"*—it doesn't necessarily have to be for wisdom. It can be for the sincere desire of your heart, whatever it is. It can be only to heal the desolate longing in your soul—a relief from pain, sorrow, poverty, stupidity or any human weakness. Then is that promise that will stand forever and forever, that if you will ask, He will never rebuke, condemn nor turn from you. It is so much easier to reach Him than any earthly dignitary, pontiff, governor or ruler.

Oh come, all ye ends of the earth, and He will gather you tenderly under the protecting love of His wings, even as a hen gathers her chickens, that you might be shielded and protected from the great storms that are gathering over the face of the whole earth.

"And the Spirit and the bride say, Come. And let him that heareth say, Come. And let him that is athirst come. And whosoever will, let him take of the waters of life freely." (Rev. 22:17).

NOTES:

Below are listed most of the references that proclaim God to be the divine, great All in All of mighty light and power as taken from the Bible.

Jer. 23:23-24; Eph. 4-6; John 15:4, 5, 7 and 10 and D. & C. 50:43-45 to those who have access to it. Then in Gal. 2:20; Phil 4:4-7 & 9; I. Cor. 3:16-17; II. Cor. 6:16; John 4:22-24; Acts 17:27-28; John 1:1-13; Colossians 1:12-17; I. John 3:1-3; I. John 4:15-18; and John 4:14.

Now are given the references that proclaim Him a personal being who appeared to various men on the earth: Genesis, where Adam is given minute instructions upon various occasions, then the record of how he hid himself after he had transgressed—etc. See II. Peter 3:8; Gen. 5:22, 24; Gen. 12:1 and 7; Gen. 13; 14-17; Gen. Chapter 17; Genesis 32:30; Genesis 35:9-13; Ex. chapter 3 to fourteen contain a record of direct contact between God and Moses. Ex. 24:9-17; Ex. 33:9-11 and 18-20; Mark 14:62; Luke 22:69; Heb. 1:1; Acts 7:48-60; Col. 3:1; Rev. 1:13-15; and Eph. 3:10.

Now, for those who have access to the marvelous record known as the Doctrine and Covenants, I shall list the following for prayerful consideration: Sec. 63:23; Sec. 67:10-13; Sec. 88:6-13; also verses 40-41, 45-50, 67-69; Sec. 93:1-37; Sec. 84:44-47; Sec. 76:24-25; Sec. 19:16; and Sec. 76:14.

CHAPTER XIII.

THE POWER OF TRANSMUTATION

"HE WHO IS *thankful in all things* shall be made glorious; and the things of this earth shall be added unto him, even an hundred-fold, yea, more." (D. & C. 78:19).

The chemists of old were men of great courage and of deep spiritual understanding. As their souls searched for light beyond the gloom and the orthodox dogma of the dark ages they were given knowledge and understanding. Had they endeavored to reveal the great truths they had discovered in their courageous searchings, they would have paid for those truths with their lives. They knew also that the world was not ready at that time for the knowledge they had been given through years of prayerful searching. Such truth and power as had come to them was far too sacred to be placed before the profane men with greedy minds who could use it for destruction. These alchemists, true to the trust placed upon them guarded their discoveries so well that the records of the alchemists of old leave only a hint of the power they possessed.

Roger Bacon, who was one of the very foremost alchemists, was completely rejected, and branded as a heretic or one in league with the devil by those in authority of the church at that time. He had desired knowledge for the sole purpose of benefiting the world—because of the blindness of the leaders his works were never released to the world. All his books, his precious works of a life-time of research were taken out and publicly burned.

The one bit of knowledge that has survived the ravages of time and the mockery of the cynic is the information that these alchemists had the ability to transmute lead into gold. The alchemists themselves made no great boast of such an achievement, claiming only that it was the ability to transmute dross elements or conditions, into a higher spiritual quality.

136

The secrets of the alchemists, because of a world in darkness, were guarded carefully, yet a few notes have come down to the present day to give an idea of the vision they held. The figure of the transmutation of the base metals into gold symbolized the salvation of man—the transmutation of his own soul into spiritual gold, which condition was to be obtained by the elimination of all evil and the development of the good, by the grace of God. It was a symbolism of salvation or spiritual transmutation which may be described as the NEW Birth, or that condition of being known as "union with the Divine."

It was definitely known that each man had to find the secrets for himself, though Christ so clearly marked the way: "Seek ye first the kingdom of God and its *righteousness*, and all else shall be added unto you." (Including one's temporal needs). "Labor not for the things that perish." etc.

The true law of alchemy is this: Every condition in life can be transmuted into glory and made divinely beautiful, no matter what that condition is. If we accept it, bless it, thank God for it, or be *"Thankful in all things,"* we can transmute the grubby, bitter, heartbreaking experiences and conditions of life by this most perfect and exacting law of science, which is chemistry, into spiritual loveliness, we receive also the power to transmute our spiritual desires and dreams into tangible, material manifestation.

So it is that gold can be transmuted from lead, beauty from ugliness, joy from sorrow, light from darkness. These never failing laws of chemistry *are* HIS RIGHTEOUSNESS or His perfect laws in use. "A man is saved no faster than he gains knowledge." As his knowledge and understanding increase, he is saved from every dark, contentious, destructive, gloomy condition of the earthly, material level of existence.

This law of chemistry never fails. Or should we call it "alchemy," which means "all chemistry"? "All Chemistry" includes the spiritual laws of change and transmutation as well as the material laws and elements. This "all chemistry" is the power of God in action. It is the most exacting, positive science. Certain procedures always bring the same exact results. The laws of chemistry are eternal, unchanging. Since existence began, and on until eternities upon eternities end, H_2O will continue to be the formula which produces water. Every formula that has been tried and proven to be true at one time, has always been true, and will always be true.

The laws of "all chemistry," which include also the spiritual substance and elements, are just as exacting and just as positive in their results as the combination of H_2O which includes two substances which can not be handled nor seen, yet combined produce a positive, tangible element which is most necessary to existence. Thus the laws of the spiritual chemistry of all existence is just as exactingly perfect as any chemical laws used in a laboratory constructed and equipped by man. It is the eternal law of God being put to use to transmute any condition, any element, any loneliness, any heart-break, any suffering or tragedy.

As one applies the law of "all chemistry," the road of life becomes a highway of light, and in his soul is an eternal song of ecstasy that never dies. The fountain of light enfolds him with its melody of gracious glory and there can be no more sorrow or distress in his life.

As one first begins to apply the laws of divine chemistry, he will find a joy such as life never before held. This ecstasy of soul will become permanently his when he learns to hold his place in the realms of light—or to hold his complete awareness of the Spirit of God, and keep himself in tune with it. This is at first difficult. It requires a constant check on one's attention, one's thoughts and an intense holding of one's desires upon the very highest goal of existence and perfection. One has to learn to use constantly the most delicately refined radio in all existence—the spiritual contact in his own soul—the divine microphone in his own heart until he has "ears to hear" —and "eyes to see." It is such a heavenly, breathtaking joy to be in the kingdom of higher thought or spiritual vibration, and such a lost feeling of darkness to withdraw from it, especially after one has once contacted it. Each time one finds his way back into the realms of light, the more tangible and real it becomes, and the haunting memories that linger in the heart when left to himself make one feel that the darkness is intensified. Again and again one may enter and depart before it becomes possible for him to understand completely and receive the fullness of the light, and Spirit of God. But there is one thing that is eternally certain, and that is, that the light of His righteousness is always there for us to enjoy, or the power by which we can rightly use His light. We withdraw from the light by errors of one sort or another, by our lack of humility, our selfishness or anything that may grieve the Spirit of the Lord, for it cannot endure even the appearance of sin—and Sin is any thought, word, act or vibration that one sends forth that is out of tune with the heavenly laws of peace, love and light. As we learn to hold to light we soon discover that it dispels darkness. Love destroys hate and discord and fear. Peace banishes confusion. Thus as we learn to draw to us the light all evil is conquered.

The law of chemistry works speedily and completely. There are no half-way measures or guessing needed. The laws of "all chemistry" are just as positive, and as one turns his thoughts to God, he will instantly feel that light enfolding him, changing the conditions around him. It is a dangerous thing to climb into the realms of light and then forsake them. The new element of spirituality that has touched the hem of one's robe with the fingers of light may be the very element that can intensify the darkness and confusion if one rejects it.

The law of "all chemistry" or "Spiritual chemistry" is for the noble, those with deep desires and far vision. It is for those who wish to overcome all things that they might rise above all things. It is for those who love the Lord and their fellow men. But it is also for those who have not yet developed the gift of love, those who have not yet stepped foot upon the road of light, for it will bring strength and power to any who will hold with determined hands to the course. It will develop vision in the eyes that have not seen, courage in the heart that has seemingly failed, hope in the breast of the hopeless, power in the soul of the weak. Light and glory was meant for every child of earth, thus as one distils the evils of life, the sorrows and the tears, with a prayer, with a whispered, loving message into the little radio set adding to it a song of praise and glory the great transmutation of sordid conditions into joy and peace begins to take place.

It is a glorious experience to learn that the kingdom of light, peace, glory and achievement is always there, waiting for us to step into it and take our place in the realms of light. It is just as possible to receive of these higher blessings as it is to receive any degree in college, and so much more satisfactory. When we learn to know and understand the divine power that is being manifest every day in our lives, when we learn to appreciate it, and work with it, then we will know also that the great gifts and powers Christ is waiting so anxiously to bestow upon us, become instantly ours. Then it is that we learn the power of the words, "Be still, and know that I am God." And "Behold, I stand at the door and knock, and if any man will hear my voice and will open the door, I will come in and sup with him, and he with me." "We will take up our abode with him." "These are my choice gifts (health, happiness, joy, peace, plenty and power not only to rule on this earth, but power to reach out into eternity) that I am so anxious to bestow upon my children as soon as they are prepared to receive them."

So are His words, and so is the power of fulfillment locked within each mortal man who desires to apply the laws of "spiritual chemistry" and in humble prayer turn the keys of the universe and open the realms of light.

This power of light is what people are unconsciously, and without full understanding, asking for, when they repeat the Lord's Prayer. "*Thy Kingdom come,* Thy will be done on earth as it is in heaven." After one finds this kingdom he brings it back to earth with him, or brings it forth from the inner realm of Spirit to be made manifest in all the outer conditions of his life, and forever thereafter he abides in it, and God's will is done in and through him even as it was through Jesus Christ.

This law of "spiritual chemistry" is the law of transmuting all conditions, all vibrations, all darkness into beauty and music and light. One must learn to speak the language of the angels, or "speak with new tongues." He must learn to speak from the soul and never from the lips, or even from the mind.

He who speaks from the lips chatters. He who speaks from an empty mind adds confusion to discord. He who speaks from a full mind feeds the minds of men. He who speaks from his heart wins the confidence of mankind. But he who speaks from his soul heals the heartbreaks of a world and feeds the hungry, starving souls of men. He can dry the tears of anguish and pain. He can bring light, for he will carry light.

The language of the soul is a sacred language, and most beautiful. It can never hurt or injure. It can only bring a benediction of glory, for it is the language of the eternal spheres and the language of Gods. It is the gift of the Spirit known as "new tongues."

"Do you not remember that I said unto you that after ye had received the Holy Ghost ye could speak with the tongue of angels? And now, how could ye speak with the tongue of angels save it were by the Holy Ghost? Angels speak by the power of the Holy Ghost." (2 Nephi 32:2).

The world is filled with dull speakers who weary the minds, hearts and souls of their listeners. It is also filled with those who pour out their worldly wisdom to glorify themselves. But how few there are who have even a small crumb of spiritual food, distilled in their own souls, and then sent forth to feed the starving souls of men. Learn to know the language of your speakers and you will know whom to trust, and who is sent of God, for everyone who is sent forth by the power of God upon him will speak with the voice of angels—the language of the angels is the language of the soul, and is given through the gift and power of the Holy Ghost. This language has long since been lost and forgotten except by a few on this earth. It is a language of compassion, of love so tender, so merciful, so healing it will help to heal a world and enfold it in light. It is a language also that can go forth as a flame of fire to rebuke those who resist the light of God, but this must never be used except under the definite command of God, and then the power of love must be increased ten-fold as it is used. Learn to speak no word except it comes from the depth of your soul. The power of God goes with this language. It is never wasted.

As one truly learns to speak the language of the angels, he

finds he can also walk and talk with God, and he can hold
his place in the realms of light. He casts out all fear and
darkness from his soul. He learns the majestic power of learning to pray for those who injure him. He knows that lip
prayers have no meaning, and he prays for his enemies from
the depths of his soul, and the love that passeth understanding
fills his being. Thus any condition of discord, hate, confusion
or misunderstanding can be transmuted into peace. Thus one's
life becomes a melody of eternal praise, glory and devotion.
Every breath becomes a song, for "If any man offend not in
word, the same is a perfect man, and able also to bridle the
whole body."

Men, for years, have rebelled at and resented the idea of
being "wage slaves." The knights of the road testify of this
rebellion. The thousands upon thousands of men who struggle
with their daily labors in a weariness of soul too deep to express, shout their protests louder by their beaten despondency
than words could ever convey. They are truly slaves, beaten
slaves of drudgery. As the keys of understanding are placed
in their grasp and they begin to use them, lifting their heads
to a higher vision, with thankfulness to God, becoming truly
"Thankful in all things," the soul will awake in song and the
shackles drop away. They need no longer be slaves. They are
masters. Masters over the elements they handle. Masters over
their work, and as they continue they will soon be lifted into
a higher service, and the things of this earth will be added
unto them, yea a hundred-fold, and more.

With the language of the angels and the keys of transmutation one travels the highway of eternal life. It is the power
and the kingdom in which the greatness of God can come
again into a life—a church—a world.

As each day unfolds we have the power to gather it into our
arms, to bless it, to glorify God for letting us live it, instead
of permitting it to live us, as is so often the case. Then with
blessing the day we seal it with glory and send it forth to
glorify God forever. Then when evening gathers her silver
shadows, we can send the day on into eternity a glorified light
because our lives touched it, our souls caressed it, and because

we lived it. This is our power, to transmute each day to the glory of God—so shall every condition of our lives be transmuted into glory and we shall become the children of light.

When the mind can be turned into a shock absorber, or a transforming center, and we can take every thought and transmute it into beauty and love for the Lord, so that every condition can be blessed, and every discordant word and thought can be turned into light, then man is ready for the greater things. This great power of transmutation in its fullness is ours only when we have learned to abide in the light of the Spirit of God.

"For behold, God hath said a man being evil cannot do that which is good; for if he offereth a gift, or prayeth unto God, except he shall do it with real intent it profiteth him nothing.

"And likewise also is it counted evil unto a man, if he shall pray and not with real intent of heart; yea, and it profiteth him nothing, for God receiveth none such." Moroni 7:6 & 9.

The power of transmutation is the power to contact the center of the soul, through the heart. This method alone holds the power of fulfilment and of perfection. It is the point of conception and of fulfilment.

CHAPTER XIV.

THE SUBSTANCE OF ETERNAL ELEMENTS

SINCE the tangible things we hold to so desperately are only shadows that will not last, or vibrations, as science classifies them, let us take another step.

In this world, or stage of existence, we live by symbols. We use either written symbols or sound symbols to express every thought or feeling, or to identify every person, place or object. Words are only symbols. Names are only symbols. Our alphabet is only a host of small symbols that can be organized into words—then words into sentences—sentences into thoughts —and thoughts into knowledge. God claims the title of the "A" and the "Z" of the alphabet, or the "Alpha and Omega" which includes all the other letters in between and can express or contain all knowledge.

Symbols only represent the things for which they stand, not the reality itself. Money is considered the most important factor in life by many because it represents power and security. Of itself, money has no value whatsoever, though through it, it is possible to purchase the comforts and luxuries of earth. Some have forgotten the true meaning behind the symbol, the blessing of plenty as a gift of God, and they worship the symbol instead. Thus the idol has become the god as it receives the tribute of adulation. Even grubby, wicked, ignorant, mediocre people who possess it are extolled and catered to by the ignorant, envying masses as they swagger through life holding aloft their symbol of self-importance and vulgar ostentation.

These symbols of earth grow daily less important under the searching eye of science, and we learn that all materials, all substance, all solids, all existing objects and things are only vibrations of light expressed on a material, or perhaps symbolical plane. There is as much difference between the symbol and the reality as there is between the letters of the alphabet

144

and the great thoughts that can be woven into tangible form through those tiny little letters. Thus we have clung to our nursery blocks as the symbols of existence, instead of stepping into the realm of reality.

In the next stage of existence we may no longer use symbols but deal in the actual, eternal substance of vibration itself. The vibration of light and love will be the eternal elements of our existence—and back of all vibration is the force of thought or intelligence that created the vibration originally.

When we arrive at the point where we will no longer be dealing in symbols but in eternal substance of thought and vibrations, each individual will be measured, not by what he has, or even by what he knows, or who he is, but by WHAT HE IS. He will find that he is the personification of all the thoughts and vibrations he created and sent forth in life.

Vibrations, even on this plane, play a much larger part in our lives than science has at the present time been able to weigh or measure. Evil, discordant thoughts are known positively to produce high blood pressure, to cause strokes and even death. Hate generated in an individual can bring all manner of illnesses and can most assuredly destroy life in time. Some people have dug their graves with their tongues, or their hateful, evil moods, nagging habits, uncontrolled evil thoughts of discord, jealousy, malice, self-pity or discontent. Individuals who permit moods of evil thoughts to rule them invariably develop physical handicaps and diseases, or at least old age and ugliness of features and expression. Asthma, heart ailments, liver troubles, cancer or any other physical discomfort can and have been developed by uncontrolled tempers and tongues. Hence Christ's continual admonition to those whom He healed, "Go thy way and sin no more lest a worse thing befall thee."

Unkind, domineering individuals, devoid of love or understanding carry their burdens with them, and their load is indeed heavy.

Happy, joyous thoughts send a rhythmic current of singing health vibrations surging through one in the same manner, and automatically keep the physical being in balance, for the physical body, if seen in its true spiritual or scientific sense, is vibration or Spirit. "For man is spirit. The elements are eternal, and spirit and element, inseparably connected, receive a fullness of joy. The elements are the tabernacle of God: yea, man is the tabernacle of God, even temples; and whatsoever temple is defiled, God shall destroy that temple." (D. & C. 93:33-35).

Cement can be poured into any shape desired, stone can be chiseled, but man has to be formed, slowly, thought by thought, word by word, act by act. Thus man himself is the *book of life*, for within him is engraved the complete record of all his thinking and his doings—and he is the record and he is also the recorder.

Vibration is the eternal, actual substance of existence. Those who have created continual vibrations of evil and discord by their thinking and speaking habits will automatically inherit kingdoms of lower vibrations of darkness unless they turn to the light and begin to live in it and use it for their own transformation and advancement. Always behind the vibration is the power of the thought that released or created the vibration. Hence the great necessity of understanding and using the dynamic force of creation intelligently, that is stored in our minds and souls, for we are no more or less than the thoughts we hold and the vibrations we send out into the universe.

These are the things Christ was endeavoring to teach when He displayed the great gifts He was so anxious to bestow upon the inhabitants of the earth as soon as they were prepared to receive them; health, happiness, wealth, prosperity and not only power to rule conditions on this earth but power to reach out into the universe and assist in the realms of glory and dominion.

The smallest, loving child with its heart filled with trust will be far more important than the greatest scholar, scientist, artist, inventor or ruler who greedily clutches to himself personal glory at the sacrifice of others, who is selfish or unkind, distributing only vibrations of discord. Thus the admonition to worship "God with all one's might, mind and soul and to love one's neighbor as oneself," and "to forgive one's enemies."

These contain the keys of glory and dominion and light and life and reach beyond earth into the spiritual realm of vibration, holding the very power of reality and creation.

It is human nature to desire everyone else to be perfect, while we love our own faults, or closing our eyes to them, walk a road of bigoted self-righteousness. This is human nature. But human nature can be conquered and glorified, as symbolized in the sphinx of Egypt. This ancient symbol has stood since the early ages of the world's history, signifying that the intelligence of man can rule over his animal instincts and passions—and crowned with the ancient headdress of divinity survive and surmount all things, rising above the storms, triumphant forever. No earthly symbol can possibly hold more meaning than that message eternal, rising above the sands of time as a witness of the power within man.

It is our right and our privilege and within our power to rise above the low, mortal vibrations of earthly, animal instincts and transgressions with their confusion and discord if we are to inherit all that the Father has for us, which includes health, happiness, peace, joy, progress, achievement and glory. This does not mean just in eternity. It means *here* and *now,* above the sands of time, yet in our earthly sphere.

Self-righteousness is always wickedness. It is critical. It is bigoted. It is unChristlike. It is cruel. And surely it has no place in the highest realms of thought. To feel self-righteous one has to feel superior to his fellow men. He has to mentally place himself as a judge over them, and view with condemning attitude their weaknesses.

This accusing business is very dangerous. In Revelations 12:10 we are given this startling bit of information: "And I heard a loud voice in heaven saying, "Now is come the salvation, and the power, and the kingdom of God, and the authority of his Anointed One because that accuser of our brethren, who accused them before our God day and night has been cast out." Thus we learn that Lucifer, or the devil was cast out of heaven because he saw no good in his brethren, even in heaven, but saw only their weaknesses. After a while he became all the evil he beheld in others and was cast out of the heavenly realms to the earth.

From the pure Greek original record we find that the word devil is translated or means accuser.

"Then the Jesus was led into the desert by the Spirit, to be tempted by the accuser.

"Then takes him the accuser into the Holy City.

"Again takes him the accuser into a mountain high—

". . . Lord the God of thee thou shalt worship, and to him only thou shalt render service. Then leaves him the accuser." (Matt. 4:1, 5, 8, 10 and 11).

"Go from me the having been accursed into the fire age-lasting that having been prepared to the accuser and to the messengers of him."

Then in Luke the fourteenth chapter, verses 2, 3, 5, 6, 8, 13 also use the word accuser instead of devil.

"Those by the path are those hearing; then comes the accuser, and takes away the word from the heart of them." (Luke 8:12).

"Jesus answered them, did I not choose you, the Twelve, and one of you is an accuser?" or devil. (John 6:70).

"You are from your father, the accuser (or judger), and the lusts of your father you wish to do. He was a man-slayer from the beginning and has not stood in TRUTH. Because there is no truth in him." (John 8:44).

If within our hearts or minds there is the power to accuse, condemn, or judge or belittle our fellowmen then are we also accusers and will as surely lose the way of divine light and mercy as Lucifer did. If we express our criticizing thoughts in words then our fault is double.

Then there are those who will cheat their fellowmen to obtain money so they can make a big show before God, that they might give Him great donations, and take high seats in the congregations. This is mockery. "For behold, God hath said a man being evil cannot do that which is good; for if he offereth a gift, or prayeth unto God, except he shall do it with real intent it profiteth him nothing." (Moroni 7:6). There are also those who preach fine sermons but who never live up to them. There are those who will work their hired men like slaves through the Sabbath that they themselves may be free to attend church and worship on the front seats. Such things are a double mockery before God and most certainly not acceptable unto Him.

The devotions of the most humble illiterate, meek, poorly individual plugging out his life in the factory or the fields is a greater glory to God than all the self-righteous offerings of those who bask in their superior importance.

To be truly the greatest, one must be the servant of all—not in self-righteous actions, but in love, in mercy, in compassion and tenderness of soul and meekness of heart. One must truly be "his brother's keeper," with a love that is far above "self." "He that is ordained of God and sent forth, the same is appointed to be the greatest, notwithstanding he is the least and the servant of all.

"Wherefore, he is possessor of all things; for all things are subject unto him, both in heaven and on the earth, the life and the light, the Spirit and the power, sent forth by the will of the Father through Jesus Christ, his Son.

"But no man is possessor of all things except he be purified and cleansed from all sin.

"And if ye are purified and cleansed from all sin, ye shall ask whatsoever you will in the name of Jesus and it shall be done." (D. & C. 50:26-29). Only such as have fulfilled these laws and received these powers can possibly consider themselves great—and after they have received them they will feel themselves to be the least, and become most humble.

Below are listed a few of the unwritten laws that should be understood in order to perfect the earth and create vibrations that will glorify a world. They have never been written because no city, state or country has ever lived by them excepting the city of Enoch that was so perfect it was taken from the earth. Only by applying the higher laws can man hope to escape the reaping of the discord, the greed, the selfishness and wickedness that has been planted on the earth. These deeper, unwritten laws must begin to find a place in our way of life—the laws of the fullness of the Gospel of Jesus Christ, not as they are taught—but as He lived them.

There are those who know just how to live the lives of others, their children, their parents, their brothers and sisters, their neighbors and acquaintances; in fact, everyone's life but their own. Sometimes to live to dominate the life of another can be worse than taking that individual's life by murder. The body may be preserved, but if the mind and the power to LIVE, to progress and to BE is destroyed then truly they are submerged in a condition far worse than death. Yes, there are many things worse than death—to lose one's right to think and live as his inner soul dictates is much worse than a physical death. Children of God, filled with light, love, understanding and tenderness would never seek to force their minds or opinions upon others. That was Lucifer's way. He desired everyone of us to live just as he thought we should, both before we came to earth and now. But Lucifer will be destroyed along with the dictators of human conscience who imprison the minds of men.

There have been many more souls destroyed than saved by the righteous intentions of the domineering people who think they know how to live the lives of others, and then by force of will, begin to take over those lives. Life is a sacred thing— and life itself is the right to BE, to live, to learn the hard way if necessary, but to gather experience in one's own way. Our precious word "freedom" came from two Anglo Saxon words, "Free doom". Yes, even complete free doom is any man's right who desires it. Advice is always the cheapest thing on earth—and to force advice, through a domineering will is one of the most detrimental services ever rendered. Only true, unselfish love is of real value, love that can feel the need of others, and lovingly supply that need.

There have been so many unhappy homes and broken hearts caused by match-making relatives, parents and friends who have dared to take upon themselves one of the most sacred obligations of God.

Every individual on this earth has the right to live his own life, unrestricted by anyone as long as he is not trespassing on the lives and rights of others. All men are born free, and equal in this right, and any who have deprived another of this right will have to give an accounting for his usurpation of such authority.

"Let your light so shine before men that others seeing your good works may glorify your Father in Heaven." Letting one's light shine is a beautiful, tender admonition, and most certainly does not mean to take one's light and gouge it into others searing them with the burning flame of forced opinions. The method of force is always wrong, and is devoid of light and love, for love only can build truth into a glorious structure that will radiate a light that can be seen and desired by all. Any individual or people who would radiate that light would never need to go out to give it—the world would come eagerly to seek it. The greatest sermons ever preached have never been put into words—it can be a sermon of divine love portrayed in a simple act of kindness—it can be a flaming glory of unexpressed joy singing from a man's soul—it can be an understanding pat on the shoulder—a smile—a handclasp—a thought.

Those who become wealthy through the labors of their fellow beings are dooming themselves into eternal slavery, for they will have to repay, and they shall not be free from the debt until they have repaid the utmost farthing of tortured service. Every individual working in any business or industry has the right to share in the profits of the establishment he helps to make successful by his labors. For every individual, or group of stockholders who gain their wealth through the underpaid, drab drudgery of their fellow men will regret it. And the time will come when they will throw their wealth into the canyons and the ravines and plead for the rocks to fall on them to blot out their lives and their crimes. Yet if the rocks did fall upon them it would only blot out their mortal lives, not the deeds they have committed. On the plane of higher, intensified vibration they will have to face the vibrations they set in action by their selfishness, their greedy and often dishonest procedures. Those things that were back of their actions, the selfish motives, the greed and dishonesty, the desire to rule above their fellowmen are vibrations that will continue into eternity and on forever until the repentance of the individual is sufficiently intense to recall those vibrations. Only the person who released such vibrations, who created them in the first place has the power to recall them—to change and transmute them, and blot out the transgressions that have been committed. This power is the law and the gift Christ gave us —the power to repent, which means "recall." This gift is unspeakable in its power, but is of no avail to the person who thinks that all that is necessary is to say he "believes in Jesus Christ." He must begin to live life as Christ lived it in order to use the gifts. Repentance is the power to "recall" the vibrations we have released in error and selfishness, through a burning desire to correct the mistakes. It is the gift Christ gave to a world, to every human being who desires it—the power to have our sins and mistakes blotted out. It is a perfect glorious law—the law by which we can overcome, and though our sins be as scarlet they might become white as snow. He gave us the law—but we have to use it.

It is an eternal fact that we will have to abide in the very vibrations that we ourselves create—thus we can dwell in heaven or hell, according to our works. We not only have to abide in those vibrations, but we become the vibrations that we create—cement can be poured, steel and iron can be melted and poured into any mold—stone can be chiseled—but man is moulded thought upon thought—act upon act. He is the architect of his own soul.

Both capital and labor are releasing continual vibrations of discord and confusion upon the inhabitants of this world and adding to the present day difficulties, making adjustment impossible. This great problem of not only human happiness and security, but human existence, can never be answered in the strikes of the laborers, nor in the greed of the employers as they continually raise prices to meet the new labor demands. With the rise in prices comes new need to strike again and yet again for more pay to exist. Thus a vicious circle is in motion that will destroy the culture and civilization of our age unless vision begins to penetrate into the darkness, and selfishness and greed and the prejudices and hates are eliminated through an understanding of just what is being done.

Every man who contributes of his time and strength to any labor whatsoever has the right to live in happiness and security regardless of how humble his task. He has the right, if he gives of his abilities, to have his needs supplied and to be free from want and fear. He has the right to share in the profits of his labor, not in miserable, beggerly "two-bit" Christmas bonuses, but in *all* profits.

With such a business organization, or concern, every individual would always put his best into his work. He would feel that he belonged, and the very vibrations of congenial workmanship and co-operation going into such an establishment would begin to release the very blessings of heaven. The owner of such an establishment would indeed be the "greatest" for by his greatness "he would truly be the servant of all," or be "his brother's keeper." That is the only way a man can possibly be greater than his fellow men, is to become the great servant of all. Thus the greatest would receive the love and respect of every individual who ever heard of him, instead of being the recipient of hate, jealousy and distrust. He would receive a superior share in the profits with all the happiness and satisfaction life could possibly bestow. Thus would be established a universal brotherhood of understanding and good will.

There have been such industries. They have always been and always will be successful. This rule was lived in the City of Enoch "Where there were no poor among them." There were none unhappy. They all possessed wealth, happiness and security, and love for, and confidence in each other. The vibrations released by human beings working under such a system could glorify a community and a people—and if expanded far enough—a world.

This law of co-operation is an unwritten law—yet, if it is not accepted, the prophecy of Orson Pratt concerning England shall soon be fulfilled; "The poor shall rise against the rich, and their storehouses and their fine mansions shall be pillaged, their merchandise and their gold and their silver and their rich treasures shall be plundered. Then shall the lords and the nobles and the merchants of the land, and all in high places, be brought down and shall sit in the dust and howl for the miseries that shall come upon them." Orson Pratt prophesied this over a hundred years ago, concerning England, and unless they repent, as he warned, it will be fulfilled as surely as God lives, and it will be fulfilled in every city and land and business and industry that does not repent and begin to work toward a greater day of righteousness and understanding.

This spirit of understanding and co-operation of capital and labor is the very opposite of Communism. It is not enslaving a people to exalt the few, or the nation, or to build up a great concern or government at the price of individual submersion. The true law of God for a church, an establishment or a nation is to assist in glorifying the individuals, not the few who stand at the head, not the church, or the nation, but every humble member of society. No church or nation is greater than the individuals who make it up and of which it is constructed. Churches that use the members to glorify the church, business concerns that use the employees only to build up the business or give wealth to its head, or nations that enslave the people to build up the nation will fall. The very vibrations released in such a procedure will bring nothing but ultimate unhappiness, calamities and ruin to all concerned.

The only possible way a nation can become the greatest nation on the earth is to be the greatest servant of mankind, to seek to bring happiness and security to the entire human race, with all selfish politics eliminated. The only way any church could possibly be the greatest church would be to bring the greatest love, light, glory and power into the lives of its members, as it assists each person to reach his own highest manifestation and fulfill his own perfection. And the only way any man could become the greatest would be to become "the greatest servant of the human race." To give more love, more understanding, more kindness, more confidence and greater satisfaction would be the only way to become the greatest on earth—Christ fulfilling that law in all its perfection, was the greatest.

Thus the only greatness that can be achieved by any individual, church, business or nation is the attempt, the ability and the work of lifting the sons and daughters of God to a higher level of happiness, understanding and progress. This alone of all the works of man is lasting. This alone fulfills all the laws and all the promises. "This is my work and my glory to bring to pass the immortality and eternal life of man." To assist in this work is the only possible way to become "the greatest." Christ did more for the human race than any other since the world began. And throughout all generations of time the good He sowed will go on bearing fruits. And so it is with every truly great man, "Their works follow them." Lift your fellowmen and you are assisting in lifting the whole world into a higher bracket of existence.

Another unwritten law is a law that would restrict "braggarts" and "gossips" from stripping the flesh from the spiritual frames of their associates to feed their own over-stuffed egos. He who feasts on the weaknesses or imagined failings of his fellow beings is an "accuser" or devil. He may not mean to be. He may only be trying to find his place in the sun— but he is endeavoring to be great without comprehending the laws of "greatness," and the very breaking of these laws bring misery and disappointments.

It does not matter what one does, what he knows, who he is, or what he possesses—it only matters what he is. And he is the vibrations of all the thoughts and emotions he has released into eternity.

He who cheats his neighbor out of a dime may be selling his own soul for that dime. He may also be selling the soul of his neighbor, for he may awake thoughts of discord that will ripen into malice and hate, and thus his neighbor will create continual vibrations of confusion and where the injuries end we cannot yet possibly know.

Doctors who grow rich from the suffering of humanity, who have gathered their wealth from the anguished, agonized pains and physical suffering of their fellowmen will perish with their gains. Lawyers who grow fat on the misunderstandings or injustices of mankind will have none to defend them.

Men who lust after gold, or fame, or a woman's lips to whom they have no right, or the most dangerous of all lusts, the lust for power over their fellowmen, are creating an everlasting horror of regret unless they can repent and overcome such weaknesses, for they are all of the lower kingdom of existence and have no place in the realms of light. And thus it is possible for man to be a creator of darkness and confusion as well as a creator of glory and light.

The sneer of the righteous can truly be more wicked than the transgressions of the sinner. A sneer can pierce the heart like a two-edged sword. It can kill the soul. It is a murderous weapon that only persons with undeveloped vision and understanding could possibly stoop to use. It can be more deadly in its sting than the fangs of a rattler. Yes, it is true that a sneer is only an expression of the face—but behind the sneer are belittling vibrations that are more deadly than poison and more injurious to the souls of men than many weapons. No one could possibly sneer who truly loved his fellow men— love, the great balm; love, the tender, compassionate healing fluid of eternal light. Yea, he who loves his fellow men instead of himself would rather perish than set a tiny shadow of a sneer across his face, or a belittling smile.

These higher laws must be understood and lived by those who wish to survive the days ahead—they will have to be lived by those who remain to welcome the Redeemer of the world when He appears in His glory. These are the laws of the millennium—if you can apply them in your own life, then you may be assured that you are ready for the greatest advent of this earth—"For when He appears, we are to be like Him." If you think you cannot live these laws, yet desire to that you might have a part in the great and glorious new day which is ahead—then let that desire grow—as it grows in your heart it will bring the power of fulfillment. This is not a book to be read—it is a book written under the hand and inspiration of the Almighty—and is a book to be *lived*. Live these laws and you will know the truth and power of them. Break these laws and you will reap the consequence of the vibrations you send forth.

Back of every condition is vibration, and back of every vibration that caused the condition are thoughts of individuals, communities, countries or of a world. Selfish, wicked thoughts of men and nations cause wars and earthquakes and disasters, and the poverty and unhappiness that exists in this world to-day. God does not bring calamities. Men bring them. Men who are created in the likeness and image of God, and who have been given the great power of thought, men who can create anything, any condition. And men themselves will have to bring to pass the new condition of light and glory by beginning to understand their own powers of thought. Vibrations and the thoughts that sent the vibrations into action are the eternal realities. And ere long we will be dealing entirely with the realities.

It is possible to tune in on the higher vibrations of faith and the realm of celestial glory and it is also possible to learn to hold one's thoughts on that vibration level of glory and light. When one learns to hold his place in that realm or "on the beam" of those glorious vibrations he also helps to create and strengthen the vibrations of light and spirituality that compose the very kingdom of Almighty God. Thus he not only has the power to assist in balancing and ruling and glorifying this world, but also has power to reach out into the realms of eternity and leave his mark and influence while still a humble mortal man. Thoughts and vibrations, longings and desires are the true realities. Loves and hates are factors that are so far beyond man's present comprehension that he would stand trembling in fear at the very thought of discord if he only understood. Thoughts mingled with emotions are the creators of vibrations, and vibrations are the cause of all conditions. Control thought and only glorious vibrations will emanate from you, and the elements and all earthly conditions will eventually bow in subjection at your feet and will obey your commands.

Eternal value is not so much in action as in the vibration accompanying the action. Those deep, unanalyzed purposes hidden within us must be observed, checked and controlled. Only by a continual self-analysis can we progress along the highway of perfection. When we get to the point where we know it all and can no longer be taught or learn anything new, we are damned, and progress for us is stopped. For those who have reached this point the treasures of the eternal storehouse of knowledge is locked and sealed. For those who keep their minds, hearts and souls wide open knowledge and more knowledge, light and more light, and power and more power will be as much a part of existence as breathing and speaking. Only humble, open minds and hearts can keep in contact with the Light. And Light is the full perfection of all vibration.

We may be amazed to find that we have often lied to ourselves, and learned to believe our own lies. But we will never be able to lie to God. We will stand before Him the completed vibrations of our motives and our thoughts, our desires and our hopes, or our hidden degenerate lusts we have fostered. We will stand for all the world to read—our own book of life.

We will be astonished to find that it is not so much what we have done, but how we have done it; not what we possess in money, talents, knowledge, fame or power, or *who* we are—but WHAT we are.

The greatest tribute we can possibly pay to God, or the greatest vibrations we can possibly release from within us is to offer an ascending flame of love and devotion, "For the prayers of the saints ascend as incense before the Lord." (Rev. 5:8 and 8:3). Incense must be lighted before its essence is released. The soul and heart of man must be lighted by love, desire or deep feeling to be released as incense before the Lord. Lip prayers have no meaning, send out no vibrations, and are wasted.

Love is the ruling power in the realms of eternal light. Love is the most powerful vibration that can possibly be released from a human heart. Love is allied with joy and happiness and light—thus to love God and our fellowmen fulfills all the laws and truly keeps all the commandments. It casts out fear. It casts out hate, jealousy, pride and prejudice. It conquers darkness, ignorance, discord, disease and holds the keys of eternal happiness here and forever more.

Learn to control vibrations by controlling thoughts and you

will hold the keys of eternal life in your hands. The eternal energy surging through all matter, the power of existence in atoms with their whirling molecules and electrons in all earthly substances are nothing more or less than vibrations condensed to the point of slow, heavy, mortal tangibility. Control vibrations and the power to control substance and material energy will eventually be given, that is, the keys of handling eternal life, for energy is life. And life and light and love and energy are the eternal elements and are vibrations created by mental thinking.

Every thought sent forth is a never ending vibration winging its way across the universe to bring us back just what we sent forth. We can control the vibrations that emanate from us —and we can thereby control our destinies.

Thus science and religion can at last join hands and step across into the spiritual realm of eternal progress and happiness together. One reaches the higher knowledge through a complete understanding of the material elements which melt into light and energy and vibration through investigation; the other through its direct search into the spiritual, for both the material and spiritual are one, expressed in varied degrees of intensity and vibration.

Chapter XV.

THE THREE GREAT TESTS

THE HIGHWAY one must travel to ascend unto the heights is one of tests, and trials and overcoming. As one journeys upward he will at last be given the three great tests—even as Jesus was—the test of *power*—the test of *self-righteousness* —and the test of *wealth*. They may not come in just that order, but they will come. Somewhere along the upward climb they will be met by every man who travels far enough. Some may be born with wealth instead of receiving that test as the last and final one. But the test will be there, somewhere along the journey into light. One may completely pass it by as Jesus did, or he may become completely immersed in it as the rich young man.

The test of power will come when one is granted the feel and the knowledge of the power vested in him, and like Moses, smites the rock to bring forth water, then takes the glory unto himself. He may be given power to lay hands on the sick and feel that glorious surge of the healing power of the Almighty flowing through him, out from his finger-tips and then gathering the memory of that moment to himself, feel in his pride that the credit was his own. He may be given the power of some great talent and be destroyed by his own vanity in the gift. He may be given the power of speech, and use it, not under the direction of God, but to unfold his own beliefs and learning, or to take over the minds of men. A thousand ways can be used to test one's ability and worthiness to handle power. But you may be sure that if you travel far enough the test will come. If you cannot pass it your progress will be stopped, for you will have found your level, at least for the time being. No man will be able to go farther than the strength and vision that his own soul permits him to go. He sets his own gauge as he prepares himself.

The public ministry of Jesus bespeaks the greatness of His conquest of this human trait to misuse power. In every act of His life he so humbly gave God the entire glory for the works He accomplished. Even for His own relief and satisfaction he refused to use the power He knew was vested in him. And since He did not misuse the power by changing the stones to bread, angels came and ministered unto his needs—and greater power was given—power to turn water into wine, to multiply a thousand fold the fish and bread, to restore withered bones and flesh, the eyes of the blind, the life of the dead.

The test of self-righteousness will also come to every individual who seeks to fulfill the laws of righteousness. There will come a moment in his life when he will desire to show forth the power of his great goodness, a moment in which he will desire all to behold his high place more than he will desire to fill that place for the glory of God. Only great love and perfect humility can carry one above the point of feeling that he, in some way, is a little superior to his fellow travelers. Having reached a point above them in his upward climb he will want the world to give him credit for his achievement and goodness, and will be filled with a false belief that he has a special claim, or monopoly on the divine favors and attention of God. He may glory in the exalted heights of his lofty position, his high seat of office, his position in the congregation, his place upon the temple pinnacle and the power to make it the envy of those beneath him in the upward climb. And thus he will misuse his calling and position to awe the minds of men, that they might look to him instead of to God. Any who thus use the power of position to hold the minds of men, to keep them from going direct to God in their upward climb into the light, have failed; and they will stand while the humble seekers for light and the true knowledge of God will silently pass them by against their own knowledge, for they have lost the vision of God in the vision of their own greatness.

The other test, the test of fame, learning, wealth or worldly possession will be within the power of every man who ascends unto the heights—and he will have to choose as the rich young man who came to Jesus by night, whether it is a kingdom of this world he desires, or the greater kingdom that is not of this world—the kingdom of heaven, in which all wealth and all power will be added. And that kingdom of heaven does not mean necessarily a kingdom after death—it is the kingdom right within man—and man must find it. Few ever pass this test, but assume that the Lord has especially rewarded them for their righteousness, they glory in their worldly possessions, heaping unto themselves the gifts of earth, her honors and her talents, not realizing that the only true gold is that which is bought of Him—gold that has been tried in the fire, or tested in the furnace of life—which pure gold is man himself as he emerges purified and unscathed from the testings along the way—and has passed by the angels and will enter into his rest—or the peace that is beyond the powers of earthly friction and confusion.

"Man" in the original language means "steward." Every person who possesses anything on this earth is not the owner —he is only the steward. He is the steward of his talents. He is the steward of the dollars he falsely claims to be his own. And he will be judged on how well he manages his stewardship. In the next stage of existence we will progress into the realm of ownership if we have been able to pass by the angels or tests of this life. But in this life no man really owns anything. "For the earth is the Lord's and the fullness thereof." No man can claim a single particle of it as his own. If he does, then death will come and pry his fingers lose and he will go empty and alone into the great beyond. Any man who basks in his bank account, his great storehouses of wealth while his brother is without is a poor steward and will be called to give an accounting of his stewardship. He has accepted willingly and perhaps gladly the kingdom of the earth to rule—and has failed to attain unto the kingdom that is not of this world. He has chosen instead, to rule over acres of land, houses and dwellings, dollars and cents—and having been unfaithful in ruling over a few things he can never be permitted to be a Ruler over many.

The greatest warning ever given against these pitfalls or tests is as follows:

"Behold, there are many called, but few are chosen. And why are they not chosen?

"Because their hearts are set so much upon the things of this world, and aspire to the honors of men, that they do not learn this one lesson—

"That the rights of the priesthood are inseparably connected with the powers of heaven, and that the powers of heaven cannot be controlled nor handled only upon the principles of righteousness.

"That they may be conferred upon us, it is true; but when we undertake to cover our sins, or to gratify our pride, or our vain ambition, or to exercise control or dominion or compulsion upon the souls of the children of men, in any degree of unrighteousness, behold, the heavens withdraw themselves; the Spirit of the Lord is grieved; and when it is withdrawn, Amen to the priesthood or the authority of that man.

"Behold, ere he is aware, he is left unto himself, to kick against the pricks, to persecute the saints, and to fight against God.

"We have learned by sad experience that it is the nature and disposition of almost all men, as soon as they get a little authority, as they suppose, they will immediately begin to exercise unrighteous dominion.

"Hence many are called, but few are chosen." (D. & C. 121:34-40).

These three special tests that are given to each in his upward climb may be scattered anywhere along his mortal life. He may either be born with wealth, or he may be given it later because of his righteous endeavors—and he may be immersed with it—or pass on to higher and loftier attainments according to his desires and his vision.

The test of wealth may only be an opportunity to gain it at the sacrifice of one's better instincts. It may even be offered at the sacrifice of one's integrity. It may be offered as the price of one's soul. This test of wealth does not necessarily mean that everyone who climbs the great highway of light into the higher realms will have wealth bestowed upon him, for like Jesus, he may completely pass it by. But the opportunity to receive wealth will be given—and the wealth itself may be placed in his hands so that he can be detained by the feel of it in his fingers.

These tests may literally be called THE angels by which man must pass if he is to reach the greatest glory. It is not the symbols or the tokens that are so important in a man's progress—it is how well he lives the higher laws of righteousness to which they belong. Will he abide by the law and the covenant of being willing to give *all* that he possesses, his time, talents, worldly possessions, even his very life, if necessary, for his "search for the kingdom of heaven" and its righteousness—or the right-use-ness of its laws of perfection in his own life? And will he seek to make that kingdom manifest on the earth through his own devotion to it? Is he willing to overcome all personal lusts, unvirtuous desires of the flesh that his body might be purified and prepared to "Know God?" For the "righteousness" of the kingdom of heaven is the "right use" of its laws of perfection right within his own life. To fulfill these higher laws one must cease speaking evil of the Lord's anointed—and every child born into the world anointed with the precious anointing of LIFE must be included. Not only must one's lips refrain from evil, but his mind and his heart must become the ruling power of love behind the lips.

These tests are truly the angels in disguise to try the souls of men. They will be stationed somewhere along each man's path. He will meet them somewhere along that upward highway of eternal light to test the very fibres of his soul, his love for purity, his desire for righteousness, for these are the eternal realities behind the symbols—by these will he be judged.

If one is found worthy and can pass these tests of "right-use-ness" of the true laws of light and heaven, or by the angels set to test him, or into his true sonship, nothing will be impossible to him, for he shall truly be permitted to receive the Second Comforter and behold the face of God—and to enter the kingdom of heaven—to know *all* Truth—to receive *all*

light, yea, to be filled with it—not just in eternity—BUT IN THIS
LIFE. This is the promise of the Second Comforter as given in
the fourteenth chapter of John. It is the promise of Jesus
Christ. It is the promise of the Gospel in its fullness. It is the
very life and power of the sacred temple service. It is for all
who will avail themselves of these blessings in this life. And
for those who have already passed beyond the stage of mortality these gifts can be handed across to them. But for all
alike, NOW is the time to fulfill them. *Now* is the time to perfect love. *Now* is the time to reach into the light. *Now* is the
time to prepare to meet God—"For He will unveil His face
unto you, and it will be in His own time and in His own way,
and according to His own will."

"Blessed is the man that endureth temptation; for when he is
tried, he shall receive the crown of life, which the Lord hath
promised to them that love him." (James 1:12).

"Verily, verily, I say unto you, darkness covereth the earth,
and gross darkness the minds of the people, and ALL flesh has
become corrupt before my face.

"Behold, vengeance cometh speedily upon the inhabitants
of the earth, a day of wrath, a day of burning, a day of deso-
lation, of weeping, of mourning, and of lamentation; and as a
whirlwind it shall come upon all the face of the earth, saith
the Lord.

"And upon my house shall it begin, and from my house
shall it go forth, saith the Lord.

"First among those among you, saith the Lord, who have
professed to know my name and have not known me, and have
blasphemed against me in the midst of my house, saith the
Lord." (D. & C. 112:23-26).

This power to behold God is the purpose of the Melchizedek
Priesthood. "The power and authority of the higher, or Melchizedek Priesthood, is to hold the keys of all the spiritual
blessings of the church—

"To have the privilege of receiving the mysteries of the
kingdom of heaven, to have the heavens opened unto them, to
commune with the general assembly of the First born, and to
enjoy the communion and presence of God the Father, and

Jesus the Mediator of the New Covenant." (*Ibid.*, Sec. 107: 18-19). If one desires that power and that priesthood for himself and for his posterity, then he must fulfill the laws of it, and not just partake of the symbolism that enfolds it. He must be able to pass his tests—or pass by the angels placed to test him. It is not a testing of his knowledge of the symbols. It is a testing of his soul on whether he has abided by the covenants of righteousness— and this testing will not come in some far distant time after death. The testing and the angels may be anywhere along the road of life. Any time. One may be met down the block from his own home, another in one's own chapel, in his own dwelling, in his neighborhood—on his brother's farm. They stand at the cross-roads of life and we know them not because of pride, worldly desires, or greed.

Not everyone arrives at these three great tests herein mentioned. Many have been sidetracked or detained, or shall we say entertained, by angels long before these tests are reached. These three are the greatest—and few have ever passed them, for few can stand the test of actually knowing God.

When the veil of mortal concept is "rent" or parted, after one has "fulfilled all righteousness" and abided by the covenants instead of being concerned with the symbols that clothe them, when he has "cleansed the inside of the cup (himself) as well as the outside," then he is prepared to receive "The fullness of the Father." Then he will realize that he himself is indeed the temple of the living God. Then will he know and understand just how literal and real are the angels that he had to wrestle with. Then he will no longer be wrapped in the veil of deep sleep, but will know that the greatest joy, the complete perfection can only be achieved while in the flesh. (D. & C. 93:32-35).

Joseph Smith said, "Would to God, brethren, I could tell you who I am! Would to God I could tell you what I know! But you would call it blasphemy and want to take my life!" (Life of Heber C. Kimball, p. 333). This is more true today than it was 120 years ago when he was talking to a group of the most spiritual men on the earth. Christ was trying to tell the same things when He was giving his last-minute instructions to his apostles: "I have yet many things to say unto you, but you cannot bear them now." (John 16:12). No man can reveal these greater things to another. Christ would have, had it been possible, if his chosen ones had prepared themselves to receive such great light, but no man can reveal it to another—each man must live the laws, apply the lessons and be given the tests on his own. He must pass them by himself. And man himself is the testing ground and within his own being must every test be made—the gold refined and purified. Therefore no man can reveal to another the great things that are beyond that veil—every man must pass into it by himself. Others can assist him to the door, but he must enter alone, when he has been completely purified and prepared for so great a glory.

No law, or power, or knowledge will glorify any individual or group unless they live by the laws, fulfilling all righteousness, "For I say unto you, unless your righteousness exceeds that of the scribes and pharisees, ye shall never enter the kingdom of heaven." (Matt. 5:20).

"Be ye doers of the word, and not hearers only, deceiving your own selves." (James 1:22).

Since it is not the symbols that are so important, but the deep principles of Truth behind the symbols, we should begin to realize that it is time for us to leave the toys of childhood and step into reality, and live by the deeper, truer meaning. It is possible to leave all symbols and fulfill all the laws and all the prophets in just two forward steps of dynamic progress.

The great, unspeakable power of the Gospel of Jesus Christ is contained in those untried, unlived portions of His teachings. And the fullness of His Gospel means every word He ever spoke, not just the sayings we select for our own convenience, to fit our small capacities or understandings. The Gospel of Jesus Christ means every promise He ever gave and the power that fulfills those promises. It means the Sermon on the Mount, taken LITERALLY. It means all the love and forgiveness that is possible to exercise. It means to pray for one's enemies—to not only give when asked, but to give double. It means literally and forever, "Forgive us our debts as we forgive our debtors." It means those two great and Dynamic Commandments: "Thou shalt love the Lord thy God with *all* thy heart, with *all* thy soul, with *all* thy mind, and with *all* thy strength," LITERALLY. Try it.

It means, "Thou shalt love thy neighbor as thyself" and since both of these Commandments are shown forth in their fullness of glory elsewhere in this record we shall only again remind you. The glory of the Gospel of Jesus is in those untried, unlived portions that will reveal the full power of His promises when taken into one's life. It is these untried portions that cleanse the inside of the cup—and the inside must be cleansed and man must be purified in order to do the works that He did.

(New Testament Apocrypha, Testament of Naphtali 1:24-27):

"Sun and moon and stars change not their order; so do ye also change not the law of God in the disorderliness of your doings.

"The Gentiles went astray, and forsook the Lord, and changed their order, and obeyed stocks and stones, spirits of deceit.

"But ye shall not be so, my children, recognizing in the firmament, in the earth, and in the sea, and in all created things, THE LORD WHO MADE ALL THINGS, that ye become not as Sodom, which changed the order of nature.

"—When the Lord has thoroughly tested a man and finds that he is determined to serve Him at all hazards then the man will find his calling and election made sure, then it will be his privilege to receive the other Comforter which the Lord promised to the Saints according to the record of John."

Tests were never meant to be a burden nor a detriment to man any more than the tests given in school were meant to retard the progress of a student. The tests must be given for they are the gauges by which progress is made. Every test passed is a step higher, a more advanced stage of development. Those who do not pass the tests must remain behind.

For those who are satisfied with the low grade of common, mediocre mortality not too much is required. But for those who hunger and thirst after righteousness and divine knowledge the inner quest for Truth must continue, and for those the lessons become increasingly advanced and the tests greater. Those whose souls will never be satisfied with anything less than ALL TRUTH must be able to pass all tests—they must be tested and tried in all things. But if their understanding is deep, their hearts pure, their minds steady and serene they may not always be aware of the testing.

Tests are an opportunity to those advanced in righteousness, not a stumbling block. To such, every Word of God becomes music, not a harsh command to resent and rebel against. Every heartbreak, every seeming set-back, every trying circumstance, every temptation conquered, every weakness left behind can be and is, an opportunity and a glory when rightly understood. Every law complied with is a blessing of added strength. Every Word of God that has been made flesh, or become an integral part of the very fibres of one's being, is power.

This world contains every grade of souls from the lowest to the highest, and often those who consider themselves at the top are at the bottom of their class, and their class may be only beginning. In the grading of souls the material standards do not exist. Wealth, education, earthly honors or fame have no value whatsoever, but a man is judged by those inner qualities—those merits of faith in God, his power of love and devotion, his degree of compassion, mercy, humbleness and his power to forgive, his willingness to learn and his desire to obey those higher laws of Righteousness.

In the souls of those who truly desire to fulfill ALL the laws of righteousness that they might "live by every Word of God" and fulfill the command, "be ye perfect even as your Father in heaven is perfect" there are no tests too great to retard them. With their eyes "Single to the glory of God" they will reach beyond all temporal laws, overcome the very powers of hell, and passing by the angels rend the veil to behold the face of God, to know ALL TRUTH that they might be forever free, fulfilling every law, receiving every promise. Glory to God for such as these for no power on earth can stop them, no devils, no mortals nor angels bar their way.

Blasphemy, you say? God never intended man to be perfect

in this sphere of progress? So said those also who crucified Christ. He was rejected for having attempted to teach the great "Mysteries of Godliness", those laws of inner perfection.

"Yea, who can stand the test of knowing God?"

The promise is and has always been that when man overcomes the evils of his life and purifies himself through abiding by the secret, inner covenants of his soul he shall behold God. The veil of darkness that must be rent is the hardness of his own heart, the blindness of his own mind which has caused him to remain in a state of unbelief, sealing the heavens. (Ether 4:12-16).

"This is life eternal, to know Thee the only True and Living God, and Jesus Christ whom thou has sent." "And upon my house shall it begin, first among those among you who have professed to know my name and have not known me, but have blasphemed against me in the midst of my house, saith the Lord." (D. & C. 112:25-26)

The promise has been given in the scripture that those who fulfill the laws of righteousness should comprehend the great mysteries of godliness. To understand the mysteries of godliness one would have to become godly. The mysteries of godliness would contain the power of comprehension to the degree that every law and every power of godliness would be understood and could be used.

In the Sermon on the Mount this is verified. "Seek ye first the kingdom of God and HIS righteousness" etc. Every one can comprehend that God is perfect and divine and all powerful. But to seek for His righteousness means definitely to seek to in-corporate the righteousness of God into one's own life— to love as God loves, to think as God thinks, to serve in such infinite compassion of tenderness that one literally becomes One with God in ideals, in desires, in love and goodness. Then it is that all things will be added and all powers.

Yea, "Be ye perfect, even as the Father in heaven is perfect."

Chapter XVI.

LOVE, THE GLORY OF THE UNIVERSE

So few understand the Two Great, and all-inclusive, Commandments: "Thou shalt love the Lord, thy God, with all thy heart, with all thy soul, with all thy mind, and with all thy strength—and, thou shalt love thy neighbor as thyself." This first commandment has been taken up elsewhere in this work, so we will go on to the second, to clothe it in its full robe of shimmering glory.

Learn to love. Let love vibrate from your hands. Let your fingertips sing with it. Let every little fibre of your being magnify it and your soul perfect it. Let love pour out from you and as it does it will heal and bless and enlighten all those whom you contact, either in thought, or by actual meeting. Never let anger rage in your heart. Never hold grudges. Forget injuries instantly. Never let discord cling to you. Never cling to discord.

Along with this great love comes the perfect gift and *privilege of forgiving*. It is beautiful beyond expression, for in it is contained the very glory of God. Read carefully the Sermon on the Mount which is contained in the fifth, sixth and seventh chapters of Matthew. At the end of chapter five is given the admonition to love your enemies, to pray for those who spitefully use you and persecute you—in other words, think love, speak love, give love, and live love—and be willing always to go the second mile—*that you might be perfect, even as your Father in heaven is perfect*. Yea, be the servant willingly, with deep, eternal love, and as sure as you live you will become one of the great and noble of the earth.

If this Sermon on the Mount sounds like so many words, then please pray about it and study it often. Then begin to live it and you will know of the doctrine, whether it is just words or whether Christ was putting the truths of eternal power

171

and glory into the hands of man. These teachings are truly living principles, filled with the power and glory of the Almighty. They are the laws of those who desire to become "Saints", which means "holy ones." No church can make a person a Saint. That has to be done by the individual as he becomes obedient to the laws of God. None can become holy only as they live in holiness, and those glorious laws of perfection become not only their creed, but their very lives.

At first this Sermon on the Mount may seem terribly difficult and even impossible to live, or at least not worth the great effort required to give love for hate. It is so much easier to love our grudges and weaknesses than it is to love our enemies. It is always easier to hold to our human faults than it is to forgive them in our neighbor, which if done, would cancel every flaw in our own characters as well as heal our foes. As one's soul opens to comprehend the divine power contained in these teachings he will rejoice in the majestic glory of these perfect privileges, for he will prove to himself for all time that it is indeed a privilege and a glory to forgive. It is the complete cauterization of an otherwise incurable ulcer on the soul, and no matter how painful the process it will bring healing, pure and glorious.

You will glory in the divine knowledge, that you too, can forgive sins that they stand not before God. You too, can share in the work of the Savior, in that you too, can begin to do the works and take upon you the sins and mistakes of the world, that they might be blotted out, that the love and light and the power of God might begin to flow through you to bless and heal and enlighten. "Verily, verily, I say unto you, he that believeth on me, the works that I do shall he do also; and even greater works than these shall he do because I go unto my Father." (John 14:12). His greatest work was the healing power of His compassion and mercy—His forgiving tenderness. In order to have the perfect power to heal and bless He had to have the power in His own heart to forgive, which was always used in connection with the healing, for more often He said, "Thy sins be forgiven thee," than "be thou whole."

As one stands thus above the discordant vibrations of the

hates and discords around him he has "overcome" and all
power is given to such a one. He walks the earth in majesty,
doing the greater works for they automatically follow.

If you do not believe this, then try it. Live it and you will
know of its power and you will need none to teach you for
God Himself will be your Instructor for you will be *one with
Him.*

As one holds to these laws of love and forgiveness, he will,
in a short time, find that they are easy and an eternal glory
to his soul. Even as he begins to understand and to do the
works of love he discovers that every word of discord, every
disagreeable condition becomes an opportunity and a privilege to meet and transmute into glory. These obstacles are no
longer insurmountable barriers, but the steps by which he
climbs into the light. With this higher knowledge he learns to
value the admonition, "He who is thankful in all things shall
be made glorious." And he fulfills that law with a power that
lifts him above every difficulty. Soon he will feel light and
love and warmth fill his being—and before too long it will
begin to pour forth from him, and the great and mighty
promises of the scriptures will begin to be fulfilled unto him.

"And now I speak unto all the ends of the earth—that if
the day cometh that the power and gifts of God shall be done
away among you, it shall be because of unbelief.

"And woe be unto the children of men if this be the case;
for there shall be none that doeth good among you. NO NOT
ONE. *For if there be* ONE *among you that doeth good, he shall
work by the power and gifts of God.*" (Moroni 10:24-25).

Only with this divine gift of love allied with faith can any
man go forth to do good. This perfect love can right all
wrongs. It can heal and restore. It can bless and glorify and
blot out all mistakes both for oneself and his neighbor. One
will even develop the power to send this light and love back
down the dark, dismal hallways of the past, to the injuries
and heartbreaks that *have been*—and enfolding them in love,
enshrine them in the purity of healing light. And thus even the
darkness of the past can be transmuted into light for the glory
of God. Love can heal every injury, past or present, and en-

fold one in such a glorious flame of light that the future can only be a melody of loveliness.

As we begin to perfect this power of love and forgiveness we find that it is possible to take upon us the sins of the world. This is done by accepting the hurts and mistakes of others without retaliation or bitterness—then they can be immediately dissolved through our love and forgiveness, forgotten and blotted out. It is the balm that can heal every cancerous ulcer of the soul and heart, both for ourselves, and those who do not yet know the law.

Job's comforters, or rather, accusers could not be restored to favor with the Lord until Job himself prayed for them as instructed by the Almighty.

"I will forgive whom I will forgive, *But of you it is required to forgive all men.*" With all this scripture of glory it is a shame that we have gone through life so blind to its literal meaning and thus have sealed our own sins upon ourselves, for, according to the Lord's Prayer, we cannot be forgiven our trespasses unless we forgive others their trespasses. Our sins can only be forgiven as we forgive. This is the key of forgiveness, and *those whom God will not forgive are those who forgive not.*

Often the true meaning of the scripture is veiled by words rather than revealed by them. At least the great meaning of the second commandment has been lost in the words:

"Thou shalt love thy neighbor as thyself." For many people it requires no love at all to love their neighbors as themselves. They have lost all love, all respect, all regard for themselves, and usually not without cause. When a man "lets himself down" so that he can no longer have faith in himself, his fellowmen or in God he is pretty close to the bottom. For such individuals to love their neighbor as themselves would require nothing at all, if taken at its face value. To others it is only a gathering together of words without meaning. Yet behind it stands a law of utter glory.

If you love your neighbor as yourself, then you are to love him as you love that inner, divine self. You are to love him as your own soul, overlooking his weaknesses and his mistakes.

You are to love him literally as though he were your VERY SELF —and you were he. There is a divine self in each man and it is that divine self that must step forth and love that divine soul of his neighbor. In doing this he has fulfilled all the laws and kept all the commandments and brought forth divinity in himself and planted that vision in the soul of his neighbor. If you would be perfect then always see your neighbor as perfect. See him in his divine power of creatorship, a son of God. Look into his soul, beyond the outer wrappings of mortality and see that Divine spark of eternal life, and you will help to awaken it and bring it forth. This is the greatest service that can be rendered to the human race. It is the gift divine. It will help to heal a world and enfold it in light.

This great, understanding, divine love, when put into practice, truly makes you and your neighbor ONE, as Christ so persistently taught and prayed for. This love can heal and bless and enlighten and enfold until darkness has no power before it. This divine love has to forgive, and in its forgiveness is the power of the Almighty.

If there are those who are so wicked they will not respond to this love, who set up a resistance against it as it pours forth in great light, they will destroy themselves, for they are fighting against the light of God if it is the pure, unselfish Christlike love of enfolding glory. However, there are few on earth who will fight against it for even the most hardened criminal will respond to this love and desire to be enfolded in its healing rays of penetrating warmth, and will often open up his heart and soul to it when no third degree on earth could break him down. Love is the wand of the magician, it is the greatest gift and the most powerful force that man can use. It is the gift divine.

Long before the sun was visible to this earth, or the moon shone, when God began His work of creation as it had been conceived in His mind, He said, "Let there be light; and there was light." And that light was the love and glory of God that conceived a world and filled every atom of it with light and a desire to expand and reach, "And light is life." (Compare

Genesis chapter 1:34 with verses 14-15. Also see Moses 2:23 and verses 14-15).

Within each man this divine spark of light, or life and love is enfolded, waiting to be brought forth by the understanding or command of each individual as he steps forth to take his place in the higher realms of divine progress. It can fulfill every desire, accomplish any task and glorify a world.

Such is the power of love, and the power of man to send it forth.

It is not sufficient not to hate, not to dislike, not to retaliate to hurts. These can be inactive, even negative conditions under some circumstances. Love must be sent out with power, knowingly and with direct purpose. It must be sent out as a musician sends out his melody. Just because one refrains from inharmony does not make him a musician. To be a musician one must send out melody; and to be a master of music requires hours of practice. So to be a master of the divine gift of love one must practice, and he is both the instrument and the musician, for upon his own being is the divine melody played, first within himself, then within the hearts of others. And love is the theme song of the universe. Sing that song and you can never be out of tune. It is the melody of heaven.

With an understanding of this great and perfect gift of love one learns the power of using his mind, his heart, and soul as one, to send it forth. Controlling one's thoughts is no longer a struggling burden of trying to eliminate the undesirable thoughts, but becomes a practice of keeping the perfect thoughts of love always there. When one is learning to play some masterpiece he often makes a slip—and then he plays that one measure repeatedly until he has perfected it. So it is in the exercise of perfecting the melody of divine, Christ-like love. If for a moment the thoughts have strayed into discord and confusion, it is easy to stand quietly for a few minutes, and intensifying the vibrations of love, send them forth as a power of light to the very ends of the earth, scattering the darkness completely. Soon the melody will become a perfect glory and there will be no tones of discord, for one will find himself a great master of the most marvelous harmony of all existence. Love is the melody that will vibrate across the entire universe, in perfect tune with it. It will play a symphony on the stars. Love is the light that will reach into the very darkest corners of human hearts—and those hearts and minds of mankind can sometimes be much darker than the forgotten corners of the earth. Love is as necessary in the life of every individual as is sunlight, food or drink. Lives grow warped and ugly without it.

Pour out love and watch a hungry, starving world respond. Pour it out as light, while you work, as you walk along the streets, and as you stand in throngs, or sit in quiet churches —send it out as light from every little cell and fibre of your being—a "pure love, unfeigned"—a love that is felt in every little tissue of the heart. Give love like this and your highway of life will become a highway of divine light, and you will know that you walk with God.

This great love automatically rises above all ego, all pride, all selfishness, all discord, fear and confusion. It is perfection that steps beyond the weaknesses without even having to give them a thought. They are left behind. It is this love that blends with the holy desires of heaven and opens wide the portals to the storehouse of eternal knowledge, and all weaknesses, darkness and ignorance are dissolved as the morning sun melts the hoar-frost.

Then one knows that in exalting his neighbor he exalts himself. In forgiving his neighbor he has received the power to be forgiven. He will know that in the beginning, he was with God, even *The Spirit of Truth*; as surely will he know this as he knows that love is a reality, more beautiful than many forests and great wealth. Love is the glorified string of pearls that belongs to every individual who desires to possess it. It is the greatest gift. As one wears this precious gift he will know also that his brother too is "The Spirit of Truth"—and he will understand that through his great, tender compassionate love he can help restore that vision to his brother. Perhaps not in words—but love plants its own glory. Then he will know that he and his brother, under the divine light and love can again become ONE—the glory of the Almighty.

This love is all-inclusive perfection. It is music and glory and life and light, and with it no man could possibly seek to climb to glory over the heads of his fellowmen, for a deep reverence for all mankind fills his soul, and a deep humility. With the most reverent attitude he finds his place of service in assisting in the glory of the Father, in helping to bring to pass the immortality and eternal life of man. Then he will understand that no creed or dogma can glorify him or lead him to exaltation unless he has fulfilled both the First and Second Commandments of eternal, perfect love. This is the Word of God—and that Word must become flesh—our flesh —for we ourselves must become the very essence of love.

"Though I speak with the tongues of men and of angels, and have not charity, I am become as sounding brass, or a tinkling cymbal.

"And though I have the gift of prophecy, and understand all mysteries, and all knowledge; and though I have all faith, so that I could remove mountains, and have not charity, I am nothing.

"Charity suffereth long, and is kind; charity envieth not; charity vaunteth not itself, is not puffed up.

"Doth not behave itself unseemingly, seeketh not her own, is not easily provoked, thinketh no evil.

"Rejoices not in iniquity, but rejoiceth in truth;

"Beareth all things, believeth all things, endureth all things.

"Charity never faileth; but whether there be prophecies, they shall fail; whether there be tongues they shall cease; whether there be knowledge it shall vanish away.

"For we know in part, and we prophecy in part.

"BUT WHEN THAT WHICH IS PERFECT IS COME, THEN THAT WHICH IS IN PART SHALL BE DONE AWAY.

"When I was a child, I spake as a child, I understood as a child, I thought as a child; but when I became a man, I put away childish things.

"For now we see through a glass, darkly; but then face to face; now I know in part; but then shall I know even as I am known.

"And now abideth faith, hope, charity, these three; and the greatest of these is charity." (I. Cor. 13:1-13).

Thus faith, hope and charity are the only three enduring things or conditions. Everything else will fail. Only these three are eternal.

There is no word big enough in our modern English to take the place of or give the full meaning of the old Anglo-Saxon word "Charity." "Charity" did not mean giving out alms, as we have translated or interpreted it. "Charity" originally meant love, plus compassion and gentleness and understanding with a complete willingness to give or share one's self and possessions in service.

This definition is given in Moroni chapter seven, verses forty-seven and forty-eight: "But *charity is the pure love of Christ,* and it endureth forever; and whoso is found possessed of it at the last day, it shall be well with him.

"Wherefore, my beloved brethren, *pray unto the Father with all the energy of heart, that ye may be filled with this love, which he hath bestowed upon all who are true followers of his Son, Jesus Christ; that ye may become the sons of God; that when he shall appear we shall be like him, for we shall see him as he is; that we may have this hope; that we may be purified even as he is pure. Amen.*"

One can never become fanatical or unbalanced if he possesses this great love. It is the perfect balance of mind, body and soul. It renews continually the fountains of the heart, the power of the soul, the vigor of the mind, the life of the cells and tissues. No one can ever go insane who consciously sends out its light of living glory to benefit a world. It heals and restores all things. This jewel alone possesses the keys of all light and glory. It is the heavenly melody each man must learn to play on his own soul before he can fulfill the great destiny God designed for him.

No human being is so lowly, so miserable, so destitute that he cannot perfect this one master gift—and thus receive all gifts. It costs nothing for the lessons, and man himself is the instrument. As one learns to understand all that this one great gift contains he will view in a measure the very grandeur of

heaven. He will know that love is more precious than sunlight, or gorgeous blooming flowers. He will know that it is
more beautiful than the song of the birds or sparkling mountain streams. It is more powerful than the oceans and more
superb than high mountains, for it is life. It is light. It is
eternal, indestructible, glorious perfection of existence. It is
more precious than jewels, more powerful than wealth. It is
the very power of heaven placed lovingly into man's hands—
the divine symphony of eternity.

Every thought carries with it its own vibration just as every
key on the piano has its own tone. The vibration sent out by
each man must first go through his own body, for he is the
instrument, and on him is engraved the eternal record of the
divine melody he creates or the eternal discord and confusion
he pounds forth. And since vibration is the reality, or the
eternal substance of existence, man himself is a creator. He
creates every condition on earth—good or bad. He, in a way,
creates himself—a record of eternal glory, a master of all
conditions, all harmony, perfection and success, or a groveling
thing of darkness, confusion and failure. "Man, know thyself,
for in thee is hidden the treasure of treasures." And "Man,
with all thy getting, get understanding." Man, thou replica of
the Divine, thou creator of thy heaven or thy hell, thy success
or thy failure! Oh, glorious man, son of God, step forth and
claim thy birthright, for it is waiting for thee HERE and NOW!

"And to know the love of Christ, which passeth knowledge,
that ye might be filled with the fullness of God." (Eph. 3:19).

Chapter XVII.

"THERE SHALL BE NO MORE DEATH"

IF THE PRECEDING chapters have held for you new and amazing thoughts, I approach this dynamic chapter in deepest humility as I ask that you keep a prayer in your hearts as you read and study it. I stand in breathless awe before this work God has placed in my hands. And to God be the credit for the sublime, breath-taking wonder of these great and mighty truths this record contains. Much of it has been written in tears—all of it in prayer. I lay no claim to this work. I only bow my head in deepest gratitude that such glorious knowledge could come forth in this day and age, and that my fingers have been privileged to touch so sacred a work, and my mind behold it.

In the Apocryphal New Testament, Nicodemus 18:12-13, is the account of the angel of death condemning Lucifer for crucifying the Son of God—there are several chapters on Christ's death and entrance into hell to release the prisoners, but I shall quote only two verses, which are as follows: "O Satan, Prince of all evil, author of death, and source of all pride, thou shouldst first have inquired into the evil crimes of Jesus of Nazareth, and then *thou wouldst have found that he was guilty of no fault worthy of death.*

"Why didst thou venture, without either reason or justice, to crucify him, and hast brought down to our regions a person innocent and righteous, and thereby hast lost all the sinners, impious and unrighteous persons in the whole world?"

From this it is suggested that death has no claim on those who have not sinned. This thought is verified in the old Chaldaic writings of the Hebrews given before the Egyptian bondage, but never included in our scripture: "On those overcoming all weaknesses and abolishing all sin from their lives, death has no claim." (Rabbi Bendovan, a Levite record keeper).

This doctrine was verified in the City of Enoch. A great multitude, working together for perfection, living in love and unselfishness, and serving God with all their hearts, minds and souls were not subject to death. The whole city was taken into heaven. This great event was not contrary to law, but in accordance with law. I might also add that they were living at a time when there was greater wickedness on the earth than at any other time in the history of the world except the present day.

Moses, according to Josephus, was taken into heaven without tasting death. So was Elijah. And John the Beloved is another on whom death has had no claim.

From the ancient records of America, from those who built a civilization of beauty and magnificence surpassing our own, is given even more individual cases to substantiate the fact that death is unnecessary if one overcomes all sin. Alma, the younger, was taken into heaven without tasting death. (Alma 45:18).

In 3 Nephi 1:3 also 2:9 there is a record of a man named Nephi who received the power to overcome death. "Behold, the power of God was with him, and they could not take him to cast him into prison, for he was taken by the Spirit and conveyed away out of the midst of them. And it came to pass that thus he did go forth in the Spirit, from multitude to multitude, declaring the word of God." (Heleman 10:16-17).

The prophet Ether's last words were a suggestion that he might be translated. Ether did not have the Bible record of Moses or Elijah because his people had come to the American continent at the time of the Tower of Babel, long before the time of either Moses or Elijah. Neither did he have the account of Alma and Nephi because he lived around four-hundred and fifty years before either of them. Therefore if he understood this higher law, it must have been revealed by God to him to prepare him for this change.

There is also the account of the "Three Nephites" who were permitted to tarry on the earth without death having any claim on them. There are those of this generation who have been contacted by one or more of them, and these individuals can testify, along with the ancient records, of their actual existence.

This makes eight, nine if Ether is included, who being identified by name, were delivered from death by the righteousness of their lives. To these individuals must be added the whole city of Enoch, and the righteous who were taken up to that city from the time of its ascension until the floods descended. How many are included in this group we do not know. It does not matter. How many have since that time been given power over death has not been revealed. They could have been legion.

According to the New Testament Apocrypha, there is one Teckla, a convert of Paul's who was translated because of the righteousness and devotion of her life—and from that early record it is apparent that the saints of the early days of the Christian Church were quite familiar with this power which was called, "translation."

From the New Testament records, John the Beloved was not the only follower of Christ who was given this power. Note the following from the original Greek record: "And he (Christ) said to them, Indeed I say to you, that there are SOME of those standing here, who will not taste of death till THEY see God's Royal Majesty having come with power." (Mark 9:1; Matt. 16:28 and Luke 9:27). And since Christ has not yet come in His power these individuals have escaped the power of death.

How many have been given this great privilege does not concern us. The thing that does concern us is: Does the law apply to us? "The last enemy to be overcome is death." Then surely if we can overcome all weaknesses, discords, confusions, fears, hates and darkness it would be possible to overcome death. And in overcoming death one can either be caught up into heaven, or be permitted to remain on this earth according to the will of the Lord, or the desire of the individual.

"We consider that God has created man with a mind capable of instruction, and a faculty which may be enlarged in proportion to the heed and diligence given to the light communicated from heaven to the intellect; and that the nearer man approaches perfection the clearer are his views, and the greater his enjoyments, till he has overcome the evils of his life and lost every desire for sin; and like the ancients, arrives at the point of faith where he is wrapped in the power and glory of his Maker and is caught up to dwell with him." (Joseph Smith).

We will now have to turn again to the teachings of Jesus Christ who, of course, is always the infallible authority for any doctrine.

"Verily, verily, I say unto you, if a man keep my sayings, he shall never see death." (John 8:51). Or according to the perfect Greek translation: "Indeed, indeed, I say to you, if anyone the word of mine shall keep death he shall not see until the end of the age (or world)." Christ was instantly challenged on this doctrine by the multitude in these words: "Now we know that thou hast a devil. Abraham is dead, and. the prophets; and thou sayest, if any man keep my sayings, he shall never taste death. Art thou greater than our father Abraham, which is dead?" To such a rebellious group Christ did not attempt to explain this sacred, higher law. He only justified his words by saying, "Verily, verily, I say unto you, before Abraham was, I am." Even this truth caused them to pick up stones and attempt to stone him to death.

"And whosoever LIVETH AND BELIEVETH IN ME SHALL NEVER DIE. Believest thou this?" (John 11:25). Christ was not speaking of life beyond the grave. He was not talking of the resurrection. He was talking to Martha concerning Lazarus, who was already buried, but one on whom death seemed to have no claim. Lazarus' going to the other side had been permitted undoubtedly as a sign and a testimony to the people. And you may be assured that Lazarus never again tasted of death.

The sixth chapter of John contains more on this subject than any other chapter of scripture: "Verily, verily, I say unto you, He that believeth on me hath life age-lasting." This again is the translation from the original Greek, and also means to the end of the age or world.

"I am the bread of life.

"Your fathers did eat bread in the wilderness and are dead."

This speech was brought forth because the multitude had boasted that their ancestors had been fed manna by God, and Christ carefully pointed out that though they had been fed manna by God, yet they had all died. Those old Hebrew Fathers under Moses had not all died a spiritual death—so in speaking of this age-lasting life that he promised, he was definitely not speaking of just the life beyond the grave, or a life after death, for their fathers did possess a life beyond, for according to the record of Peter, even those who had been disobedient in the days of Noah, had that, for Christ went to preach to them during the three days and nights his body lay in the tomb. This record is verified in Nicodemus 18.

"This is the bread which cometh down from heaven, that a man may eat thereof *and not die* (as had their ancestors who had lived on the coveted manna).

"I am the living bread which came down from heaven; if any man eat of this bread, *He shall live forever*: and the bread that I will give is my flesh, which I give for the life of the world." (John 6:47-51). I would recommend the prayerful study of the whole chapter, for here Christ promised that those who partook of the sacrament would have this great gift if they would truly believe in him. Then he said, *"It is the spirit that quickeneth; the flesh profiteth nothing: The words that I speak unto you, they are spirit, and they are life."* (John 6:63). In other words, He is saying that the ordinance of the sacrament is merely symbolical of the deeper meaning He is trying to teach—that it is not the sacrament that will profit anyone, but the Spirit of Christ that is to be desired and received, that one might truly be quickened into Life. John definitely comprehended his words and their meanings. And according to the records there must have been others.

Now let us examine the covenants of the sacrament and the promises given that make it so extremely important. Each time one is privileged to partake of it, he covenants that he will ALWAYS remember the Son of God, even Jesus Christ. ALWAYS to remember Him would demand that one's thoughts would have to be in control, that one's mind would have to be almost a constant prayer. He would have to live every law given by the Master, and the Sermon on the Mount would become as much a part of his life as eating and breathing. If we partake of the sacrament without keeping this covenant, or even attempting to, we are liars before God. Many are ill and many have died because they have failed to try and understand this covenant and to live by it. When we take upon us the flesh and blood of Jesus Christ, keeping our part of the covenant, we are partaking of the spiritual emblems of eternal life—even as Christ had life in Himself, so will He give to us the power to have life in ourselves. Thus we will have His power to be upon us, and His Spirit to be with us always, insomuch that our lives can become a living glory, directed in righteousness, truth, peace and progress. We will know what to say and when to say it. We will be able to perform the works that He performed, "even greater works." This is the promise. If we understand the great privilege that is ours and live by the covenants we make, then we will not only have His Spirit to attend us always, but we need never die. This is the positive promise given in the sixth chapter of John, unless, of course, we are called to lay down our lives to seal our testimony and thus further glorify Him.

We also covenant in the sacramental prayer that we are willing to take upon us the Name of Jesus Christ. This will be explained later. But unless we begin to comprehend the great truths behind the symbols we will continue to live in our human niches of distress, and eventually perish from the earth.

"Therefore leaving the principles of the doctrine of Christ, LET US GO ON UNTO PERFECTION: not laying again the foundation of repentance from dead works, and of faith toward God, of the doctrine of baptism, and of laying on of hands, and of resurrection of the dead, and of eternal judgment." (Heb. 6:1). In other words, the first principles of the Gospel, as Christ taught it, are the milk. Faith, repentance and baptism, and the laying on of hands for the Gift of the Holy Ghost are as much a part of His teachings as love, and forgiveness and perfection—in fact, they are the stepping stones to the others.

But after they have been fulfilled no individual has the right to sit in security, thinking he has done all. From there he must go on towards perfection, fulfilling the higher laws. The very Gift of the Holy Ghost is to lead one into *all* truth—even as the Melchizedek Priesthood is to reveal the mysteries of the kingdom of heaven and reveal the face of God. Therefore unless one goes on to perfection through the great gifts of the Gospel "all is vain."

In Nephi's farewell speech to his people, and to all men, he gave the admonition to repent and be baptized, that the promised blessings might be received. He mourns because of ignorance, unbelief and wickedness of the people—and ends by saying, "And now, my beloved brethren, after ye have gotten into the straight and narrow path, I would ask if all is done? Behold, I say unto you, Nay: for ye have not come thus far save it were by the word of Christ with unshaken faith in him, relying wholly upon the merits of him who is mighty to save. Wherefore ye must press forward with the steadfastness in Christ—FEASTING UPON THE WORD OF CHRIST." (Feasting means to partake of, and digest, or in this case, study. The only way his teachings can be digested is by making them a part of one's being even as food becomes a part of one's body). He goes on to say that if men have obeyed the first words of Christ, they should be able to speak with the tongue of angels, because angels speak by the power of the Holy Ghost. He further says: "IF YOU DO NOT UNDERSTAND, IT IS BECAUSE YE DO NOT ASK OR KNOCK—FOR IF YE WOULD HARKEN UNTO THE SPIRIT WHICH TEACHETH A MAN TO PRAY, YE WOULD KNOW THAT YE MUST PRAY: for the evil spirit teacheth not a man to pray, but teacheth him that he must not pray." (2 Nephi chapters 31 and 32).

When one can make every breath a prayer of praise and glory and rejoicing, he will find he truly abides in Christ—then it will be that "he shall have whatsoever he saith."

Every attribute that God the Father possesses is also possessed in an embryo state by every child of earth. Every son and daughter of God when told of the gifts that should follow those who truly believe, are commanded to desire to prophesy.

Paul said that he would to God that all men could prophesy. And the promise is given that the Spirit of the Lord will cover the earth as the waters cover the sea, and our sons and our daughters shall prophesy. No one having the power of God upon him will be silent, or inactive—the very power demands activity that will continually glorify Him—that His name might be made known and magnified upon the earth.

It is impossible to reach too high, unless one is reaching to take hold of the power of God that he might bask in his own glory, and surpass his fellow men. Such an individual in reaching for light and power will not be prepared to take hold of it and it will consume him. Only deep humility, perfect love and a burning desire to glorify God can fulfill the highest vision.

When Ammon, the son of king Mosiah, had completed his mission to the Lamanites, who had been converted by the thousands to a belief in God, through Ammon and his brothers' preaching, he said: "Yea, he that repenteth and exerciseth faith and bringeth forth good works, and PRAYETH CONTINU-ALLY WITHOUT CEASING unto such is given to know the mysteries of God; yea, *unto such it shall be given to reveal things which never have been revealed;* yea, and it shall be given unto such to bring thousands of souls to repentance, even as it has been given unto us to bring these our brethren to repentance."

Paul admonished the saints of his time to *lay hold of every good gift.* To lay hold of a gift one must understand it, must desire it—and must not only reach for it, but hold his mind upon it until it is fulfilled unto him, or until his faith has become sufficiently strong to receive it.

"Let the same mind be in you which was also in Christ Jesus:

"Who, being in the form of God, thought it not robbery to be equal with God."

Along with this great power of God that comes through fulfilling the laws and perfecting love—is the power to abide in Christ, to become one with Him, even as He and the Father are one—to be instructed and directed by Him and that all achievements will be done in and through Him, and nothing in our lives can then fail. This great power also carries with it power over death, except for those who are called to give willingly their lives as martyrs for the glory of the Father and His Son.

"He that loveth not his brother abideth in death." (I John 3:14).

"The wages of sin is death, but the gift of God is eternal life." (Rom. 6:23).

"We believe that men will be punished for their own sins and not for Adam's transgressions." If this be true, and I know that it is, men do not die because of Adam's transgressions which brought death to him. They die because of their own sins. Adam brought sin into the world, and by sin came death—the sin that every individual commits because we partake of sin. But the sins for which we are punished and die are our own sins and not Adam's.

When we overcome sin we can overcome death, the last enemy.

"To him that overcometh I will cause to eat of the tree of life which is in the midst of the Paradise of God." (Rev. 2:7).

"To be carnally minded is death, but to be spiritually minded is life and peace." (Romans 8:6).

"Behold, I shew you a mystery: We shall not all sleep, but we shall all be changed . . ." (I Cor. 15:51).

"But everyone shall die for his own iniquities." (Jer. 31:30).

"The last enemy to be destroyed is death." (I Cor. 15:26 and Rev. 2).

"Wherefore they have foresworn themselves, and by their oaths, *brought upon themselves death, and hell.*" (Moses 6:29).

"Oh death, where is thy sting? Oh grave, where is thy victory? *The sting of death is sin,* and power of sin is the law." (I Cor. 15:55).

"Enoch was translated that he should not see death, and was not found because God translated him, for before his translation he had this testimony *that he pleased God.* But without faith it is impossible to please him, for he that cometh to God must believe that he is, and that he is a rewarder of them that diligently seek him." (Heb. 11:5-6).

Death is definitely to be banished during the Millennium, for every promise of that day that is just before us, is that there shall be no more death—that those who are mortal will be changed in "the twinkling of an eye from mortality to immortality" when they have reached the age of a tree. Trees vary in age from a few years to centuries, so will the change taking place in mortals vary in time, for it will be when each individual has thoroughly prepared himself for it and not before. That preparation can begin at any time when the individual gets the understanding of the law, or catches the vision of it.

We, too, have the right to lay hold upon these greater blessings. God is no respecter of persons. It is not robbery to seek to share in such a glorious privilege and calling. It is not an over-estimated assumption. It is not a wicked desire. It is an everlasting invitation to those who will abide the higher laws.

"But behold, that which is of God inviteth and enticeth to do good continually; wherefore, everything which inviteth and enticeth to do good, and to love God, and to serve him, is inspired of God." (Moroni 7:13).

"And as sure as Christ liveth he spake these words unto our fathers, saying: "Whatsoever thing ye shall ask the Father in my name, which is good, in faith believing that ye shall receive, behold it shall be done unto you." (*Ibid.,* verse 26). There is no need to ask for the things that already exist, but there is a need to ask for the gifts that we have not yet received.

When one's mind lays hold upon the idea of being able to serve the Lord with all one's time, talents, strength, energy, mind, and body and soul, the spirit of the Lord will testify, or bear witness to that individual that if he continues he shall have the privilege of serving to that extent under the direction and inspiration of God. After the Spirit of God bears witness to one's soul of this great promise, it becomes very real and very dear to his heart, and is not nearly as strange as the thought of death itself. Even the doctrine of the resurrection is a more difficult one to understand, though so perfect and beautiful in its power, mercy and comprehension. Lucifer is the author of death and if we can completely throw off his powers of sin and darkness death cannot possibly have any claim on us, and thus our last enemy "death" can be overcome.

"Come unto me, O ye house of Israel, and it shall be made manifest unto you how great things the Father hath laid up for you, from the foundation of the world; and it hath not come unto you, because of unbelief. Behold, when ye shall rend the veil of unbelief which doth cause you to remain in your awful state of wickedness, and hardness of heart, and blindness of mind, then shall the great and marvelous things which have been hid up from the foundation of the world from you—" be made known. (Ether 4:13-15). In other words, when we have overcome the wickedness of our lives, the hardness of our hearts, and the blindness of our minds and thrown out all sin, great and unspeakable blessings, such as the world has never known shall be ours—blessings that have been hidden "from the foundation of the world."

Perhaps I can explain it a little more thoroughly this way: after one has learned to make his mind a constant prayer of love and devotion; when his heart has become a continual melody of praise and glory and his mind is at last permitted to reach through into the great storehouse of Eternal Truth, or the fourth dimension, then it is only logical that after abiding in that condition for awhile his body gradually being filled with light should be able to follow into it also.

"In that day two shall be grinding in a field, and one will be taken and the other left." "Two shall be sleeping in a bed, one shall be taken and the other left." From this we know that it will be necessary to live higher laws of obedience or glory in order to be taken up that one might escape the great and final judgments of the consummation of earthquakes, bombings and destruction of nations.

Within the soul of man is the atomic energy and power to lay hold upon all the great gifts and blessings of God. This power can only be used through great humility, dynamic desire and great love, and when the mind has been brought to obey and becomes a continual prayer of tender devotion of light and glory. "Without vision the people perish." They have died down the centuries because they did not have this vision.

The demand made on our pioneer forefathers was a challenge on their physical and moral fortitude—ours is a demand upon our mental and spiritual strength. Mentally we have to awaken—to think—to *feel*—to vision—to desire—and finally to KNOW. And only he can know who has paid the price of knowing. That price is paid by living the laws of righteousness, by opening wide the mind and soul to feel—by humble, earnest prayer, to seek—and by increasing righteousness. "If you will live the laws you will know if they be of God, or whether I speak of myself." That is just as true now as it was when Christ gave it.

You ask me how I dare to write such unorthodox things, and how I know them? I know them to be true because God showed them to me before I came to earth. I was taught by Him—and death was explained to me—and the laws by which it could be overcome. And again in life was it verified unto me—and the promise was given that I was to have the gift and power of the "Three Nephites", that I would be able to go forth, under the Spirit and power of the Almighty, to serve mankind and help bring a world to light. And that same promise is yours if you will only lay hold of it—if you will only believe, if you will only ask and seek and desire.

"There was a man of the Pharisees, named Nicodemus, a ruler of the Jews; the same came to Jesus by night, and said unto him, Rabbi, we know that thou art a teacher come from God: for no man can do these miracles that thou doest, except God be with him.

"Jesus answered and said unto him, Verily, verily, I say unto thee, except a man be born again, he cannot see the kingdom of God. Nicodemus saith unto him, How can a man be born when he is old? Can he enter the second time into his mother's womb, and be born? Jesus answered, Verily, verily, I say unto thee, except a man be born of water and of the

Spirit, he cannot enter the kingdom of God. *That which is born of the flesh is flesh: and that which is born of the Spirit is Spirit.*

"Marvel not that I said unto thee, ye must be born again.

"THE WIND BLOWETH WHERE IT LISTETH, AND THOU HEAREST THE SOUND THEREOF, BUT CANST NOT TELL WHENCE IT COMETH, AND WHITHER IT GOETH: SO IS EVERY ONE THAT IS BORN OF THE SPIRIT." (John 3:1-8).

Those are not my words, those are the words of Jesus Christ, and they are not mistranslated. They mean exactly what they say. They mean that anyone who has been born of the Spirit will be able to come and go without anyone being able to tell where he came from, or where he goes. And Christ Himself proved the words many times in His own life.

"And he that was healed wist not who it was: for Jesus had conveyed himself away, a multitude being in that place." (John 5:13).

"If I do not the works of my Father, believe me not.

"But if I do, though ye believe not me, believe the works: that ye may know, and believe that the Father is in me, and I in him.

"Therefore they sought again to take him: but he escaped out of their hand,

"And went away again beyond Jordan into the place where John at first baptized; and there he abode." (John 10:37-40).

"While ye have light, believe in the light, that ye may be the children of light. These things spake Jesus and departed, and did hide himself from them. But though he had done so many miracles before them, yet they believed not on him." (John 12:36-37).

"And he said, Verily I say unto you, No prophet is accepted in his own country.

"But I tell you of a truth, many widows were in Israel in the days of Elias, when the heaven was shut up three years and six months, when great famine was throughout all the land;

"But unto none of them was Elias sent, save unto Sarepta, a city of Sidon, unto a woman that was a widow" (and a Gentile).

"And many lepers were in Israel in the time of Eliseus the Prophet; and none of them was cleansed, saving Naaman the Syrian, (also a Gentile).

"And all they in the synagogue, when they heard these things, were filled with wrath.

"And rose up, and thrust him out of the city, and led him unto the brow of the hill whereon their city was built, that they might cast him down headlong.

"But he passing through the midst of them went his way." (Luke 4:24-30).

"Jesus said unto them, Verily, verily, I say unto you, before Abraham was, I am.

"Then took they up stones to cast at him; but Jesus hid himself, and went out of the temple, going through the midst of them, and so passed by." (John 8:58-59).

After feeding the five thousand—"Therefore they gathered them together, and filled twelve baskets with the fragments of the five barley loaves, which remained over and above unto them that had eaten.

"Then those men, when they had seen the miracle that Jesus did, said, this is of a truth the prophet that should come into the world.

"When Jesus therefore perceived that they would come and take him by force, to make him a king, he departed again into a mountain himself alone." (John 6:13-15).

Later, that night, he joined His apostles, walking on the sea of Galilee.

"The "iron rod" which we are admonished to hold to is the "word of God" and it will lead us to partake of the love of God, or the fruit of the tree of life, "Which is shed forth in the hearts of the children of men; wherefore it is the most desirable above all things, and the most joyous to the soul." (I. Nephi 11:22-23).

"And it came to pass that I beheld that the iron rod, which my father had seen was the word of God, which led to the fountain of living waters, or to the tree of life; which waters are a representation of the love of God; and I also beheld

that the tree of life was a representation of the love of God."
(*Ibid.*, verse 25).

The foregoing information is most clear and beautiful. It
so plainly tells that if we desire to partake of the fruit of the
tree of life, which is the pure love of God, we must hold fast
to the "iron rod" which is the word of God.

The word of God, as it has come down to us from the prophets is a continuous record of promises. This is especially true
of the teachings of Jesus Christ. The Four Gospels are so
filled with dynamic promises that we have completely failed
to comprehend them—yet if we hold to them, believe in them,
seek to fulfill them, they will lead us to the perfect love and
we shall be permitted to partake of the fruit of the tree of life
located in the midst of the paradise of God, and we need not
die.

This is verified in Rev. 2:7— ". . . To him that overcometh
will I give to eat of the tree of life, which is in the midst of
the Paradise of God."

Thus as we seek diligently for the kingdom of God and its
righteousness, believing in the promises, we shall at last receive all things, or have all things added unto us. We are told
that the kingdom of heaven is within us. Now we are informed
that the fruit of the tree of life, which represents the love of
God, is His love that is shed forth in our hearts. If that is so
then the power to attain unto this gift of eternal life has to be
right within us.

Now, going back to Genesis, to study carefully the record
of Adam and Eve being driven from the garden: "And now,
lest Adam put forth his hand, and take also of the tree of life,
and eat, and live forever in his sins . . . he placed at the east
of the garden of Eden, Cherubims, and a flaming sword which
turned every way to guard the way of the tree of life." (Gen.
3:22 and 24).

The gate to the garden was sealed and man went forth to
earn his bread by the sweat of his brow in a lone and dreary
world, shut out from the presence of God. Cherubim drew a
veil over his consciousness and the flaming sword which turned
every way to guard the way to the tree of life is the flaming

burden and anguish of our physical, mortal conceptions and traits. These very weaknesses of the flesh guard the way to the tree of life more surely than could legions of angels.

Thus by his changed, mortal concept of thought Adam was not permitted to partake of the fruit of the tree of life lest he live forever in his sins. Neither are we permitted to partake of it lest we live forever in our sins. But when we have overcome our sins the fruit of the tree of life, which is the great and perfect love of God bestowed upon us in all its fullness and power, we may partake of the fruit of the tree of life and death will no longer have any claim on us.

And sin, according to the scriptures, is the cause of death. Sin is every thought, feeling or vibration that is out of harmony with man's true pattern of life, or out of harmony with the divine melody of the perfect love and peace of the universe.

"Verily, verily, I say unto you, he that heareth my word, and believeth on him that sent me, hath everlasting life, and shall not come into condemnation; but is passed from death unto life." (John 5:24). These higher laws and powers are the gifts of Christ. They are the gifts He was trying to prepare the people of his day to receive—and the same blessings stand waiting for us today. They belong to you if you can only believe—if you can hold to the "iron rod", the word of His promises. Not only remember always, but *know* that to him that believes nothing is impossible. And know also that for him who reaches and asks, there is no rebuke. To the "Three Nephites" his answer was: "*More* blessed are ye, for ye shall never taste of death; but ye shall live to behold all the doings of the Father unto the children of men, even until all things shall be fulfilled according to the will of the Father, when I shall come in my glory with the powers of heaven." Here He plainly told them that they were *more blessed* because they had desired so great a thing of Him. The greater one's vision, the greater will be his desires.

The greatest work of Christ was breaking the bands of death. That can also become our greatest work, for if we believe in His words we are to do the works that He did. He is not to do them for us. He only showed the way. They are for us to accomplish.

"Verily, verily, I say unto you, *he that believeth on me the works that I do shall he do also, and greater things than these shall he do* because I go unto my Father." (John 14:12).

And so I leave this chapter with you, asking only that you continue to pray as you study and ponder it in your heart, for only as the Spirit of God unfolds it unto you can you know of its great truth and receive of its blessings.

Chapter XVIII.

THE TRUE PATTERN OF EACH INDIVIDUAL LIFE

Light is life, and life is intelligence, or Spirit. It is energy. It is motion and activity—and it is the power of God. By it and OF it all things were created—the universe—the stars —the worlds—and mankind.

". . . The light of Truth.

"Which truth shineth. THIS IS THE LIGHT OF CHRIST. As also he is in the sun, and the light of the sun, and the power thereof by which it was made.

"As also he is in the moon, and is the light of the moon, and the power thereof by which it was made;

"As also the light of the stars, and the power thereof by which they were made;

"And the earth also, and the power thereof, even the earth upon which you stand.

"And the light which shineth, which giveth you light, is through him who enlighteneth your eyes, which is the same light that quickeneth your understandings:

"WHICH LIGHT PROCEEDETH FORTH FROM THE PRESENCE OF GOD TO FILL THE IMMENSITY OF SPACE—

"*The light which is in all things, which giveth life to all things, which is the law by which all things are governed,* EVEN THE POWER OF GOD, who sitteth upon his throne, who is in the bosom of eternity, *who is in the midst of all things.*"

The law by which all things are governed, which is in the *midst* of all things, or in the very center of all things, is one of the most remarkable explanations ever given. The law which governs man is his conscience, deep in the *midst* of him. It is most assuredly true, "That the light shineth in darkness, and the darkness comprehendeth it not; nevertheless, the day shall come when you shall comprehend even God, being quickened in him and by him." Or when we learn to hear clearly

and distinctly the voice of God as it speaks out of the depths
of our own souls.

"Behold, here is the agency of man, and here is the condemnation of man; because that which was from the beginning
is plainly manifest unto them, and they receive not the light.

"And every man whose spirit receiveth not the light is under condemnation." (D. & C. 93:31-32).

This Spirit that has been in man from the beginning and is
plainly manifest is the voice of conscience that whispers out
of the *"midst"* of him. Those who reject this voice are under
condemnation for they follow not the light of its guiding, and
groping in darkness fail to fulfill their full pattern of life.

I once asked a group of young people what repentance is.
A very beautiful young woman answered, "It is that wormy
feeling you get when you do something you shouldn't."

I think that is one of the most complete answers ever given
in one sentence. Repentance is truly a wormy feeling, but it is
beautiful with all its "worminess," when understood, for it is
the only true guide to life. By giving ear to that Spirit of
Christ, in hearing its rebukes, then letting its fires purge out the
results of the mistakes committed, leaving the slate clean, and
the pattern of life close to the touch. This voice is the only
true guide to perfect living. That is why no one can possibly
live the life of another—and no two lives have the same pattern—the same mission and destiny. Each person must get the
vision and the courage to live his life as he sees it, regardless
of what "the neighbors say," or what anyone says. He must be
directed from "within" to meet his highest destiny. This voice
of conscience is not always disapproving, or a rebuking voice.
It is also that loving voice of approval—that divine voice
within us—the voice of God. It contains our true pattern of
life, revealed to us day by day, moment by moment as we live
by it. This voice will as surely lift a man from mediocrity as
it will lift the plant from the seed. It alone can bring the full
flower of fulfillment into the life of each individual. No person was ever born without it. None are so lowly, none so insignificant, so devoid of gifts and talents, so friendless and alone
that they cannot fill a perfect pattern of their individual ex-

istence if they will learn to contact that "Still, Small voice within." This voice is the true Word of God that will lead to the life abundant, perfect and free.

Only as one learns to live by this infallible guide can he possibly live true to himself, or true to God. This voice is the "Spirit of Truth" speaking within him. It never flatters. It never condemns without cause. It is the one true, unfailing, all-knowing, dependable friend.

All the days of my life, kindly intentioned people have been giving me advice on how to live my life. They are well-meaning individuals who wish to help me live my life as they live theirs, and I love them for it, and their advice is just perfect for their lives—*and for what they would do if they were in my place.* But they are not in my place, therefore their advice is all wrong for me, and for my life. In fact, it is darkness to me. Only that inner voice can possibly guide me in my mission in life—and only that voice can truly guide you to reach and fulfill your highest destiny, be that destiny what it may.

Every great person has had to live true to that inner voice or they would never have achieved greatness. Abraham Lincoln, with no opportunities and no backing of friends, except that guiding voice within, reached his high destiny in honor and directed America through its most crucial period.

The complete pattern of your life in all its divine power of fulfillment is contained as completely within that all-knowing center as the pattern of the flower is within the seed. Only you have contact with your pattern of life—only you can keep that contact open. No one can do that for you. Neither can you do it for another. Each individual must learn to live true to his own pattern in order to truly reach his magnificent dignity of complete fulfillment.

If you wish to give advice, to comfort, to help—then teach those whom you contact, or who come to you for help, how to find God—teach them how to listen to that voice within their own souls. That is the greatest service you can possibly render anyone. Teach them how to "be still" and know God.

That same "wormy" voice of conscience that can make

you feel like the very "lowest thing on earth" is also the first
to pat you on the back when you do the noble, or the splendid,
unselfish thing. Its very approval sings out in a melody of
glory at every task well done. It never lies. It never flatters.
It never over-estimates. It just *knows* and *is*. It is the very
Spirit of Truth or of "Light that enlightens every man that
cometh into the world." It is the truest friend man ever had.
Listen to that voice and you will never fail in anything. You
will never feel deserted and alone as long as you listen to that
voice, or the Word of God planted deep within your own soul.
You will go forward from one achievement to another as you
learn to hold to it, even as to an iron rod. Thus you will
climb the ladder of destiny—your own great destiny—for
within every human being the seed of greatness lies waiting.
Only by and through the direction of this voice can you go
from grace to grace as new levels of progress unfold.

There is no such thing as glory without effort, salvation
without price. And in order to reach the light, one must learn
to walk in the light. "And he whose spirit refuseth to receive
the light is under condemnation."

Learning to heed this voice does not rob one of his free-
agency, for it is his willingness or unwillingness to follow or
heed it that makes life a glory or a failure. Every man is
entitled to "free doom". His free-agency is used in making
the choice of unfolding his life in its true pattern of perfection, or marring it continually with his mistakes. In following
the glorious voice of his true inner self, that knows and comprehends all things, he lives above the groping, blundering
conscious mind, with its lack of understanding, its changing
whims and moods, its instabilities. He lives in contact with the
super-conscious mind at all times. And with this growing understanding, and divine contact he will soon find that the
voice not only speaks after he has acted in blind, blundering
ignorance—but will speak before the act is done, before the
harsh or false word is spoken. Thus all mistakes can be eliminated. Two of the ancient Greek scholars claimed that whenever they even began to speak the wrong thing they would be

stopped, or warned—and by following the warning their works have lived down the centuries.

This glorious *voice of approval* that pats one on the back with such warm affection, filling his whole being with that "good feeling" within, is not the voice of ego with its blare of self-importance or self-righteousness. Ego is of the conscious mind entirely, and is completely mortal and of the flesh. That glorious voice of conscience is of the soul. It is the Spirit of Christ that is born in every man. It is the voice of God that Christ followed so lovingly and so gratefully. It is the vine, yielding life and strength and power to us, for of ourselves, truly we can do nothing of value. Only as we abide in the vine can our lives and our works become glorious. (John 15).

The trouble with most of us is that when we get that "good feeling" over something we have done, we wish to hold on to it by retelling what it was we did—and just how we did it, even magnifying our goodness in the telling. This is a very grave mistake. That feeling is the abiding voice of God in the secret chamber of our own souls. It is the sacred voice that comes to each of us, individually, as we enter the Holy of Holies, or our own closet, or inner soul, to pray to God. This inner approval is an individual and sacred experience and is not meant to be shared openly, else if it is, we have received our reward—the empty praise of the world. When that public acclaim or approval means more than the reward which only the Father can give, then we may have the public acclaim— but it will be empty and meaningless compared to that loving direction that will lead us on up the high stairway of achievement so that it may be made apparent openly by the power of Almighty God Himself. Any man who "toots his own horn" will fail utterly in receiving great honors from His Father in heaven.

Thus understanding just how this glorious power or law of God works in our lives we can understand just why it is not good to tell our left hand what our right hand does, for by so doing we have received all the reward we are entitled to—the reward of the flesh, and have forfeited our right to the greater reward—the reward promised by our Father. The very telling of the good we have done becomes boasting and immediately places a false standard before us. This method causes us to lose contact with that inner voice which contains our true pattern of life. Gradually the flattering praises of men become the only voice we live for, and the greatness that was meant for us has been sacrificed upon the altar of vanity.

Christ was never known to repeat in words any good He ever accomplished—but living true to the voice within he was rewarded openly—two thousand years of homage paid by the loving devotion of a world.

Only the approval of that inner voice matters in anyone's life. No outside opinion counts, for the full, glorious pattern of each individual's life is enfolded minutely within that seed of all-knowing, locked waiting within each man's soul. It can only be brought forth gradually as the seed grows into the plant, and the plant is glorified by the unfoldment of its own blossoms. If man desires to get in step with the great forward marching glory of the whole universe then he will have to do so by learning to heed that voice of conscience, or that "still small voice" within—that guiding voice of light that stands knocking on the door of his consciousness, waiting to be admitted. This is the light that was apparent from the beginning —and man rejected the light. Follow that inner voice or guide and you will ascend to a life of honor and fulfillment as surely as the flower rises from the seed, the oak from the acorn, or the bird comes forth from the egg.

Know with all your heart and soul that you have His approval and your road will become a road of high honor though it leads to the gallows—and though you lose your life, yet shall you find it, for all things shall be added unto you and your works will stand forever as a beacon light to those who wish to stand above the low, common, mediocre way of life.

It takes great courage to stand alone against the world, to live true to your own destiny and calling for the simple reason that so few have dared to step forth and live their own lives in the complete freedom in the perfection of God's sublime direction. But as one understands the road of his own high destiny courage will be given, it will enfold him as a shining armour. It is the Joans of Arc, the Columbuses, the Magellans, the Roger Bacons and the Patrick Henrys who were willing to give their lives for what they *felt* to be true that have been the truly great of the earth.

The late Robert Henri, the great artist with a living soul, said, "Each genius differs from the mass in that he has found freedom for his greatness: the greatness is everywhere, in every man, in every child. What our civilization is busy doing, mainly, is smothering greatness—we fear people who live simply and beautifully—then condemn them. It is only if they are great enough to outlive our condemnation that we accept them . . . The great revolution in the world which is to equalize opportunity, bring peace and freedom, must be a spiritual thing in each one. Our education has led away from the realization that the mystery of nature is in each man. When we are wiser we will not assume to mould ourselves (or let others mould us), but will make our ignorance stand aside—hands off—and will watch our own development. We will learn from ourselves."

In other words, we will learn to live by the pattern that is contained within each one of us—I by my pattern—you by yours. We will cease trying to fit everyone into the same mould. We will each respect the other in his work and calling and will be respected ourselves as we fulfill our own individual pattern of life, attentive to that all-knowing, all-loving voice from within.

Learn to listen to that voice, love it. This is the "feeling after God" mentioned in Acts 17:27. Thank that deep inner-knowing for its rebukes. Apologize to it for your mistakes, and promise it that you will try to do better—and then live true to that promise. You will soon glory in the amazing closeness of that divine contact. Even a discordant thought or vibration is felt by it, for it is all-knowing, ever present, and completely aware of every thought and feeling within one. This light of Christ, or Spirit of Christ is the inner reality of each individual.

"Therefore it is given to abide in you: the record of heaven; the Comforter; the peaceable things of immortal glory; the truth of all things; that which quickeneth all things, which maketh alive all things; *that which knoweth all things, and hath all power,* according to wisdom, mercy, truth, justice and judgment." (Moses 6:61).

"Wide is the gate and broad is the way that leadeth to destruction and many there be that go in thereat.

"For narrow is the gate and straight the way that leads to life, and few there be who find it." (Matt. 7:13-14).

"I am come that they might have life—and have it more abundant."

This abundant life for each individual is learning to live in contact with the abiding light and power of that divine contact with the Spirit of Christ, which is within. Ask this "voice of conscience", this "still, small voice" for help and understanding when you stand upon the threshold of the tempest and it will respond, and legions shall fly to do your bidding. Rejoice with it over its approvals, and enjoy that glorious "good feeling" to the very tips of your toes as its light tingles in every fibre of your being with that divine, inner satisfaction. Learn to follow that voice to the very seat of its inner chamber —and it will lead you to the Christ—and He will reveal the Father to you as given so often in the record of St. John.

"We have also a more sure word of prophecy; whereunto ye do well that ye take heed, as unto a light that shineth in a dark place, until the day dawn, and the day star arise in your hearts." (II. Peter 1:16-19).

Love that voice within. Praise it. Honor it, and it will become a constant glory in your life. Seal your ears against it and you will ensnare your soul in darkness and your life with failure.

Two boys can steal a bag of marbles. Both will hear that rebuke from within. One heeds it and permits that "wormy" feeling to have its cleansing work. And you may be sure that that boy will not steal again. The other, by refusing to be rebuffed, and by hardening his heart and sealing his mind, rejoices that he was not caught. Later he will steal, perhaps a knife—a purse—a car—a gun—anything and everything he can possibly take. This is the road of all criminals—the road away from the true pattern of life within. For this is "The light that was plainly manifest from the beginning, and man rejected the light, and is therefore under condemnation." And being without this great directing principle of tender, loving, all-knowing light is the greatest condemnation that is possible to bear. This in itself is a burden of utter darkness. No one becomes a criminal by one act alone No man becomes a saint by any one act of goodness. But every act is a step along the road of destiny.

> "Plant a thought and reap an act—
> Plant an act and reap a habit—
> Plant a habit and reap a character—
> Plant a character and reap a destiny."

It is when the conscience is seared with a red-hot iron so that the inner voice is silenced within one that "he is without hope—and he who is without hope must needs be in despair—and despair cometh because of iniquity." (Moroni 10:22). And iniquity is the sin of losing contact with that inner voice —it is every thought, feeling, act or vibration that is out of harmony with the true pattern of one's own divine existence.

> • "There is a way—and ways—and THE way.
> And the high man travels the high way,
> And the low man travels the low—
> And in between, on the misty flats
> The rest drift to and fro.
> But for every man that goeth
> There's a high way and a low—
> And every man decideth
> The way his soul shall go."

It is most certainly true that "we aren't what we think we are —we are only what we *think*." If we think according to the rhythm and pattern of our own melody of life there can be no failure, no darkness, no dismay. There can be only unfolding light and glory and joy and happiness.

"And Christ truly said unto our fathers: if ye have faith ye can do all things which are expedient unto me.

"And now I speak unto all the ends of the earth—that if

the day cometh that the power and gifts of God shall be done away among you, it shall be because of unbelief.

"And woe be unto the children of men if this be the case; for there shall be none that doeth good among you, no, not one. For if there be one among you that doeth good, he shall work by the power and gifts of God.

"And woe unto them who shall do these things away and die, *for they die in their sins,* and they cannot be saved in the kingdom of God; and I speak it according to the words of Christ; and I lie not."—"And except ye have charity (love) ye can in nowise be saved in the kingdom of God; neither can ye be saved in the kingdom of God if ye have not faith; neither if ye have no hope." (Moroni 10:22-26-21).

This hopelessness that is spoken of, that comes because of iniquity is a condition that comes to one who has lost contact with his own pattern of perfect unfoldment and achievement—when he has ceased to be guided by that inner light or voice—when he has failed to find its approving whisper, its guiding direction and is left unto himself to grope blindly in the mud and darkness. As long as one lives by this unfailing, infallible guide there can be no darkness, no despair, no hopelessness. It is when this guide has been forsaken, or ignored, or silenced by transgression or the hardness of one's heart that one is truly under condemnation. Thus life becomes a drab, mediocre thing of outer show and inner frustration. It becomes a thing of failure instead of an experience of increasing joy and unfolding glory.

This inner voice should also be identified with the voice of faith that soon becomes *"knowing"* as one follows it to its fulfillment. "For faith promises all things—and it fulfills all things."

In the beginning, this whole glorious force of faith, or light, through which and by which the worlds are and were created and which is the light thereof and the power thereof, and is also the light that is within man was called "Christ," and that is the great and glorious *Word* of all-power. This is also "The Father within" that Christ was always giving such humble credit and honor to. It is absolutely the only true guide to perfect, glorious living.

For those who insist on unrestricted freedom to live their own lives as they desire, without any suggestions from any source, I would like to say, that is their privilege. Every one is entitled to his "free doom." But the "free" should be left out, for there is no such thing as free doom. The price of doom is the highest price that can be paid for anything. The price of doom is the price of one's self respect, the price of his strength, his peace of mind, his joy, his glory of achievement, and eventually the very highest price that can be paid for anything—*the price of his own soul.* "And if a man should gain the whole world and lose his own soul what would it profit him?"

No, doom is not free. For it there is required the highest price of all. And the thing bought at such a cost? What is its true value and of what does it consist? It is the burned out ashes of regret—the dregs of a cup—the bitterness without the sweet. It is failure and remorse. It is outer-darkness, misery and death.

Only as one learns to follow the infallible guide within his own soul—that "Still small voice" of love and gentle tenderness, of knowledge and power, which is given to abide within each man, can he fulfill his destiny in honor.

"For it is given to abide in you; the record of heaven; the Comforter; the peaceable things of immortal glory; the truth of all things; that which quickeneth all things, which maketh alive all things; that which knoweth all things, and hath all power, according to wisdom, mercy, truth, justice and judgment."

Chapter XIX.

"IN THE NAME OF JESUS CHRIST"

OUR GREAT and glorious older Brother, Jesus Christ, the
First Born of the Spirit children of our Father, the most
perfect, the most loving, the most noble because He followed
in every thought, word and act, the voice of the Christ, or
light, or intelligence within. Thus He fulfilled *all* the laws of
perfection, in all things. For this very reason He was chosen
before the foundations of this world to be its Redeemer, or
guiding teacher—its leading example. "He was the Lamb slain
from the foundation of the world." The only individual who
never committed sin—who never for a moment lost contact
with His own true pattern of life.

No one has ever equalled Him in goodness, in love, in meekness and perfection. It is impossible to praise and honor Him
enough. His unselfishness, His love, His understanding and
compassionate mercy has so completely glorified light—or the
"Spirit of Truth" even that very "Spirit of Christ," of which
all things are composed, including us, that He will stand forever a complete embodiment of it—its eternal symbol—symbol of light.

"Christ" means "Anointed" and *"Anointed"*—the English
translation of the Greek word "Christos" is given to Jesus on
account of his being "Anointed" with the Holy Ghost—and because of His Holy calling. He was anointed unto this end
before the foundation of the world—that anointing was reaf-
firmed in the flesh just following His baptism. It was after
he had fulfilled this last, final law of righteousness that He
received of the *"fullness of the Father,"* or the fullness of the
power and light of God.

Having followed that inner voice from grace to grace, or
from one bit of instruction to another, until he had fulfilled
all the laws and kept all the commandments, He received the
fullness of light, and all power, both in heaven and on earth.

His work and mission was not to take away our free-agency and exalt us into glory by us simply saying we believed on Him, or to say that we know that He existed, or, that he is the Son of God. Such an idea is preposterous—yet is the common belief of many. His entire mission was to show us just how the great power of that inner light worked, and how we could, by following the pattern He gave, receive the same power and do the very works that He did, even greater works.

Ask any Christian on the earth if he believes in Jesus Christ, and he will most emphatically answer, "Yes." Ask him to prove his statement and he will fail utterly. "If you believe in MY NAME, ye can ask anything and it will be done unto you." Is that statement false? Is His promise or word, a mistake, or a lie where He declared, "Verily, verily, I say unto thee, that if you believe on me, the works that I do shall ye do also— and greater works than these shall ye do—because I go unto my Father. And whatsoever ye shall ask *in my name*, that will I do, that the Father may be glorified in the son. *If ye shall ask anything in my Name, I will do it.*" Not for one instant are these statements or promises false. They are the most true promises ever uttered. It is man who has failed—failed to understand or believe in THE POWER OF THE NAME.

The name "Jesus" is the Greek derivation of "Joshua" or according to the ancient Hebrew "Jehshua" or "Yehshua." "Jah" or "Yah" means literally, "I shall be." And "shua" means, "powerful." Thus Jesus is a promise—the promise, "I shall be powerful." And the word *"Christ"* means "Anointed" or "Anointed with light" thus completing the promise and power of the name. "I shall be powerful when anointed with light." Or in its complete fullness: *"I shall be powerful when I am anointed with light!"* Do you believe in *that name?* Have you ever believed in it? Or has any man ever understood or believed in the *powerful name of Jesus Christ?* If he has believed in that name then he has fulfilled that name within himself, and can do the works that Christ did. But most emphatically mankind has not understood its meaning and has not received the powers attached to it. They have believed the great Personage who symbolized the fulfillment of that power is the One who is to lift them into glory while all that is necessary is to sit weakly back and let Him do it—all of it—not realizing that *each man* must fulfill that NAME in his own life. He must follow that voice of light, faithfully, diligently, until all weaknesses and mistakes are eliminated—and until he can, through his own faithfulness, also be "anointed with light."

It was through this "Christ" or "Light" that the worlds were and are created—and most of them are far older than this little earth of ours. It is one of the youngest of the planets. It is the baby of the spheres, comparatively speaking. Yet it was not until *just before the foundations of this earth* of ours, that Jesus Christ, the individual who bears the NAME, was chosen to be the Redeemer of this world, the guide, the Great Shepherd, the Savior, by showing the way of salvation to all who would follow Him. The Shepherd never has to carry the sheep into the fold. They have to go in on their own power— and it is done as they follow the shepherd. He was chosen before the foundations of the earth for this very mission and purpose, and the world will forever owe Him a debt of love and gratitude that can never be completely repaid. But this great "Light of Truth" or "Spirit of Truth" or "light of Christ," of which we are a part, and were a part, even from the very beginning (and there is no beginning, and no end), existed long before that time. For we too were with God before the works of creation began, "The Spirit of Truth." This will be explained more fully in the following chapter.

This light of life, or spark of the Divine Spirit of Christ, is the original source of our existence. That divine spark is often imprisoned in mortality instead of being clothed or endowed with mortality. This body is the kingdom bequeathed to this spirit for fulfilling the laws of progress and advancement in the past. This mortal heritage is a great and precious gift, and was meant to be glorified by the Spirit, even as the Spirit was meant to be glorified by the flesh. These two, inseparably connected can receive a fullness of joy—or a fullness of the Father—or power and light.

This destiny can only be completed in glory as we learn to let the voice of the Spirit direct the "without" as it abides in

the "within." Or, as given in the Apocrypha: "For the Lord
himself, being asked by a certain person, when his kingdom
should come? answered, When two shall be one, and that which
is without as that which is within." His kingdom, or the kingdom of heaven will be revealed to every man when he learns
to abide by the laws of that inner kingdom, or the voice of
the Christ, or light within.

For each person who learns to listen to that inner voice at
all times, who heeds its loving, tender instructions until he has
fulfilled all the glorious laws of righteousness, is to have the
great privilege of Jesus Christ, the Redeemer, to appear in
person to him from time to time—and even He will reveal
the Father to him.

Jesus Christ chose the way of the crucifixion to prove that
this great light and power of the Christ Light could fulfill all
things—and had life eternal, or was life eternal—boundless,
indestructible—and as He fulfilled all the laws of righteousness and glorified that light within Himself He had the power
over death—that He could lay down His life and take it up
again if he chose.

"On account of this the Father loves me, because I lay down
my life, that I may receive it again.

"No one takes it from me, but I lay it down of myself. I
have authority to lay it down and I have authority to receive it
again." (John 10:17-18).

"For as the Father has life in himself, so he gave to the son
to have life in himself." (John 5:26).

So He gives to every son to have life in himself who is
truly born of the Spirit, if he will follow the pattern and fulfill all the laws.

Being born of the Spirit is being baptized into the very
name of Jesus Christ, or anointed with light—so that with full
consciousness one realizes that "In Him we live and move and
have our being." Thus as we live with a full understanding of
the meaning of His Name, and truly believe in it—we too
shall begin to be able to do the works which He did—even the
greater works. Yea, "I shall be powerful when I am anointed
with light," or "Spirit." Thus we begin to take upon ourselves

that name and the power of it. When we truly believe in *The Name of Jesus Christ* and fulfill that name within ourselves our lives will no longer be barren and unfruitful, but will unfold in complete fulfillment of all the promises ever given— and the divine pattern within us will be brought forth in all its unfolding glory. It is only the voice of that "Light within" that can guide us to this complete fulfillment.

The name "Jesus Christ" is the great key-word of power. *Learn the power of the Name.* The only name under heaven where mankind can be saved—saved from their weaknesses as well as from their sins. *Use the Name.* Think it. Love it. Magnify it—and Walk with Him in Light. How else could the following promise possibly be fulfilled? "For as many as are led by the Spirit of God, they are the sons of God—the Spirit itself beareth witness with our Spirit, that we are the children of God; and if children, then heirs of God, joint-heirs with Christ." (Romans 8:14, 16, 17). And if we are "joint-heirs" then we must be equal with Him, if we fulfill that NAME in our lives, even as He did.

It is only as we each follow our own true pattern of life that we can hope for this complete perfection within us. The voice of the multitude, the praise of the world, the desire for wealth and fame so often sidetrack us from our own design of life. Despair or failure can never come to us as long as we live true to the pattern, not any more than it could come to Jesus. Every heartache, every trial was a stepping stone upward—even the crucifixion—the great, triumphant, final victory over death—the victory awaiting all who will "overcome."

"He that hath the Son hath life, and he that hath not the son of God hath not life." (I John 5:12).

"When the Anointed may appear, the life of us, then also you with him shall appear in glory."

"Let the same mind be in you which was in Christ Jesus, who being in the form of God, thought it not robbery to be equal with God."

"The light that shineth in darkness, and the darkness comprehendeth it not; nevertheless, the day shall come when you shall comprehend even God *being quickened in him and by him.*"

"Behold, that which you hear is as the voice of one crying in the wilderness—in the wilderness because you cannot see him—my voice, because my voice is Spirit; my Spirit is Truth; Truth abideth and hath no end, and if you abide in it you shall abound." (D. & C. 88:66).

"For no man has seen God at any time in the flesh, except quickened by the Spirit of God." (*Ibid.*, 67:11).

"Therefore it is given to abide in you; the record of heaven; the Comforter; the peaceable things of immortal glory; the truth of all things; *that which quickeneth all things,* which maketh alive all things; that which *knoweth* all things; and *hath all power,* according to wisdom, mercy, truth, justice and judgment." (Moses 6:61).

According to the dictionary, the word "Quicken" is given the following definition: "To revive; to cheer; to increase the speed of; to sharpen; to stimulate.—(Verb); "To become alive; to move quickly, or more quickly." This is truly the inner voice within. It is the voice of conscience that cheers and approves our actions. It is the voice of the Christ, the very Light of God that is in the MIDST of all things. It is the power that will sharpen, quicken, stimulate and glorify our lives.

Thus to be quickened by the Spirit of God means to have our vibrations increased from the slow, mortal tempo to the Spiritual that we might be prepared to receive our anointing of light. This increasing of vibrations will be the power that will prepare us to comprehend even God—to receive a fullness of His joy and power. This quickening power can translate us from mortal beings into translated beings, on whom death has no claim, unless, we like Christ, permit it. This quickening comes from within, and is the source of all high inspiration, for this is the divine light and life of the Christ light, the very power of God pouring through us as we prepare ourselves to receive it. It is given to abide in us, but we must bring it forth by a conscious awareness of it, and by our understanding of it and the glorious laws under which it operates in our lives. This is the only possible way we can PROVE that we *believe in the name of Jesus Christ, and fulfill that name in our own lives.*

"Behold, the Lord passed by, and a great and strong wind rent the mountains, and brake in pieces the rocks before the Lord; but the Lord was not in the wind: and after the wind an earthquake; but the Lord was not in the earthquake:

"And after the earthquake a fire; but the Lord was not in the fire: and after the fire a still small voice.

"And it was so, when Elijah heard it, that he wrapped his face in his mantle, and went out, and stood in the entering of the cave." (I. Kings 19:11-13). Such is the power of God and His manner of speaking through that still small voice within.

We are told repeatedly throughout the scriptures, that we are the temples of the living God. Perhaps it would be well to give a brief description of the Holy of Holies in the temple of Jerusalem at the time of Christ's ministry. "The Holy of Holies in the temple of Herod retained the form and dimensions of the Oracle of the Temple of Solomon. It was therefore a cube, twenty cubits in each principal measurement. Between this and the Holy Place hung a double veil, of finest material, elaborately embroidered. The outer of the two veils was open at the north end, and the inner at the south; so that the high Priest who entered at the appointed time once a year could pass between the veils without exposing the Holy of Holies. This sacred chamber was empty save for a large stone upon which the high priest sprinkled the sacrificial blood on the Day of Atonement. This stone occupied the place of the Ark and its Mercy Seat." However, originally this spot belonged to the Ark and the record or Testament of the Lord that was contained therein. This had disappeared at the time of the Babylonian captivity 589 B. C. This Holy of Holies was the room, or sacred chamber within the temple where the voice of the Lord was heard when He had some message for the people. It was in this room where Zacharias received the announcement of the birth of his son, John, who was the forerunner of Christ. It was originally the place where the laws of the Lord were contained, the laws that had been written by

His finger, in the days of Moses. (*The House of the Lord,* by Talmedge, p. 59).

The above is quite adequate to give an idea of this inner sanctuary of God. It is interesting to note that it is the place in which the laws of the Lord were kept—that it was entered only by the one appointed to officiate in the temple—and on keeping the *Day of Atonement* or "At-one-meant."

We are the temples of the Living God, and within each one of us is the Holy of Holies, the Oracle, or place where God can contact us in the depths of our own souls. It is the place where His laws are engraved. It is where the voice of conscience dwells—even "the Light of Truth." When we become sufficiently silent, sufficiently humble to hear that voice, and then have the courage to follow it at all times, it will become audible to us, and be a guide to us in all that we say and do, so that we, like Jesus will say nothing except it is given to us of the Father, and do nothing except He commands us. We will speak only His words, for His Holy place in our own souls is where our own true pattern or law of life is contained. This is a complete, individual pattern for each man. No two will unfold alike—no two will have the same exact work to do, or mission to fill, or the same exact road to follow. I cannot live by your pattern, neither can you live by mine. We must each live by our own pattern, and follow it to its complete unfoldment of glory—and thus we are eventually "anointed" with light, and the complete understanding and fulfillment may be accomplished.

"My little children, of whom I travail in birth again until Christ be formed in you." (Gal. 4:19).

". . . But we know that when he shall appear, we shall be like him, for we shall see him as he is—(and as we are).

"And every man that hath this hope in him purifieth himself, even as he is pure." (I John 3:2-4).

Christ never purifies any man. Each man must purify himself by following that Christ light of conscience within himself, as he learns to stand before God, rejoicing in a clear conscience that is perfected within him, as "the Spirit of Truth." Thus to be saved by grace is to be saved by obedience to the continued instructions that come daily from God, through the Vine—or voice within. This voice is truly the "Word of God" —and those to whom it comes "are gods."

It is not necessary for any man to ever seek to justify himself by words in anything he does, whether it be good or bad. If one has done wrong it can never be justified by words. If he has done right God will justify him in time, and his justification will be made apparent to the whole world.

If you have wondered, as I used to, what the writings of Jesus would have been like had He left a written message, you should rejoice as I have rejoiced in the "Odes of Solomon," from the New Testament Apocrypha. They were not written by King Solomon, but by a Gentile convert of the first century of Christianity, whose name remains a mystery. "All those will be astonished to see me. For from another race am I." (41:8).

"These writings contain the most beautiful and inspired words the world possesses. They have come down to us in a single and a very ancient document in Syriac language, and evidently the document is a translation from the original Greek. There has been much debate around these Odes. And there does not seem to be anything about which the scholars all agree unless it be that the Odes are of singular beauty and high spiritual value." All agree however that there was nothing else like them ever written, either in the Old Testament or in the Gospels. They were written by a man who believed in the *Name* of Jesus Christ and fulfilled that *Name* in his own life. I shall only quote a few of them.

ODE 12:7-13

"For as the Word of the Lord is, so is its end: for it is light and the dawning of thought;

"And by it the worlds talked one to another; and in the Word there were those who were silent;

"And from it came love and concord; and they spake one to the other whatever was theirs; and they were penetrated by the Word:

"And they knew Him who made them, because they were in concord; for the mouth of the Most High spake to them; and his explanation ran by means of it:

"For the dwelling place of the WORD *is man;* and its truth is love.

"Blessed are they who by means thereof understood every-thing and have known the Lord in His Truth."

Ode 13

"Behold! The Lord is our mirror; open the eyes and see them in Him: and learn the manner of your face;

"And tell forth praise to His Spirit: and wipe off the filth from your face: and love his holiness, and clothe yourself therewith:

"And be without stain at all times before Him."

Ode 15:8-11

"I have put on incorruption through His name; and have put off corruption by His grace.

"Death hath been destroyed before my face; and Sheol hath been abolished by my word;

"And there hath gone up deathless life in the Lord's land,

"And hath been made known to His faithful ones, and hath been given without stint to all those that trust in Him."

Ode 17:7-10

"And He who knew and brought me up is the Most High in all His perfection. And He glorified me by His kindness, and raised my thoughts to the height of His Truth.

"And from thence He gave me the way of His precepts and I opened the doors that were closed,

"And brake in pieces the bars of iron; but my iron melted and dissolved before me;

"Nothing appeared closed to me; BECAUSE I WAS THE DOOR TO EVERYTHING."

Ode 21:2-4

"And I put off darkness and clothed myself with light,

"And my soul acquired a body free from sorrow, or afflic-tion or pain.

"And increasingly helpful to me was the thought of the Lord, and His fellowship in incorruption."

Ode 26:10-12

"Or who can rest on the most High, so that with HIS mouth, he may speak?

"Who is able to interpret the wonders of the Lord?

"For he who could interpret would be dissolved and would become that which is interpreted."

Ode 30

"Fill ye waters for yourselves from the living fountain of the Lord, for it is opened to you;

"And come all ye thirsty, and take the draught; and rest by the fountain of the Lord.

"For fair it is and pure and gives rest to the soul. Much more pleasant are its waters than honey;

"And the honeycomb of the bees is not to be compared with it.

"For it flows forth from the lips of the Lord and from the heart of the Lord is its name.

"*And it came infinitely and invisibly; and until it was set in the* MIDST *they did not know it.*

"Blessed are they who have drunk therefrom and have found rest thereby."

Ode 36

"I rested in the Spirit of the Lord; and the Spirit raised me on high;

"And made me stand on my feet in the height of the Lord, before His perfection and His glory, while I was praising Him by the composition of His songs.

"The Spirit brought me forth before the face of the Lord; and although a son of man, *I was named the illuminate, the Son of God:*" (Received the anointing of Light or of Christ).

"While I praised amongst the praising ones, and great was I amongst the mighty ones.

"*For according to the greatness of the Most High, so He made me; and He* ANOINTED *me from His own perfection*:

"And I became one of His neighbors; and my mouth was opened like a cloud of dew:

"And my heart poured out as it were a gushing stream of righteousness.

"And my access to Him was in peace; and I was established by the Spirit of His government." (or by fulfilling His laws).

ODE 41:11-17

"And His word is with us in all our way.

"The Savior who makes alive and does not reject our souls;

"The man who was humbled and exalted by His own right-eousness.

"The Son of the Most High appeared in the perfection of His Father.

"And Light dawned from the WORD that was beforetime in Him.

"The Messiah is truly one; and He was known before the foundation of the world,

"THAT HE MIGHT SAVE SOULS FOREVER BY THE TRUTH OF HIS NAME."

No man could possibly write such messages of divine glory unless he had fulfilled those very things in his own life, and unless he wished to help others to do the same.

"And the Word of the Lord is Truth, and whatsoever is truth is light; and whatsoever is light is Spirit, even the Spirit of Jesus Christ. It is this Spirit that is the guiding voice that will *lead us to all truth.* It will lead upward to God just as much today as in days of old. It contains the laws of perfection and is the law of Jesus Christ. It is the very name of Jesus Christ as it begins to be fulfilled in each man's life.

"We have all sinned and have come short of the glory of God." We have truly all failed, and have fallen short of His glory. But He never intended us to come short of it. We were meant to obtain "all power, both in heaven, and on earth, even as Christ did." (Romans 3:23; D. & C. 50:26-29).

His glory will become our glory when we fulfill the NAME of *Jesus Christ* in our lives, and we can only fulfill it as we believe in it. Then our glory will also be His glory—"For this is my work and my glory, to bring to pass the immortality and eternal life of man." Believe in this name and you will prove that you truly believe in His words, and in the power of *His Name*, and in the power of Almighty God, and in the promises of His Son Jesus Christ, for you will be able to do the works that He did, even the *greater works*.

This most sacred anointing of Light should be the greatest, most intense desire of every man. It can only be given when each individual has prepared himself for it through the sanctification of his life through righteousness. But every one who earnestly desires it and who purifies himself from all sin, who "ASKS" for it will as surely be led to it as the river finds its way to the sea, or the bee finds its way to the flowers. This is the one, sublime gift of gifts that God is most anxious to bestow upon His children. It is the gift divine, and anyone who asks for it, and continues to ask for it will automatically prepare themselves to receive it—and to such it will be given. Anyone who can catch the divine vision of this gift will gradually be led to fulfill all the laws of righteousness, even to being led to those who have the authority direct from God to baptize in the NAME of His Beloved Son Jesus Christ. He will be led into all truth though he abides at the nethermost part of the earth, or in the heart of the African jungles—"For everyone who asks receives and he who seeks finds, and to him who knocks it shall be opened." This is the true heritage of every man. It is the greatest gift of God.

This anointing of light is not a thing of wild hysteria, of jumping and shouting and babbling. It is an anointing of divine majesty, of dignity and supreme power—a majesty of divinity such as Christ wore. It is the power and light of God in all its unspeakable, enfolding glory.

This is the complete opening of the doors to the kingdom of God, within, in which all things are revealed—and all power bestowed. It is the full and complete power of the *Name of Jesus Christ* fulfilled in man—"For when you have become anointed with Light, you shall be powerful."

So be it, in the Name of Jesus Christ, Amen.

CHAPTER XX.

OIL FOR THE LAMPS OF ISRAEL

THE ROAD of light is the road of joy, of divine glory, of ecstasy and gladness. To travel the highway of light until one at last becomes immersed with light, or "Anointed with light," one must of himself leave the darkness behind. Never for a moment must sadness or despair be permitted to lay hold of one. The door to heaven is love, but the key to the door is ecstasy or joy in all its Spiritual outflowing glory of singing power. That song of joy must never be permitted to die, not for one instant. It is the contact with the Spirit of God. It is Spirit. Love, ecstasy and that glorious spirit of anticipation is the very essence and Spirit of the power of God. It is faith's singing glory as it swings into action. It is power triumphant that will bring fulfillment—"for it promises all things, and will fulfill all things."

"And if your eyes be single to my glory, your whole bodies shall be filled with light, and there shall be no darkness in you; and that body which is filled with light comprehendeth all things. Therefore, sanctify yourselves that your minds become single to God, and the day will come that you shall see Him, for he will unveil his face unto you, and it shall be in his own time, and in his own way, and according to his own will. Remember the great and last promise which I have made unto you; cast away your idle thoughts far from you." (D. & C. 88:67-69). Eyes single to the glory of God is having power to see only the joy of His glory, to behold His light, and to cast out darkness.

"The perfect love casteth out all fear." This is the "overcoming" of all mortality, for fear, sadness, despair is of the earth and is darkness. This darkness can only be eliminated by keeping one's eyes or mind continually on the light—or by keeping his ear attuned to the joy of that voice within. This is

222

the ecstasy of the Spirit that will melt the doors of brass and
the bars of iron or any other obstruction that is holding one
back. This great joy or ecstasy does not mean empty, hilarious
nonsense, but a deep, steadfast song of power singing in one's
soul of promise and fulfillment. It is this joy, or faith of action that casts out all darkness, or "overcomes" it. No one can
do that for us. We have to cast it out ourselves. We have to do
our own "overcoming." We have to take hold of the great light
and draw it to us by love and constant awareness of it.

1. "Put all sadness far from thee; for it is the sister of
doubting and of anger. How sir, said I (to the angel), is it the
sister of these? For sadness, and anger, and doubting, seem to
be very different from one another.

2. "And he answered: Art thou without intelligence that thou
dost not understand it? For sadness is the most mischievous of
all spirits, and the worst to the servants of God: It destroys
the spirits of all men, and torments the Holy Spirit; . . .

3. ". . . Hear, said he, and understand. They who never
sought out the truth, nor inquired concerning the majesty of
God, but only believed, are involved in the affairs of the
world.

13. "But they that have the fear of the Lord, and search
out the truth concerning God, having all their thoughts towards
the Lord; apprehend whatsoever is said to them, and forthwith
understand it, because they have the love of the Lord in them.

14. "For where the spirit of the Lord dwells, there is also
much understanding added. Wherefore join thyself to the Lord,
and thou shalt understand all things.

15. "Learn now, O unwise man! How sadness troubleth the
Holy Spirit. When a man that is doubtful is engaged in any
affair, and does not accomplish it by reason of his doubting,
this sadness enters into him, and grieves the Holy Spirit.

18. "Remove therefore sadness from thyself, and afflict not
the Holy Spirit which dwelleth in thee, lest he entreat God,
and depart from thee. For the Spirit of the Lord which is
given to dwell in the flesh, endureth no such sadness.

19. "Wherefore clothe thyself with cheerfulness, which has
always favor with the Lord, and thou shalt rejoice in it. For

every cheerful man does well; and relishes those things that are good, and despises sadness.

20. "But the sad man does always wickedly. First, he doth wickedly because he grieveth the Holy Spirit, which is given to man, being of a cheerful nature. And again he does ill, because he prays with sadness unto the Lord, and maketh not a first thankful acknowledgement unto him for former mercies, and obtains not of God what he asks.

21. "For the prayer of a sad man has not always efficacy to come up to the altar of God. And I said unto him, Sir, why has not the prayer of a sad man virtue to come up to the altar of God? Because, said he, that sadness remaineth in his heart.

22. "When therefore a man's prayer shall be accompanied with sadness, it will not suffer his requests to ascend pure to the altar of God. For as wine it is mingled with vinegar, has not the sweetness it had before; so sadness being mixed with the Holy Spirit, suffers not a man's prayer to be the same as it would be otherwise.

23. "Wherefore cleanse thyself from sadness, which is evil, and thou shalt live unto God. And all others shall live unto God, as many as shall lay aside sadness and put on cheerfulness." (II. Hermas 10).

"Verily, I say unto you, my friends, fear not, let your hearts be comforted; yea, rejoice evermore, and in everything give thanks." (D. & C. 98:1).

The first and greatest mission of the Comforter is to give comfort—to speak peace, to give courage, to reveal light—and he who refuses to be comforted is rejecting the light and power of the Comforter. There is no sorrow so great, no condition so dark, no life so hopeless that the voice of the Comforter will not bring peace if that individual will not reject it, clinging rather to the darkness. Darkness is only a lack of light. Unhappiness is a condition where joy is not—and a lack of joy and hope, or faith comes because of iniquity. It comes truly because we have refused to be comforted—and have failed to heed that voice from deep within our own souls.

The very greatest tragedy that could possibly happen in any life would be transgression—poverty, want, despair, death of a loved one, loss of any kind could not possibly compare to the great tragedy of transgression. Yet the promise is always there: "He who seeks me diligently shall find me." "Turn unto me and I will turn unto you." "Though their sins be as scarlet yet shall they be white as snow to him that overcometh." "There is more joy in heaven over one soul that returns to Me than over ninety and nine just persons."

And the first and greatest outburst of joy is that glorious joy in the heaven of a man's own soul as he returns to the light.

"And if ye have no hope ye must needs be in despair; and despair cometh because of iniquity." (Moroni 10:22). Despair is a condition of the mind that eliminates the power of faith, hence shuts out that contact with the Divine, and causes one to lose contact with his own pattern of divine fulfillment.

"But the fruit of the Spirit is love, joy, peace, long-suffering, gentleness, goodness, faith, meekness, temperance; against such there is no law." Those who fulfill these higher laws and receive the glory of the divine gifts have fulfilled all laws for these are the gifts of eternal light—gifts that leave no room for darkness, discord, confusion or despair. They are light and glory and carry with them all power.

Love is truly the door to the realms of the great kingdom of heaven, and the key to the door is that inner ecstasy of joy that is always in contact with the Spirit of Almighty God, opening wide the soul to the great gift of eternal light.

"Behold, I stand at the door, and knock; if any man hear my voice, and open the door, I will come in to him, and will feast with him, and he with me. To him that overcometh will I grant to sit with me in my throne, even as I also overcame, and am set down with my Father in His throne." (Rev. 3:20-21). "If any man hear my voice"—this voice of Christ is the voice of faith and love and gladness and joy—it is that voice of approval within—the voice that will lead into all truth and all power. Learn to hear this voice of light, and open the door, for it is the door to heaven or the fulfillment of all your own great possibilities—and thus all things will be added to you.

This is truly the "Feast of the Passover." Originally it was thought only to pertain to the passing over of the destroying angel—but it was the feast also in which the children of Israel passed out of bondage into free living, under the direction of the love and power of God. To Christ it was the last supper, but it was also the Feast of the Passover—or symbolized His passing over from death into life. When we hear His voice and open the doors of our hearts, souls and minds wide to His Holy Spirit we too partake of the feast of the passover, for we pass over from mortal thinking into the realm of divine thinking—and thus He feasts with us—and we with Him.

Man himself is the doorway. He must open the door. No outside power can do it for him. It would be as detrimental to him to have some outside force open this door and release him as it would be for anyone to tear the cocoon from the moth. It has to free itself, and in the struggle to obtain that freedom it gains the strength to fly. So it is with man.

It is like that humble, glorious Saint, who wrote those inspired Odes of Solomon said,

"And He who knew and brought me up is the Most High in all His perfection. And He glorified me by His kindness, and raised my thoughts to the height of His truth.

"And from thence He gave me the way of His precepts and I opened the doors that were closed.

"And brake in pieces the bars of iron; but my iron melted and dissolved before me;

"NOTHING APPEARED CLOSED TO ME: BECAUSE I WAS THE DOOR OF EVERYTHING." (Odes of Solomon 17:7-10).

"And he who is thankful in all things shall be made glorious, and the things of this earth shall be added unto him an hundred fold, yea more." (D. & C. 78:19). Gratitude is the song of the soul. It is the joy released into vibrations that will as surely lift one into the higher realms of light as the stream will follow its course to the sea. The sea is the eternal abode of the waters—the realm of divine light is the resting place of man.

That great inner joy of the soul is the power that contacts the Holy Spirit of God and opens wide the portals to the kingdom of heaven. It is this joy of love that unites the heart, mind and soul into a power that completely fulfills all other laws. The very power of the heart, soul and mind united in this overwhelming love of devotion and joy turns the key and fulfills all the laws, opening wide the doors to all light, all power and perfection.

This kingdom of heaven is within us, but we have to seek for it, and for its righteousness, leaving the darkness behind as we step into it, thus fulfilling all righteousness, and gathering its light to us and living by that light.

We have to open the door. We have to tune in on our own radio sets—we have to learn to listen—to "Be Still and *know* that I Am, God." We must learn to commune with God—this is the Holy Communion·that is symbolized in the Sacrament of the Last Supper. And unless one learns to find this holy communion his partaking of the sacrament is a vain and useless thing. This is the "hidden manna." This is partaking of the "Waters of life freely" for which the sacrament is only the outer symbol. This is the Holy Communion, partaking of the body and life of Christ—"for my words are Spirit, and they are truth, the flesh profits nothing." (John 6:63).

We of ourselves have to open our understandings by humbling ourselves, and turning over our conscious minds, burdened with the experiences and knowledge of mortality, to the power of the Spirit mind, that is in tune with *all Truth,* knows no error, contains no discord, but is in itself the kingdom of light. We must desire the light, and seek to bring it forth as we reach for it with clean hands and pure hearts. As we take hold of this light with complete understanding we will realize that darkness is banished and thus we become completely filled with light. One cannot possibly step into the great kingdom of light while his mind is holding to his sorrows, his woes and his fears—and the love of this light, and the love of God will eliminate all fears. This is what Christ promised when He said, "Come unto me all ye who labor and are heavy laden, and I will give you rest. Take my yoke upon you (which yoke is love), for my yoke is easy and my burden is LIGHT."

With this understanding it is possible to step through the

door of ourselves, as the writer of the Odes of Solomon did, into the kingdom of heaven, and all things will be added unto us, and we will comprehend all things.

"... For the Lord himself being asked by a certain person, When his kingdom should come? Answered, When two shall be one, and that which is without as that which is within ..." (II. Clement 5:1, New Testament Apocrypha).

"Him that overcometh will I make a pillar in the temple of my God, and he shall go no more out; and I will write upon Him the name of my God, and the name of the city of my God, which is New Jerusalem, which cometh down out of heaven from my God; and I will write upon Him my new Name." (Rev. 3:12). It is only this overcoming that will let the light in us shine forth that "others seeing our good works can glorify our Father in heaven." "For it is the Father who doeth the works." As long as man is trying to do the works, and is taking credit for his strained efforts there can be no glorifying of God—for if one can bring forth this light, others can also be taught how to bring forth that same light, and thus too they will be able to glorify God—for what one can do—all can do—"For my kingdom is not in word, but in power." This is the only possible way to glorify God—to humble the "self" before Him so that His Holy Spirit can take over—and thus permit Him to do His works through us. And this is not for one, but for all. Words and speeches are meaningless, only the power of Almighty God in action has the right to speak—the power that has left all darkness, sadness, despair, anger and fear behind—the power that is light—light eternal, shining forth from within the souls of men. This is the anointing of light.

This cannot take place in an instant without some preparation or the very light of the Spirit would consume us. We must purify our minds, our bodies and our souls by divine thinking before we can be prepared to be the pure temples of God, radiant with light, having received of His fullness.

Thus we are told, "Seek ye first the Kingdom of God and His righteousness and all things will be added unto you." Seeking that righteousness is gradually bringing that righteousness into our outer lives and incorporating it into every fibre of our beings, even as Christ did. This is the growing from grace to grace, permitting a little light to enter our minds, or consciousness, then living by that light—then comes more light—and thus line upon line, precept upon precept we learn to listen to the voice of "All Truth" as it directs us into the realms of eternal light—and thus we reach our own complete fulfillment of perfection. Thus it is possible for us to receive of the fullness of the Father, which means having every attribute, and glory and power and trait of the Father fulfilled in us—until we are filled with that fullness of perfection. (D. & C. 93:17, 20, 26-28).

Perhaps it could be explained in this way. Before the gorgeous flower is revealed every perfect petal must be completed in every detail. The color must have been gathered, the perfume distilled, the satin texture spun—the full glory held in all its perfection within the enclosed green bud. Men are like rosebushes that have never bloomed—or if the green buds have appeared they have been blighted by an incomplete vision. Our true heritage is divinity and only as we unfold that divinity from within us, bringing forth the embryo qualities of our Divine, Heavenly Father, which were planted in us from the beginning, can our lives be a complete fulfillment of our title, "Sons of God."

As we reach ever toward the light, holding before our minds always the perfect pattern of our divine unfoldment and destiny can we "overcome" and receive our "Anointing of Light" "and become powerful." This is the Oil for the Lamps of the world—it is the only oil that will illuminate the soul until it can be prepared when the Bridegroom comes—those who have not brought forth this light will be cast out into darkness and there will be weeping and wailing and gnashing of teeth.

"He that is ordained of God (or anointed with Light) and sent forth, the same is appointed to be the greatest, notwithstanding he is the least and the servant of all.

"*Wherefore, he is possessor of all things; for all things are subject unto him, both in heaven and on the earth, the life and the light, the Spirit and the power, sent forth by the will of the Father through Jesus Christ, his Son.*

"But no man is possessor of all things except he be purified and cleansed from all sin.

"And if ye are purified and cleansed from all sin, ye shall ask whatsoever you will in the name of Jesus and it shall be done." (D. & C. 50:26-29).

The Keys? "Rejoice in the Lord always, and again I say, Rejoice!" (D. and C. 98:1).

This work contains the complete pattern of the fulfillment of Godhood in every child of God. You who desire to hold the keys of light and glory in your hands must fulfill these laws —and only as you pray, as you seek, as you search, and as you take hold of these divine laws with your whole souls can you know of their great, eternal power and truth. This is not a book to be read—this is the pattern of life—the Life abundant that must be lived in order to be understood. If you are tired of the crumbs of life, if a common, mediocre existence has become a burden of dreary dismay, then take this flaming banner of eternal light into your hands and open the doors of your soul to the full glory of the light of God. For so shall it be unto you, according to your faith and your desire.

Too long has the world been boasting of its light while carrying empty lamps. Too many people have held forth their individual darkness and proclaimed it light—and the blind have led the blind and all have fallen into the ditch and know it not. "Fill your lamps with oil, oh Israel! And let your lights shine forth to greet the new day, for behold the Bridegroom cometh—Go ye! Go ye out to meet Him!"

This unfolding or bringing forth of light is a slow development from within and at first is almost unnoticeable. It is first just a feeling—the feeling a seed feels in the warm earth as it begins to unfold and manifest its powers. Then one's physical surroundings begin to be more harmonized—and thus it unfolds steadily, surely, perfectly—and the light shines brighter, with greater clearness and more joy until the full flower unfolds in all its glory.

That last unfolding can take place in an instant—"The

Anointing of Light", but the full preparation of it will have to be completed in perfect, most minute detail first. It is the constant awareness of anticipation that brings it forth. One must live for it, every moment, every breath, every thought. This will shortly turn from *belief to faith,* and *from faith to knowing.*

This unfolding of light is glory unspeakable. It is life everlasting. It is power and light and love and perfection. It is the fullness of the Father, the glory and power of God, the Light of the world.

This great unfolding of power and perfection and light belongs to every man. No man has a monopoly on the light of God, for every man that cometh into the world is enlightened by this Holy Spirit and it can be unfolded in his breast. However it can only be brought forth as he desires it, as he begins to believe in it, and live for it. This power belongs to every man just as surely as the power of blossoming and bringing forth a full and ripened crop of fruit belongs to every fruit tree. It is as one learns to trust completely and implicitly the Spirit of Light, or Christ, within, which is the true vine, that he can bring forth the perfect, divine pattern of his own fulfillment of glory and perfect achievement. Man is the branch or the door through which the very power of life is manifest. It is only as he acknowledges this power of light within, as Christ did, that he can do the works of the Father. Thus as he brings forth the Christ—or "the anointing of light" from within himself he places the crown of divinity upon his own head—thus he evolves from the man kingdom to the God kingdom—and the branch develops into a vine, giving life and light forever.

"The fullness of the Father" is when the full power of God comes forth and is made manifest in the works of the individual—this is when the full power of the Father fills the individual. It is the ordination of God, the Birth of the Spirit, the Anointing with Light. The outside man is only the temple —it is the Father within that is the One who occupies the temple.

This search for light or the search for a man's soul is also

the search for God—and the search for God is also the search
for the gift of eternal life. "For this is life eternal to know
Thee, the only True and Living God, and Jesus Christ whom
thou hast sent." This is a search that will glorify man, for as
his understanding expands and his heart and soul opens he
begins to become the very thing he seeks to interpret. Thus
the greatest work of God is not to rush forth to try to save the
souls of men before one has found the seat of his own soul,
the light of his own inner knowing—the voice of the Spirit of
the Lord, and has at least begun to unfold his own true pattern of life and glory. Any who does not have this direct contact with the Almighty is walking in blindness and therefore
cannot possibly lead others into the supreme, divine light of
God. "First, get the power."

As one enters the closet of his own soul to seek God or to
be exact, contact God, he shall truly be rewarded openly. His
life will gradually unfold in beauty and completeness and the
great treasures of power hidden in his own soul shall be
brought forth to glorify his life—and to glorify God. Thus
he learns to "walk with God," even as the great one of old
walked.

He shall become purified by the most sacred of all quests,
and when he has reached that center of light in his own soul,
the Son will stand revealed—and He will reveal the Father to
him—and he shall comprehend all things—even God—and
receive of the fullness of the Father, and receive his "anointing of light—and "Be ordained of God and sent forth with
the powers of heaven in his hands—"to do the works of God."
And so it is that "His kingdom is not in word, but in power."

The very voice of the scriptures thunder forth a warning
to the world that the wicked shall be cast out into outer darkness, and our minds shiver and pass on ignoring the warning
—while we have all been living in outer darkness—in the very
darkness of our physical minds and thoughts. We have groped
through our mortal consciousness of dark perception, wallowed
in our earthly conditions, been ruled by the flesh—tossed and
churned by the mental storms of hurt, pride, fears, worries,
vanities, bigotry, confusion, ego, anger, selfishness, greeds and

jealousies. Outer darkness? Yes, the outer darkness of the flesh—and this will continue to be our abiding place until we are willing to return to our Father's house, and partake of the warmth and the light that awaits us there.

"The kingdom of heaven is within you," Son of man—how far you will have to journey from your particular place in outer darkness to that glorious realm of peace and light that you might fulfill your own ultimate glory will depend on you —what you desire to accept and fulfill—and the vision you hold in your heart—for "Faith promises all things—and fulfills all things." According to your faith be it unto you.

According to the prophecies of the Almighty the Saints are to adorn themselves as a bride as they prepare to receive the Bridegroom, the Son of the Living God.

"Can a maid forget her ornaments or a bride her attire?" (Jer. 2:32).

"I will greatly rejoice in the Lord, my soul shall be joyful in my God; for he hath clothed me with the garments of salvation, he hath covered me with the robe of righteousness, as a bridegroom decketh himself with ornaments, and a bride adorneth herself with her jewels." (Isa. 61:10).

". . . And as the bridegroom rejoiceth over the bride, so shall thy God rejoice over thee." (Isa. 62:5).

"And the ransomed of the Lord shall return, and come to Zion with songs of everlasting joy upon their heads: they shall obtain joy and gladness, and sorrow and sighing shall flee away." (Isa. 35:10).

"O Zion, that bringest good tidings, get thee up into the high mountain (the Spiritual mountain of understanding); O Jerusalem, that bringest good tidings, lift up thy voice with strength; lift it up, be not afraid; and say unto the cities of Judah, behold your God." (Isa. 40:9).

"Awake, awake; put on thy strength, O Zion; put on thy beautiful garments, O Jerusalem, the holy city; for henceforth there shall no more come to thee the uncircumcised and unclean.

"Shake thyself from the dust; arise; and set down, O

Jerusalem; *loose thyself* from the bands of thy neck, O captive daughter of Zion.

"For thus saith the Lord, ye have sold yourselves for nought; and ye shall be redeemed without money." (Isa. 52:1-3).

"And the Redeemer shall come to Zion, *and unto them that turn from transgression,* in Jacob, saith the Lord." (Isa. 59: 20).

The redeemed are those who have turned from transgression, those who have overcome by their faith in the promises of the Almighty through their love of the Lord their God.

The robe of the bride is the robe of righteousness and the adorning jewels are the gifts of the Spirit. The first is peace—the peace Christ came to bring—the great peace that can only be received by those who have learned to "BE STILL." And to be still does not mean a dead, dull, sleepy, stupid stillness. It is a condition of silence in which the conscious, warring, doubting mind learns to be quiet, and learns to *listen.* It is that stillness, or quiet, attentive listening of the soul in which one learns to hear the voice of the Spirit of Almighty God—the stillness in which the ego, outer-self is forgotten—the stillness in which one learns to KNOW that God is God, and is known of Him, and becomes one with Him.

The very first gift of this glorious, gracious contact is the precious jewel of divine peace—"The peace that passeth understanding." This gift of peace is one of the great jewels of the Almighty. It is the gift that lifts one from a common mortal to sonhood, a prince of the Royal Household of the Father. It is one of the graces which comes from God. It must be accepted graciously and worn always in full knowing of its sacred value. It is the key that opens the storehouse to the other gifts and graces and powers. Gather the unspeakable gift of divine peace to you and wear it forever as a robe of glory —the "Peace that passeth understanding."

"Peace on earth good will toward men!" So sang the herald angels at the birth of Christ—so came the gift, to be received by all who would desire it and seek to hold it as their own, from that time henceforward and forever.

"Peace I leave with you, my peace I give unto you; not as

the world giveth, give I unto you. Let not your heart be troubled, neither let it be afraid." (John 14:27; 16:33; Eph. 6:15; Phil. 4:7). This salutation of peace has been the salutation of Heavenly Messengers from time immemorial. And it is Christ's gift to the world—to each individual who is willing to give up his discords to receive it. And it is true that He did not give this divine gift of peace as the world gives gifts. He gave it as a jewel, not from the outside to be seen of men—but from within—a gift that lies buried within each man's soul and must be brought forth as one turns to Christ and finds that divine contact through developing his love for Almighty God.

This great, glorious gift of peace, peace of soul, peace of mind, peace of life is the first jewel to be received and worn as each individual prepares to meet the Bridegroom. The other jewels will follow—the jewels of the Spirit—love, gentleness, tenderness, mercy, compassion, understanding, joy, wisdom and the power to forgive. These are the jewels of the Spirit. These are the jewels that each individual must wear or be adorned with before he can be prepared for the Bridegroom. These jewels only will glorify Zion, "The Pure in Heart." These jewels only will glorify any individual on this earth, be they farmer, prophet or king. These glorious gifts, as they are incorporated into the very lives and beings of each individual are the glorifying of the Bride. They are worn on the soul and the body receives their glory and is exalted by their purity and beauty of perfection. None can enter the feast of the righteous except the righteous—those who love sincerely, deeply and perfectly, with a love unfeigned—those who are crowned with the jewel of peace and bedecked with the brilliance of mercy, understanding, and those precious gifts of the Spirit that can never be worn by the self-righteous, the proud, the haughty, the slothful nor rebellious.

"And an highway shall be there, AND A WAY, *and it shall be called The Way of Holiness;* The unclean shall not pass over it; but it shall be for *those*: The wayfaring men, though fools shall not err therein." (Isa. 35:8).

And this record is "THE WAY" and the unclean shall never

pass over it, yet it is mapped plainly and true so that children and fools need not err therein. For this record is the record of God, and is written so that a child may understand, and he who is built upon the rock receiveth it with gladness—and glory be to the Most High God forever and forever—Amen.

ODE OF SOLOMON 23

("The reference to the sealed document sent by God is one of the great mysteries of the collection.") And now the mystery is revealed, for this record is the document—and as you read the words of this ode, pray, and you will understand.

"Joy is of the saints! And who shall put it on, but they alone?

"Grace is of the elect! and who shall receive it except those who trust in it from the beginning?

"Love is of the elect! and who shall put it on except those who have possessed it from the beginning?

"Walk ye in the knowledge of the Most High without grudging: to His exultation and to the perfection of His knowledge.

"And His thought was like a letter; His will descended from on high, and it was sent like an arrow which is violently shot from the bow:

"And many hands rushed to the letter to seize it and to take and read it:

"And it escaped their fingers and they were affrighted at it and at the seal that was upon it.

"Because it was not permitted to them to loose its seal: for the power that was over the seal was greater than they.

"But those who saw it went after the letter that they might know where it would alight, and who should read it and who should hear it.

"But a wheel received it and came over it:

"And there was with it a sign of the Kingdom and of the Government:

"And everything which tried to move the wheel it mowed and cut down:

"And it gathered the multitude of adversaries, and bridged the rivers and crossed over and rooted up many forests and made a broad path.

"The head went down to the feet, for down to the feet ran the wheel, and that which was a sign upon it.

"The letter was one of command, for there were included in it all districts;

"And there was seen at its head, the head which was revealed even the Son cf Truth from the Most High Father,

"And He inherited and took possession of everything. And the thought of many was brought to nought.

"And all the apostates hasted and fled away. And those who persecuted and were enraged became extinct.

"And the letter was a great volume, which was wholly written by the finger of God:

"And the name of the Father was on it, and of the Son and of the Holy Spirit, to rule for ever and ever. Hallelujah!"

PREFACE TO THE FOLLOWING CHAPTER

"For the Lord shall rise up as in Mount Perazim, he shall be wroth as in the valley of Gibeon, that he may do his work, his strange work; and bring to pass his act, his strange act." —Isa. 28:21.

"For the preparation, wherewith, I design to prepare mine apostles to prune my vineyard for the last time, THAT I MAY BRING TO PASS MY STRANGE ACT, THAT I MAY POUR OUT MY SPIRIT UPON ALL FLESH.

"But behold, verily I say unto you, that there are many who have been ordained among you, whom I have called but few of them are chosen.

"And they who are not chosen have sinned a very grievous sin in that they are walking in darkness at noon-day." (D. & C. 95:4-6).

"What I have said unto you must needs be, that all men may be left without excuse;

"That wise men and rulers may hear and know that which they have never considered;

"That I may proceed to bring to pass my act, my strange act, and perform my work, my strange work, that men may discern between the righteous and the wicked, saith your God." —D. & C. 101:95.

CHAPTER XXI

"YE ARE GODS"

"Knowledge Is For The Strong"

THE FOLLOWING CHAPTER is truly only for the strong. It is for those who can follow the vision given and fulfill it in their own lives. It contains a "knowledge of truth as it was, as it is, and as it is to come," and the key to use that knowledge that one might be free from the binding shackles of earth's burdens of sorrows and tears—free from the bondage of other's beliefs and opinions—free to know and partake of the Light of Eternal Truth. In it is contained the mysteries of the power of "godliness." So if you are afraid of Truth then do not read it, for if you trample it under your feet you will be brought into judgment.

"It is given unto many to know the mysteries of God; nevertheless they are laid under a strict command that they shall not impart only according to the portion of his word which he doth grant unto the children of men, according to the heed and diligence which they give unto him.

"And therefore, he that will harden his heart, the same receiveth the lesser portion of the word; and he that will not harden his heart, to him is given the greater portion of his word, until it is given unto him to know the mysteries of God until he know them in full.

"And they that will harden their hearts, to them is given the lesser portion of the word until they know nothing concerning his mysteries; and then they are taken captive by the devil, and led by his will down to destruction. Now this is what is meant by the chains of hell." (Alma 12:9-11).

The chains of hell are the chains of a sealed mind—a mind that has shut out light—a "hardened mind" and heart that has lost the power to kneel humbly before the Lord to *know* truth, but rather judge according to their own understandings.

"Verily, thus saith the Lord: It shall come to pass that every soul who forsaketh his sins and cometh unto me, and calleth on my name, and obeyeth my voice, and keepeth my commandments, shall see my face and know that I am;

"And that I am the true light that lighteth every man that cometh into the world:

"And that I am in the Father, and the Father in me, and the Father and I are one—

"The Father because he gave me of his fullness, and the Son because I was in the world and made flesh my tabernacle, and dwelt among the sons of men.

"I was in the world and received of my Father, and the works of him were plainly manifest.

"And John saw and bore record of the fullness of my glory, and the fullness of John's record is hereafter to be revealed.

"And he bore record, saying: I saw his glory, that he was in the beginning, before the world was:

"Therefore, in the beginning the Word was, for he was the Word, even the Messenger of salvation.

"The light and the Redeemer of the world: *The Spirit of Truth,* who came into the world because the world was made by him, and in him was the life of men and the light of men.

"The worlds were made by him; men were made by him; all things were made by him, and through him and *of him;*

"And I, John, bear record that I beheld his glory, as the glory of the Only Begotten of the Father, full of grace and truth, even *The Spirit of Truth,* which came and dwelt in the flesh, and dwelt among us.

"And I, John, saw that he received not the fullness at the first, but received grace for grace.

"And he received not of the fullness at first, but continued from grace to grace until he received a fullness.

"AND THUS HE WAS CALLED THE SON OF GOD, BECAUSE HE RECEIVED NOT OF THE FULLNESS AT THE FIRST.

"And I, John, bear record, and lo, the heavens were opened, and the Holy Ghost descended upon him in the form of a dove, and sat upon him, and there came a voice out of heaven saying: this is my beloved Son.

"And I, John, bear record that he received a fullness of the glory of the Father.

"AND HE RECEIVED ALL POWER, BOTH IN HEAVEN AND ON EARTH, AND THE GLORY OF THE FATHER WAS WITH HIM, FOR HE DWELT IN HIM.

"And it shall come to pass, that if you are faithful you shall receive the fullness of the record of John.

"I give unto ye these sayings, that you *may understand and know how to worship, and know what ye worship; that ye may come unto the Father in my name, and in due time receive of his fullness.*

"*For if ye keep my commandments ye shall receive of his fullness, and be glorified in me as I am in the Father.*

"And now, verily I say unto you, *I was in the beginning with the Father,* and am the Firstborn.

"YE WERE ALSO IN THE BEGINNING WITH THE FATHER: THAT WHICH IS SPIRIT, EVEN THE SPIRIT OF TRUTH.

"And truth is a knowledge of things as they are, and as they were, and as they are to come.

"THE SPIRIT OF TRUTH IS OF GOD. I AM THE SPIRIT OF TRUTH. And John bore record of me, saying; He received a fullness of truth, yea, even of all truth.

"*And no man receiveth a fullness unless he keepeth his commandments.*

"He that keepeth his commandments receiveth truth and light, until he is glorified in truth and knoweth all things.

"MAN WAS ALSO IN THE BEGINNING WITH GOD, INTELLIGENCE, OR THE LIGHT OF TRUTH, WAS NOT CREATED OR MADE, NEITHER INDEED CAN BE." (D. & C. sec. 93).

The above record plainly reveals the knowledge that man was also in the beginning with God, even that glorious *Spirit of Truth* of which Christ was. That even as Christ, man can grow from grace to grace unto a fullness of joy and perfec-tion—that the *Spirit of Truth* in the beginning was called "Christ" or the "Word", and every man partook of that Spirit, or was definitely that Spirit, hence Christ, or the Spirit of Truth, dwells in him. This is given in Acts 17:28: *"For in him we live and move and have our being."* And this explains the meaning of the words that we were *made of him.*

"He that ascended up on high, as also he descended below all things, in that he comprehended all things, that he might *be in all and through all things, The Light of Truth.*

"Which truth shineth. *This is the Light of Christ.* As also he is in the sun, and the light of the sun, and the power thereof by which it was made.

"As also he is in the moon, and is the light of the moon, and the power thereof by which it was made;

"As also the light of the stars, and the power thereof by which they were made:

"And the earth also, and the power thereof, even the earth upon which you stand.

"And *the light which shineth, which giveth you light, is through him who enlighteneth your eyes, which is the same light which quickeneth your understandings:*

"Which light proceedeth forth from the presence of God to fill the immensity of space—

"The light which is in all things, which giveth life to all things, which is the law by which all things are governed, EVEN THE POWER OF GOD, WHO SITTETH UPON HIS THRONE, WHO IS IN THE BOSOM OF ETERNITY, WHO IS IN THE MIDST OF ALL THINGS." (D. & C. 88:6-13).

"He comprehendeth all things, and all things are before Him, and all things are round about Him: and he is above all things and in all things, and through all things, and is round about all things: and all things are by him and OF him, even GOD, FOREVER AND EVER." (*Ibid.,* verse 41).

"The earth rolls upon her wings, and the sun giveth his light by day, and the moon giveth her light by night, and the stars also give their light, as they roll upon their wings in their glory, *in the midst of the power of God.*

"Unto what shall I liken these kingdoms, that ye may understand?

"Behold, all these are kingdoms, and any man who hath seen any of the least of these hath seen God moving in his majesty and power.

"I say unto you, he hath seen him; nevertheless, he who came unto his own was not comprehended.

"The light shineth in darkness, and the darkness comprehendeth it not; nevertheless, the day shall come when you shall comprehend even God, being quickened in him and by him.

"Then shall ye know that ye have seen me, that I am, and that I am the true light that is in you, and that you are in me, otherwise ye could not abound." (*Ibid.,* Sec. 88:45-50).

As we open our minds to these great, dynamic truths, that can only be revealed to our understandings by the Spirit of God, we will comprehend the very glory of Truth, and thus we will receive a knowledge of *Truth as it was—and as it is.* We were "THE SPIRIT OF TRUTH" IN THE BEGINNING, EVEN AS CHRIST WAS THE "SPIRIT OF TRUTH." Yea, we were a very part of the Divine Spirit and Power of God. Our mission in this life is to bring forth that Spirit or light and to let it so shine that others seeing the works will glorify God, who himself will be doing the works, through us.

"My little children, of whom I travail in birth again *until Christ be formed in you."* (Gal. 4:19).

"And every man whose spirit receiveth not that light is under condemnation.

"For man is Spirit. The elements are eternal, and Spirit and element, inseparably connected, receiveth a fullness of joy.

"And when separated man cannot receive a fullness of joy.

"The elements are the tabernacle of God; yea, man is the tabernacle of God (the abiding place), *even temples*: and whatsoever temple is defiled, God shall destroy that temple" (or body, and it shall die). (D. & C. 93:32-35; see also II. Cor. 6:16).

Here is *"a knowledge of Truth as it is"*—a knowledge that man can become that very Spirit of Truth which he was in the beginning, and growing from grace to grace, receive a fullness of the glory of God, or all power both in heaven, and on earth. But it must be done while in the flesh—even as Christ did it. He is our Redeemer as He marked the exact way for us to follow, and the perfect pattern for us to become even as He is—and do even the greater works, as promised in John 14:12; "Verily, verily, I say unto you; he that believeth on me the works that I do shall he do also, and even greater works than these shall he do . . ." etc.

The following references are given to prove that this per-fection is expected of God's children—in this life.

"I am Almighty God. Walk thou before me, and be thou perfect." (Gen. 17:1).

"For I am the Lord your God, ye shall therefore sanctify yourselves, and ye shall be holy, for I am holy." (Lev. 11:44).

"Thou shalt be perfect with the Lord thy God." (Deut. 18:13).

"Be ye therefore perfect, even as your Father in heaven is perfect." (Matt. 5:48).

"And in nothing does man offend God, or against none is His wrath kindled, save those who confess not his hand in all things, and obey not his commandments."

"Wherefore gird up the loins of your minds, be sober, and hope to the end for the grace that is to be brought unto you at the revelation of Jesus Christ.

"As obedient children, not fashioning yourselves according to the former lusts of your ignorance.

"But as he which hath called you is holy, so be ye holy in all manner of conversation.

"Because it is written, Be ye holy, for I am holy." (I. Peter 1:13-16).

"And again, verily I say unto you that it is your privilege, and a promise I give unto you, that hath been ordained unto this ministry, that inasmuch as you strip yourselves of jeal-ousies and fears, and humble yourselves before me, for ye are not sufficiently humble, the veil shall be rent and you shall see me and know that I am—

"For no man hath seen God at any time in the flesh, except quickened by the Spirit of God.

"Neither can any natural man abide the presence of God.

"Ye are not able to abide the presence of God now, neither

the ministering of angels: wherefore, continue in patience *until ye are perfected.*" (D. & C. 67:10-13).

"He that is ordained of God and sent forth, the same is appointed to be the greatest, notwithstanding he is the least and the servant of all.

"WHEREFORE, HE IS POSSESSOR OF ALL THINGS: FOR ALL THINGS ARE SUBJECT UNTO HIM, BOTH IN HEAVEN AND ON EARTH, THE LIFE AND THE LIGHT, THE SPIRIT AND THE POWER SENT FORTH BY THE WILL OF THE FATHER THROUGH JESUS CHRIST HIS SON." (Compare the mission and Power of Christ as given in Sec. 93:17).

"BUT NO MAN IS POSSESSOR OF ALL THINGS EXCEPT HE BE PURIFIED AND CLEANSED FROM ALL SIN.

"And if ye are purified and cleansed from all sin, ye shall ask whatsoever you will in the Name of Jesus and it shall be done." (D. & C. 50:26-29). According to the above record no man is truly ordained of God until he is purified and cleansed from all sin—for no man is possessor of all the great, dynamic powers of the Almighty except he be purified and cleansed from all sin, or has overcome all sin. For surely baptism is of no avail to a man who continues to live in pride, arrogance, self-seeking and who fails to live the perfect laws of love and forgiveness, not just in a display of hypocritical words, but in the fullness of his whole soul. Only one who loves God with all his heart, soul, mind and strength and his fellow men, has fulfilled all the laws of perfection.

"And to know the love of Christ, which passeth knowledge, that ye might be filled with all the fullness of God." (Eph. 3:19). This is the key whereby we may receive of the "fullness of God" even as Christ received of His fullness.

"Behold, now are we the sons of God, and it doth not yet appear what we shall be; but we know that when he shall appear we shall be like him, for we shall see him as he is.

"AND EVERY MAN THAT HATH THIS HOPE IN HIM PURIFIETH HIMSELF, EVEN AS HE IS PURE." (I John 3:2-4).

"This I say then, walk in the Spirit, and ye shall not fulfill the lusts of the flesh.

"For the flesh lusteth against the Spirit, and the Spirit

against the flesh: and these are contrary the one to the other; so that ye cannot do the things that ye would.

"BUT IF YOU ARE LED BY THE SPIRIT, YE ARE NOT UNDER THE LAW.

"Now the works of the flesh are manifest, which are these, adultery, fornication, uncleanness, lasciviousness,

"Idolatry, witchcraft, *hatred, variance,* emulations, *wrath, strife,* seditions and heresies.

"*Envyings,* murders, drunkenness, revellings, and such like: of the which I tell you before, as I have also told you in the past, that they which do such things shall not inherit the kingdom of God.

"*But the fruit of the Spirit is love, joy, peace, long-suffering, gentleness, goodness, faith, meekness, temperance: against such there is no law.*" (Gal. 5:16-26).

In the above is given the things that must be eliminated and the traits that must be perfected. Usually as one reads the list of "don'ts" in the above he reads with his eyes closed and a drowsiness of mind that fogs his vision, and he thinks, with that unawakened glance, that it means all those faults. It means ANY ONE OF THEM. There are few human beings who could possibly carry the burden of all of them. And there are few mortals who do not have the burden of at least one of these weaknesses weighing upon them. In the original Greek the list is somewhat simplified, giving those little weaknesses that we take so much for granted we are almost unaware of them, at least in ourselves. Every fault, every weakness must be eliminated, as darkness is banished when the light shines forth. As one works toward the high goal of perfection he discovers the amazingly beautiful truth that as he fills his soul with light and love and goodness, the weaknesses are automatically eliminated. To overcome them, he must be honest. He must first search into his own soul without any hypocrisy of self-righteousness, and be willing to see his own weaknesses and faults—then, with a deep humility and a true determination of devotion to the Most High, he must leave the darkness and look steadfastly into the light. To hold one's weakness and faults in mind, to brood over them is not the way of glory.

The way of light is to look steadfastly into the light, and the perfection of the Almighty, knowing that perfection belongs also to His children, and that as the light comes into one's soul, the darkness is dissipated. This is the true use of faith. If one will do this, believing in the power of God, and in light and goodness, there will be no power in heaven or on earth that can keep him from his goal.

So much for the scripture that proves beyond question the status and requirements of man—or *"knowledge of things as they are."*

Now, to give added scripture concerning the light and truth, or the *Spirit of Truth* that is contained in every man that cometh into the world, being released by obedience to the laws.

"Therefore it is given to abide in you; the record of heaven; the Comforter; the peaceable things of immortal glory; the truth of all things; that which quickeneth all things, which maketh alive all things, that which knoweth all things and hath all power, according to wisdom, mercy, truth, justice and judgment." (Moses 6:61).

"And I gave unto them their knowledge in the day I created them . . ." (Moses 7:32).

"Who hath put wisdom in the inward parts? Or who hath given understanding to the heart?" (Job 38:36).

This light and truth that has been placed in the heart and soul of man, from the beginning, is the Spirit of Truth, which he already was before he was clothed in spirit form and sent out as a personality, endowed with full consciousness.

"The prophets who prophesied of the grace that was to be yours searched and inquired what PERSON or TIME was indicated, *By the Spirit of Christ within them* (long before His advent on the earth) when predicting the suffering of Christ and the subsequent glory." (I. Peter 1:10-11 R. V.).

"And the light which shineth, which giveth you light is through him who enlighteneth your eyes, which is the same light that quickeneth your understanding, which light proceedeth forth from the presence of God to fill the immensity of space—the light which is in all things, which giveth life to all things, which is the law by which all things are governed, even the power of God, who sitteth upon His throne, who is in the bosom of eternity, who is in the midst of all things."

"The light shineth in darkness (or in the flesh) and the darkness (or mortal mind) comprehendeth it not; nevertheless, the day shall come when ye shall comprehend even God, being quickened in Him, and by Him. Then shall ye know that ye have seen me, that I am, and that I am the true light that is in you, and that ye are in me; otherwise ye could not abound."

Below is the promise given to the Three Nephites who were to tarry on the earth until Christ came in His glory: "And for this cause ye shall HAVE FULLNESS OF JOY: AND YE SHALL SIT DOWN IN THE KINGDOM OF MY FATHER: YEA, YOUR JOY SHALL BE FULL, EVEN AS THE FATHER HATH GIVEN ME FULLNESS OF JOY: AND YE SHALL BE EVEN AS I AM, AND I AM EVEN AS THE FATHER AND THE FATHER AND I ARE ONE." (3 Nephi 28:9-10). Here is the definite promise that because these three men believed and because they had the vision to reach, and the faith that the vision could be fulfilled, they would become even as Christ, and He was even as the Father. In other words, they should be even as the Father—or gods.

"Unto him that keepeth my commandments I will give the mysteries of the kingdom, and the same shall be in him as a well of living water, springing up unto everlasting life." (D. & C. 63:23 and John 7:38).

"For you shall live by every word that proceedeth forth from the mouth of God.

"For the word of the Lord is truth, and whatsoever is truth is Light, and whatsoever is Light is SPIRIT, *even the Spirit of Jesus Christ.*

"And the Spirit giveth light to every man that cometh into the world; and the Spirit enlighteneth every man through the world, *That harkeneth to the voice of the Spirit.*

"And everyone that harkeneth to the voice of the Spirit cometh unto God, even the Father." (D. & C. 84:47—See also John 6:37, 39-40 and verse 65 and John 10:27-30).

Such is the record of things *"As they are,"* for within man is the Spirit of light waiting as a guiding beacon of glory to lead into Truth and a perfect life, as was intended by God, our Father.

From the ancients comes this beautiful admonition: "If man has lost the light, let him go deep within his own soul and bring it forth, for it is there as it always has been."

Now, to take up the *"Knowledge of things as they are to come."* And they will come, or be brought forth whenever man opens his spiritual eyes to see and his heart to understand.

Christ was sent as a forerunner of perfection. He was the pattern, the model, the ideal or guide to follow. And as He perfected Himself in this life, so are we to perfect ourselves —IN THIS LIFE. We are to seek to become as God, even while living on this earth, even as Christ did by his thinking and living. Thus is given the admonition, "Think as God—Love as God—Live as God." Or in other words, "Live by every word that proceedeth forth from the mouth of God." As each individual seeks to live by every word of God he becomes that *Word*—"And the word of the Lord is truth, and whatsoever is truth is light—and whatsoever is light is Spirit—even the Spirit of Jesus Christ." Thus the Word of the Lord is the Spirit of Jesus Christ, and as we apply His words in our lives, or follow that "still small voice of the Spirit" from within us until it becomes a very part of our beings, our source of light and direction and life—that Word becomes again flesh. As it becomes a living part of every cell and fibre of our bodies our bodies are exalted by the living vibrations of divine thinking—and we become even as He is.

This is the pattern Christ gave. It is the true pattern, and no one can go into perfection by any other door. Thus the words are spoken: "Straight is the gate and narrow is the way, and few there be who find it." But the day is at hand when those who survive must find it, and live by it.

"Hear, O ye heavens, and give ear, O earth, and rejoice ye inhabitants thereof, for the Lord is God, and besides him there is no Savior.

"Great is his wisdom, marvelous are his ways, and the extent of his doings none can find out.

"His purpose fail not, neither are there any who can stay his hand.

"From eternity to eternity he is the same and his years never fail.

"For thus saith the Lord—I, the Lord, am merciful and gracious unto those who fear me, and delight to honor those who serve me in righteousness unto the end." This "end" does not mean the end of one's life as many have supposed. It means the end of one's testing—"And he shall be tested and tried in all things and when the Lord has thoroughly proved him, and found that he is determined to serve Him at all hazards, then he will find his calling and election made sure— then it will be that the Lord Himself will appear unto him from time to time, and teach him face to face." etc. (Joseph Smith—also D. & C. 76:1-5 and I. Peter 1:13-16).

"For man is spirit. The elements are eternal, and spirit and element, inseparably connected receive a fullness of joy. And when separated man cannot receive a fullness of joy." This has erroneously been believed to be a condition that man is to receive in the resurrected state. Yet in the same section is the exact pattern showing how Christ received this fullness in this life, and that man also is to receive it even as He did —IN THIS LIFE.

"Great shall be their reward and eternal shall be their glory.

"And to them I will reveal all mysteries, yea, all the hidden mysteries of my kingdom from days of old, and for ages to come, will I make known unto them the good pleasure of my will concerning all things pertaining to my kingdom.

"Yea, even the wonders of eternity shall they know, and things to come will I show them, even the things of many generations.

"AND THEIR WISDOM SHALL BE GREAT, AND THEIR UNDER-STANDING REACH INTO HEAVEN, AND BEFORE THEM THE WISDOM OF THE WISE SHALL PERISH, AND THE UNDERSTANDING OF THE PRUDENT SHALL COME TO NAUGHT." (This verse proves conclusively that these promises are for this life).

"For by my Spirit will I enlighten them and by my power

will I make known unto them the secrets of my will—yea, even those things which eye hath not seen, nor ear heard, nor yet has entered into the heart of man." (D. & C. 76:6-10).

There are many unspeakable things "That can only be seen and understood by the power of the Holy Spirit, which God bestows on THOSE WHO LOVE HIM AND PURIFY THEMSELVES BEFORE HIM.

"TO WHICH HE GRANTS THIS PRIVILEGE OF SEEING AND KNOWING FOR THEMSELVES.

"THAT THROUGH THE POWER AND MANIFESTATION OF THE SPIRIT, WHILE IN THE FLESH They may be able to bear his presence in the world of glory." (D. & C. 76:116-118).

"God standeth in the congregation of the mighty; he judgeth among the Gods." (Psalms 82:1). Who are these whom God is standing among who are called gods?

"Jesus answered them, Is it not written in your law, I said, YE ARE GODS? If he called them gods, unto whom the Word of God came, and the scriptures cannot be broken; say ye of him whom the Father hath sanctified, and sent into the world, Thou blasphemest; because I said, I am the Son of God?" Now, as the scriptures cannot be broken they have to be fulfilled, for "God's word cannot return unto him void" and "He is a God of truth and cannot lie." (John 10:34-35; Isa. 55:11 and Deut. 13:14).

Again, "Is it not written in your law, I said, ye are gods: If he called them gods, unto whom the word of God came . . ." etc.—This "word of God" referred to does not mean just the scriptures. There are hundreds of Christian churches on the earth, all using the Bible, which they call the "Word of God," yet they are teaching and living by dark doctrines and under false principles, without light. There are millions of people on this earth professing Christianity, to whom the scriptures have come, who are wicked and blind and fanatical and in darkness, and the most ardent straining of the imagination could not possibly classify them as "gods." The only hypocrites on the earth are the religious hypocrites, those who hide their evil behind "The word of God" or the Bible, and their churches.

"The Word of God" referred to by Christ does not mean just the scriptures alone. It refers to those who have learned to live from the very center of their souls—who have learned to hear and heed that "Still Small voice of the Spirit" until they speak no word unless He gives it to them—and then permits Him to do His works through them, even as Christ did. These are the ones to whom the "Word of God" is a living fountain of waters, a thing of continual glory, of constant instruction, *leading into all truth.* As they develop the ears to hear, and the eyes to see, as given so many times in the Sacred, inspired Book of Revelations, they receive constant direction from God, and thus His word abides in them—and His Word is Truth, and whatsoever is Truth is Light, and whatsoever is Light is Spirit even the Spirit of Jesus Christ. Thus it is that those who receive this Spirit of Jesus Christ, or the Spirit of Truth, are called gods. Thus it is easy to understand that this "Word of God" does not mean just the inspired words of some man written many years ago, only. It means the living contact of each man with his Father—HERE and NOW. Those who have that living contact are gods. And even as Christ received a fullness of the Father by developing from grace to grace so man has the power to develop in the same way until that inner voice becomes audible and a continual source of light and living glory. Such men can be called "gods" for to them the Word of God comes continually, a living fountain of light, and they speak with "new tongues" or the "voice of angels." These are they who receive the power of the Atonement—At-one-meant—and they become ONE with the Father, in His heavenly household.

"Without revelation direct from heaven, it is impossible for any person to understand fully the plan of salvation. We often hear it said that the living oracles must be in the Church, in order that the Kingdom of God may be established and prosper on the earth. I will give another version of this sentiment. I say that the living oracles of God, or the Spirit of revelation must be in each and every individual, to know the plan of salvation and keep in the path that leads them to the presence of God." (Brigham Young).

"O Lord, I have trusted in thee, and I will trust in thee forever. I will not put my trust in the arm of flesh; for I know that cursed is he that putteth his trust in the arm of flesh. Yea, cursed is he that putteth his trust in man or maketh flesh his arm." (2 Nephi 4:34).

"And he (Christ) received not of the fullness at first, but continued from grace to grace, until he received a fullness.

"AND THUS HE BECAME THE SON OF GOD, BECAUSE HE RECEIVED NOT OF THE FULLNESS AT THE FIRST."

"For as many as are led by the Spirit of God, they are the sons of God—the Spirit itself beareth witness with our Spirit, that we are the children of God; and if children, then heirs of God (or of godhood), joint-heirs with Christ." (Romans 8:14, 16, 17).

If we are "joint-heirs with Christ" then we are equal with him, if we understand this truth and live by it, making it a very part of our lives.

This is *"a knowledge of Truth as it is to come"*—or as we bring it to pass. Each degree of glory is merely a state of consciousness in the mind of each individual, from those who live in the filth of the gutters and the slums to those who travel a highway of light. Celestial glory is a state of consciousness or awareness and understanding. It is man's heritage to look unto his Father and to claim his divine birthright. As he lifts his eyes to perfection he can no longer follow his old paths of mortal perception, of weaknesses and sins. As he lifts his heart to understand and opens his eyes to see, and learns the power of the word of God in his life, and begins to live that word, he becomes the very thing his vision holds. So be it according to each man's vision and his desires in righteousness, for the Spirit of God will bear witness to his spirit that this is true if he will but "Ask, seek and knock." "He that believeth these things which I have spoken, him will I visit with the manifestation of my Spirit, and he shall know and bear record. For because of my Spirit he shall know that these things are true; for it persuadeth men to do good." (Ether 4:11).

"For as many as are led by the Spirit of God, they are the sons of God."

And so can be fulfilled in each man's life these glorious words of promise: "Know the truth, and the truth will make you free." To know the truth one must be very humble, willing to learn and also willing to unlearn, for often he has to unlearn the narrowed, bigoted beliefs that he has accumulated through false teachings or through a lack of complete understanding.

As one reaches for truth with all his soul he will be led to the great truth that will free him—and *"Truth is a knowledge of things as they are, as they were, and as they are to come:* and whatsoever is more or less than this is the Spirit of that wicked one who was a liar from the beginning." Hence, the only great truth is the complete knowledge. It is the all-inclusive truth whereby man can know all things and be filled with light and spirit as he again reaches out and lays claim to this divine heritage. All other truths are but parts of this one great truth—they are imperfect bits of it—and every other truth, or rather, small portion of truth is but a guidepost to direct one to this all-inclusive knowledge of all Truth. It is the truth that will give man the vision to become free—free from darkness, fears, doubts, pride, hates, discords, worries and all weaknesses including either an inferiority complex or an oversized ego, for either of these last named is just as deadly to the progress of the soul as the other. One is without faith, and the other seeks only its own glory. Only truth can free man from any of these deadly weaknesses that destroy the soul. And "He that is free shall be free indeed."

"We know in part, and we prophesy in part. But when that which is perfect is come, then that which is in part shall be done away.—For now we see through a glass darkly; but then face to face: now I know in part; but then shall I know even as also I am known." (I Cor. 13:9-10 and 12).

The complete vision, the complete understanding, the complete power, with all light and all joy and all knowledge is waiting for any man who will "ask, seek and knock." Man was never intended to go blundering through life, heaping unto himself mistakes upon mistakes, burden upon burden,

misery upon misery. Man was created to be a bearer of
light and glory—to manifest power, poise and peace.

This is what Christ meant when He said, "Come unto me all
ye who labor and are heavy laden (and every mortal man is
overburdened—this IS mortality, this burden of blindness,
woes, sorrows, lack of understanding), and I will give you
rest. Take my yoke upon you, for my yoke (love) is easy,
and my burden is LIGHT"—even the great light of glory that
banishes all darkness or human burdens and man becomes
again ONE with the Spirit of Truth or LIGHT. This is the
message: "Come unto me all ye mortals, struggling under your
burdens of weaknesses, sorrows, sins, blindness, fears, worries
and heartaches and enter again into the LIGHT. Share with me
the glory which you had with me before the world was."

Even those who think they possess all, are described thus
in the scripture: "Because thou sayest, I am rich, and increased with goods, and have need of nothing; and knowest not
that thou art wretched, and miserable, and poor, and blind and
naked:

"I counsel thee to buy of me gold tried in the fire, that thou
mayest be rich; and white raiment (which signifies purity),
that thou mayest be clothed, and that the shame of thy nakedness do not appear; and anoint thine eyes with eyesalve that
thou mayest see." (Rev. 3:17-18). And regardless of how
diligently one thinks he is serving, unless he has learned to
live from his soul, and found that personal contact with the
Father, his life is a burden and a misery and a blank—and
he is poor, and wretched, and miserable, and blind, and naked.

"The glory of God is intelligence." And according to the
Doctrine and Covenants 93:29: *"Man was also in the beginning with God, Intelligence, or the Spirit of Truth,* was not
created or made, neither indeed can be."

Thus we were the glory of God, even the very spirit of
intelligence before the world was.

This agrees perfectly with the following: "This is my work
and my glory, to bring to pass the immortality and eternal
life of man." Thus *the Glory of God is man, exalted.* In the
beginning we were the very Spirit of Intelligence or Truth, and

thus the glory of God is to gather us back as gods, or deified, if we will only understand and co-operate.

"The glory of God is intelligence, or, in other words, light and truth.

"Light and truth forsake that evil one.

"Every spirit of man was innocent in the beginning and God having redeemed man from the fall, man became again, in their infant state, innocent before God.

"And that wicked one cometh and taketh away light and truth, through disobedience, from the children of men, and because of the traditions of their fathers." (D. & C. 93:36-39).

Now, taking again the eighty-eighth section of the D. & C. verses six to thirteen:

"He that ascended up on high, as also he descended below all things, in that he comprehendeth all things, that he might be in and through all things, *The Light of Truth.*

"Which truth shineth, *This is the Light of Christ.* As also he is in the sun, and the light of the sun, and the power thereof by which it was made . . ." It goes on to explain that this light of Christ, or the Light of Truth, or the Spirit of Truth is in the moon and the stars and is the light and power thereof, which is also the light that is in us—

"Which light proceedeth forth from the presence of God to fill the immensity of space—

"The light which is in all things, which giveth life to all things, which is the law by which all things are governed, *even the power of God,* who sitteth upon his throne, who is in the bosom of eternity, who is in the midst of all things."

Here is given a clear explanation that the Spirit of Christ, or the Spirit of Truth, or the Light of Truth, as you may choose to designate it, is the POWER OF GOD, and that it proceeds forth from the true and living God. Thus every man is a living witness to the power of God, for he was that very thing in the beginning. He is still that as he opens his mind to comprehend, and his heart to understand.

As one catches the vision of the glory of these truths the veil of eternity rolls back and man is no longer hampered by a race consciousness of fears, woes and blindness, but with clear vision he is free. "Know the truth and the Truth will make you free," if you will only use it and live by it.

Truth is the substance out of which eternity is composed. Every small truth, or minute portion of it is but a part of the whole. He who builds on truth ·builds for eternity. He who speaks only truth shall have his words blazed in glory and they shall live forever. Know the truth and you become free—free from earthly sorrows and trials. Live truth and you become Truth.

He who builds on falsehood builds a false structure on a false foundation and his building will crumble ·and great will be the fall of it. He who fights truth will be destroyed for he is kicking against the indestructible walls of eternity and they cannot be destroyed or changed in the least by any man's erroneous thinking. Against the false beliefs of a whole world, yea, a whole universe, truth will endure. And since truth is light and light is Spirit, the great realm of spirit rises in ever increasing splendor above the bigotry, the falsehood, the narrowness of personal views and false conceptions—the only glory for man is to become ONE with the whole, or all truth and this can only be done as he contacts the Spirit of God centered in his own soul—until the very Word it continues to speak in guiding revelation will lead him into all truth—and thus the word of God can lead him to perfection that he too might lay claim to his divine heritage.

As man overcomes the darkness of the earth and forsakes all evil, the intelligence, or light again increases within him and he returns to the status of the glory which he had with God before the world was—even as Christ, our elder Brother did. As one turns to Christ, the Spirit of Truth, he again becomes ONE with Him, and the burdens of mortality drop away and he becomes again the *Light*.

When one reaches this point he receives all power, both in heaven and on earth, and nothing is impossible to him, for he has glorified his heritage and become a god—a true son of his Divine Sire. (See D. & C. 50:26-29; also Sec. 93:17).

These are the great and marvelous things that have been hid from the foundation of the world and have been lost be-

cause of wickedness, and the hardness of men's hearts and the
blindness of their minds, as given in the Record of Ether, the
ancient historian.

And I hear you ask, "If any man say, I am without sin, he
is a liar, and the truth is not in him," what about it? The
above is certainly an exact statement, for if any man is without sin he would be the last person in existence to speak such
a thing. For Christ was the only One who lived without sin—
"We have all sinned," but it is possible to overcome sin—to
overcome our weaknesses, but after this is done the very humility of a person, his developed love and meekness would
seal his lips forever against such boasting. He would become
like the description given in the Odes of Solomon, given of
the Christ: "And His Word is with us in all our way; The
Savior who makes alive and does not reject our souls; *The
man who was humbled and exalted by His own righteousness.*"
Thus true righteousness does not make a man proud—it makes
him humble. Self-righteousness exalts one in the pride of his
heart—but true righteousness perfects his love and devotion
until he would be quite unaware of perfection within himself,
for in viewing the very goodness and glory of God he would
thoroughly understand his own incompleteness without that
divine power of God behind him.

No man could possibly be perfect without having overcome
many human weaknesses—and he will realize with all his
heart that without the help of the Almighty, without the constant direction of the "Father within," that "Still small voice"
he could never have overcome them. Such a man would never
in the world be able to boast of his goodness. He would understand that boasting itself is a great transgression—a transgression as bad as stealing, lying, hate, confusion or any of the
other sins of the flesh. Like Christ, he would say, "Why
callest thou me the good? God is the good." The power to seek
in any way to exalt himself above his fellowmen would have
been banished by his reverent love, and deep humility—*that is*
perfection.

In order to be without sin would require a divine meekness
of soul that carries its own light. Then you say, "But no mor-

tal man is perfect." That too is correct, for when man reaches perfection he is no longer a mere mortal, but becomes translated into a higher state. And this condition is every man's right, if he will only catch the vision of it—and live for it.

Step forth, ye sons of light, and with clear vision claim your heritage and thus glorify your Father forever and ever. "Let the same mind be in you which was in Christ Jesus, who being in the form of God thought it not robbery to be equal with God."

And when the "Unspeakable name of God," which the ancients knew, but which has long since been lost because of wickedness, is again revealed to your understanding you will know that these things are true. And you will know that they are true if you will only "*Ask*," for every one who asks receives. "And if any of you lack wisdom, let him ask of God, who giveth to all men liberally, and upbraideth not."

Below is the pure and perfect prayer of the Sacrament of Jesus Christ: "Oh, God, the Eternal Father, we ask thee in the name of thy Son, Jesus Christ, to bless and sanctify this bread to the souls of all those who partake of it, that they may eat it in remembrance of the body of Thy Son, and witness unto thee, Oh God, the eternal Father, THAT THEY ARE WILLING TO TAKE UPON THEM THE NAME OF THY SON, and always remember Him, and keep His commandments which He has given them, that they may always have His Spirit to be with them—AMEN.

"Behold, Jesus Christ is the name given of the Father, and there is none other name given whereby man can be saved.

"Wherefore, ALL MEN MUST TAKE UPON THEM THE NAME WHICH IS GIVEN OF THE FATHER, FOR IN THAT NAME SHALL THEY BE CALLED AT THE LAST DAY." (D. & C. 18:23-24).

Every woman who takes upon her the name of her husband is henceforth known by that name. And so it is with everyone who takes upon them the name of Christ. He is the Bridegroom. The Saints, or Holy Ones, or those who have purified themselves before him until they become holy, are called the bride, according to the scripture. At the marriage the two become ONE—and forever after the bride, or Holy Ones, are known by His name. Anyone who takes upon him a name becomes that name. And the word "Christ" meaning "The Anointed", when man becomes "Anointed with light" he enters again into that Light, or receives of the fullness—and so he receives the name of "Christ."

In childhood small boys are known by their individual, first names, but when they mature to manhood they take upon them the names of their fathers.

The name "Adam" means "many" according to Moses 1:34. The name "Christ" includes all who enter into and receive the light—for it means "THE SPIRIT OF TRUTH" and we were that very Spirit of Truth before the world began. We become that again when we lift our hearts and minds to understand and partake of the anointing which is ours, and receive of His fullness as we fulfill the laws of righteousness. Again, quoting 3 Nephi 28:10:

"And for this cause ye shall have fullness of joy; and ye shall sit down in the Kingdom of my Father; yea, your joy shall be full, even as the Father hath given me fullness of joy; and ye shall be even as I am, and I am even as the Father and the Father and I are ONE."

If these three men can become even as Christ and God the Father, then all men can if they will fulfill the laws of righteousness and perfection.

Any son who makes an idol of his father, knowing his father is all-important, all-wise, all-efficient, all-powerful and perfect and yet never attempts to become like his father will never amount to anything. God to every man should be the ideal, not the idol. An ideal is something or Someone to model one's life after. "Therefore be ye perfect even as your Father in heaven is perfect." So to become gods we must step forth and live the life and claim the birthright, for it is ours as we live for it. "Yea, all that the Father has is yours." Not just in eternity, but whenever we prepare ourselves to accept the glory of our heritage.

"Come now and let us reason together, saith the Lord; though their sins be as scarlet they shall be white as snow; though they be red like crimson, they shall be as wool—TO HIM THAT OVERCOMETH." (Isa. 1:18).

This "overcoming," mentioned so often in scriptures, has to be done on this earth and while in the flesh. This is the key that mankind has lost as the dark veil of night has wrapped itself closely around the world, and man has been lulled to sleep beneath his burden of human weaknesses and blindness. There is just one step between mediocrity and the power of the genius. There is another step between the genius and the Saint, or one who has "overcome all things." These steps are steps in consciousness, the last being taken when all fears and darkness is left behind, as one steps knowingly into the light, or is completely born of the Spirit, not in words, but in the Power of the Almighty. These steps of progress can only be taken as one learns to heed the Light of the Spirit from within.

This is the day of our probation, so we are told. Probation for what? "To see if we will do all things whatsoever the Lord shall command us." That we might receive all the blessings He has for us, which cannot possibly be bestowed upon us unless we have prepared ourselves to receive them. If such glory and power were bestowed upon us before we had overcome our weaknesses we could destroy ourselves completely. We could destroy the world. Such power can only be entrusted to those who have been tested and tried in all things and been proven worthy of so sacred an obligation and privilege. This power banishes all misery, all fears, all darkness, all evil and unhappiness completely as it is used under the power and direction of the Almighty. And God never gives a command that is impossible to fulfill. The road to attainment may be a road of sacrifice and overcoming, but it is a road of eternal glory and light and satisfaction and power that compares to nothing else on earth. It is health. It is happiness. It is eternal youth. It is service. It is light, and it is mastery and achievement and fullness of joy.

From ancient records comes this message, it was told thousands of years ago in language so simple children could read —the message is: "Man of his own free will shall leave the man kingdom and evolve to the God Kingdom."

I leave a special prayer upon this work that God may enlighten your souls, and open your eyes to see and your hearts to understand that you may walk with Him—*And be* ONE *with Him*—even gods—for the scripture cannot be broken, and if you receive the Word of God—and live it until that Word becomes flesh—then are ye gods.

"For though there are, indeed, Gods so called, whether in heaven or on earth (as there are Gods many and Lords many).

"Yet to us there is but One God, the Father, out of whom are all things, and we in him; and One Lord, Jesus Christ, through whom are all things, and we in Him." (I Cor. 8:5-6 —Greek original).

"Would to God, brethren, I could tell you who I am! Would to God I could tell you what I know! But you would call it blasphemy and want to take my life." (Joseph Smith).

And now I will say, "Would to God you can understand when I try to tell you who you are—and what you are—for these are the things to which Joseph Smith referred. And would to God I could tell you what I know, but you would call it blasphemy.

"When one's mind and lips have lost the power to hurt and wound, then shall his voice be heard among the Gods." No man's voice can be heard among the scholars until he himself, has become a scholar. No man's voice can be heard among the doctors until he himself has become a doctor. No man's voice can be heard among the scientists until he has become a scientist. And no man's voice can be heard among the Gods, until every vibration, every thought, every word is so enfolded in love that he has completely lost the power to hurt and wound —then to him the door will be opened—and he will see and know for himself and he will need none to teach him.

Our eyes can only become single to His glory when our thoughts, or mental vision is held steadfastly on His glory and perfection until we begin to fulfill that very perfection in our own lives. Then it is that we shall truly be "Born of the Spirit," or "anointed with Light," or become "ordained of the Father" and receive of "His fullness."

"The pearly gates" are open wide before you, oh son of man, the vision of godhood and glory is yours to claim. Entering the "pearly gates" is not done by dying. It is accomplished by living and loving. Entering the "pearly gates" is entering a higher state of consciousness and leaving one's weaknesses behind. The key is love—love unfeigned, unselfish, tender, compassionate, merciful, Christ-like, forgiving, and filled with divine understanding. This love is not just to be given to one's own, but it is to embrace the whole human race, the weak, the humble, the lost. Love alone fulfills all the laws and keeps all the commandments. It is the perfect, outpouring melody of love that blends forever with the heavenly choir in symphonies of eternal praise. Love is the melody of heaven vibrating across the universe, playing a symphony of eternal glory upon the stars. Love is the name of God, "For God is love," even as His name is "Endless" and "Eternal" and "Almighty." Love is the only perfecting essence that can redeem man, for though he has all faith and all power, even to raise the dead or to move mountains, and though he gives all that he has to the poor, and his body to be burned, and has not love it will avail him nothing—for such things are as sounding brass and tinkling cymbals without the divine gift of pure, Christ-like love.

Love is heaven—and "Heaven is within you," son of man, and it must grow as the mustard seed and fill your being as leaven. "Seek ye first the kingdom of God, and His righteousness (that you might bring forth that righteousness in your own life), and all else shall be added unto you." Love endureth forever. The "pearly gates" are only symbolical of pure and perfect love and light. Love is more beautiful than pearls and more eternal than precious stones. LOVE IS LIGHT. It is glory and perfection.

As one develops the gift of love to its full perfection—even as the master musician develops his art, until he not only perfects love within himself, but becomes the very essence of love he will find that "He is truly the door to everything." He will know that the gates to the kingdom of heaven is but the opening wide the portals of his own heart to light and love and gentleness. And he himself will become the very thing he seeks to interpret. "Or who can rest on the Most High, so that with His mouth he may speak? Who is able to interpret the wonders of the Lord? For he who could interpret would be dissolved and would become that which is interpreted."

Yea, love is the cohesive power of the Universe. It holds together nations, communities, families, friends, substance and atoms. It holds together body tissue and thus keeps the muscles from sagging and growing old. It keeps the flesh from disintegrating. It will perfect the body and the soul. Love! Boundless and eternal is the vibrant perfection and power of eternal life. It is the power of God made manifest in a human form—or His holy temple. Open your heart, soul and mind wide to love that the Spirit of God might abide in you and step from death into life. No occupant of a dwelling, who is not slothful and indolent, ever permits his dwelling to crumble into decay over his head. Let the Light of God and the divine love fill your being and feel its ever perfecting power renew your being. Gather this light and love to you—and you will become love and light—and you will become the door to everything.

Oh, son of man, evolve from the man kingdom into the god kingdom through the gates of perfect love, for love is the door, and heaven is your heritage—*here and now*.

In the very ancient record of Ether is given these marvelous words: "Come unto me, O ye Gentiles, and I will show unto you the greater things, the knowledge which is hid up because of unbelief.

"Come unto me, O ye house of Israel, and it shall be made manifest unto you how great things the Father hath laid up for you, from the foundation of the world; and it hath not come unto you, because of unbelief.

"Behold, when ye shall rend that veil of unbelief which doth cause you to remain in your awful state of wickedness, and hardness of heart, and blindness of mind, then shall the great and marvelous things which have been hid up from you the foundation of the world from you—yea, when ye shall call upon the Father in my name, with a broken (open or cleft) heart and a contrite spirit—" etc.

The above scripture tells plainly that the veil which shuts

us out from the great, unspeakable blessings is unbelief. It states also that this state of unbelief has caused the world to remain in its *awful state of wickedness*—hardness of heart—and blindness of mind.

This can be better understood when one studies carefully the words of another ancient prophet—"And the angel said unto me Knowest thou the meaning of the tree which thy father saw? And I answered him, saying: Yea, *It is the love of God which sheddeth itself abroad in the hearts of the children of men;* wherefore it is the most desirable above all things. And he spake unto me saying; Yea, and the most joyous to the soul. ***** And it came to pass that I beheld that the iron rod, which my father had seen was the word of God, which led to the fountain of living waters, or to the Tree of Life; which waters are a representation of the love of God; and I also beheld that the tree of life was a representation of the love of God." (I. Nephi 11:21-23 and 25).

Truly it has been the very hardness of our hearts that has not permitted this divine love of God to be shed forth in them. When we can open our hearts to this most joyous of all gifts then the great and unspeakable things that have been hidden from the foundation of the world be revealed in all their breath-taking glory. The veil that has shut us out from partaking of the very Fruit of the Tree of Life, is our own unbelief—and the perfect love of God, which can be shed forth in our hearts only when our hearts are opened, is the Fruit of that Tree.

"Beloved, let us love one another; for love is of God; and *everyone that loveth is born of God, and knoweth God.*

"He that loveth not, knoweth not God; for God is love."

"And we have known and believed the love that God hath to us. God is love; and he that dwelleth in love dwelleth in God, and God in him." (I. John 4:7-8 and 16).

CHAPTER XXII.

THE LAMB'S BOOK OF LIFE

"AND all saints who live by the Word of Wisdom, *walking in obedience to the commandments* . . . shall find wisdom and great treasures of knowledge, even hidden treasures."

The hidden treasures of knowledge are the sacred, glorifying treasures of truth that have been veiled and hidden between irrelevant passages and verses of scripture.

Take for instance I Nephi 11:22-25, given in answer to the angel's query, "Knowest thou the meaning of the tree which thy father saw?"

"And I (Nephi) answered him, saying: Yea, it is the love of God, which sheddeth itself abroad in the hearts of the children of men; wherefore, it is the most desirable above all things.

"And he spake unto me saying; yea, and the most joyous to the soul."

The above verses tell that the most precious, desirable and joyous gift of God is His love that is shed forth in the hearts of the children of men, as they prepare themselves to receive this divine gift.

Then the great, complete truth is veiled or hidden by the following verse which disconnects or breaks up the full meaning of a revelation that is breath-taking in its fullness.

The passage that veils the full truth is beautiful in its own shimmering glory, but is completely irrelevant to the subject of the tree and its fruit.

The verse that veils or draws away the attention from the full vision reads thus: "And after he had said these words, he said unto me; Look! And I looked, and I beheld the Son of God going forth among the children of men; and I saw many fall down at his feet and worship him." This verse is beautiful and filled with meaning, yet it has completely broken up the main thought of the tree and the meaning of it, therefore it is quite necessary to pull this intervening veil aside and with clear vision again take up the thought of the tree and its glorious fruit.

"And it came to pass that I beheld that the rod of iron, which my father had seen, was the word of God, which led to the fountain of living waters, *or to the tree of life;* which waters are a representation of the love of God; and I also beheld that the tree of life was a representation of the love of God."

This last verse completes the description of the fruit of the tree which was most precious and explains that the fruit of that tree is the fruit of the tree of life, and is the pure love of God that is shed forth in the hearts of the children of men. Now, the tree of life is located "in the midst of the Paradise of God." And again, "The kingdom of heaven is within you," so is the Paradise of God, and the Tree of Life—and the fruit of that tree is the great, perfect, divine love of God as it is permitted to come forth and bear fruit in the hearts of the children of men as they are led to the understanding of it by holding steadfastly to the iron rod. And the iron rod is the word of God.

Now analyze for a moment just what the word of God is. The word of God is almost a complete record of promises, from individual blessings to the greatest revelations ever given under the Spirit of Almighty God. There are also warnings to show how the great promises can fail to be fulfilled, but always the promises hold first place. And it is the promises that God is desirous to have man fulfill that he might receive the great promised blessings. His word is a record of promises so great, so dynamic, so glorious that it has been almost impossible for the minds of men to grasp or understand them— promises that *all* who *believe* on Jesus Christ should have the power to do all the works that He did, even greater works— the promise that man could have the power to move mountains, even as Enoch of old—the promise that *all who believed* and were baptized in His Name, even unto the ends of the earth, should have these signs follow them: power to cast out devils, speak with new tongues (or by the power of the Holy Ghost) —they should pick up serpents and be unharmed; drink deadly poison and be unhurt; lay hands on the sick and they would recover; restore the blind; heal the halt and the lame and cure all manner of diseases; and should have power to perform many mighty miracles in His name. These promises are the word of God, but who has held to them until they received that power? Who has even believed in them? They believe in history, in the record of those of old, *but in the word of His promise* they do not believe, for they have proved their disbelief in their very lack of power. "For My kingdom is not in word, but in power." Mankind does not believe, neither is it holding to the word of His promises, yet it is only by holding to His word that the power of God can be fulfilled. As these promises are believed in, and held to, it is possible to partake of the fruit of the tree of life, which represents the pure love of God.

In the marvelous record which follows is given some of the veiled thoughts that must be unveiled. Please note the sequence and numbering of the verses:

16.   "And, I, John bear record that he received a fulness of the glory of the Father.

17.   *"And he received all power, both in heaven and on earth, and the glory of the Father was with him, for he dwelt in him.*

19.   "I give unto you these sayings that you may understand and know how to worship, and know what you worship, that you may come unto the Father in my name, and in due time receive of his fulness.

20.   "For if you keep my commandments you shall receive of his fulness and be glorified in me as I am in the Father—

21.   "And now, verily I say unto you, I was in the beginning with the Father, and am the First born.

23.   "Ye were also in the beginning with the Father; that which is Spirit, even the Spirit of Truth.

26.   "The Spirit of Truth is of God. I am the Spirit of Truth, and John bore record of me, saying, He received a fulness of Truth, yea, even of all truth.

27.   "And no man receiveth a fulness unless he keepeth his commandments.

28. "He that keepeth his commandments receiveth truth and light until he is glorified in truth and knoweth all things.

29. "Man was also in the beginning with God, Intelligence, or the light of truth, was not created or made, neither indeed can be." (D. & C. Section 93).

Here is given the plan Christ followed—and our pattern is exactly like His. Notice in verse seventeen where it states that He received all power both in heaven and on earth. In Section 50:24-29 it gives that same exact promise to every man who will but purify himself and chase out darkness and overcome all sin:

"That which is of God is light; and he that receiveth light and continueth in God, receiveth more light;

"And again, verily I say unto you and I say it that you may know the truth, that you may chase darkness from among you.

"He that is ordained of God and sent forth, the same is appointed to be the greatest, notwithstanding he is the least and the servant of all.

"Wherefore, he is possessor of all things; FOR ALL THINGS ARE SUBJECT UNTO HIM, BOTH IN HEAVEN AND ON EARTH, THE LIFE AND THE LIGHT, THE SPIRIT AND THE POWER, SENT FORTH BY THE WILL OF THE FATHER THROUGH JESUS CHRIST, HIS SON.

"But no man is possessor of all things except he be purified and cleansed from all sin."

Study all the scriptures in this manner, with a humble heart, with earnest prayer, in the name of Jesus Christ, seeking only for truth, desiring only to glorify God, and if you are sincere, and if you are truly humble, praying always to *know* truth, the veil will be lifted. And as you find truth, those great hidden treasures, worship and adore and praise and love and give thanks continually—and live by every word that is revealed by the Spirit of God to your understanding. Guard such knowledge well, and never seek to force it on the minds of others unless directed by the Spirit of God to do so.

This book has been written under the direction of the Almighty for the sole purpose of opening the sacred Books of scripture to the eyes of those who seek. This work is to unveil the hidden treasures that have already been revealed—to make clear those dynamic promises of God and reveal some of the hidden treasures to those who keep the commandments and live by the Word of Wisdom, and to those who love the truth. The rebellious, the proud and those with wicked minds will have no power to understand or take hold of these great truths and live by them, for only by deep humility, perfect love, and constant prayer can one *know* Truth, and use it.

There are only two possible ways for those who read this book to know if it is TRUE, and the first is to pray to God the Eternal Father in the name of Jesus Christ to know if these things are true. The other way is to live these higher laws of love, forgiveness, worship, devotion and singing glory, as Christ admonished. "Live the laws and you will know whether it be of God, or whether I speak of myself."

If you will read Rev. 20:12, "And I saw the dead small and great, stand before God; *and the books were opened;* and another book was opened, which is the Book of Life; and the dead were judged out of those things which were written in the books, according to their works."

The Books have been opened. This work that has come forth under the command and power of God is to open the Books. Their great hidden treasures of knowledge have been opened to all who will receive—the knowledge of how to cleanse the inside of the cup, or the hearts, the souls, and the minds of men. The fulfilling of all church ordinances, functions and requirements are only the cleansing of the outside of the cup. The inside can only be cleansed by "Living by every word that proceedeth forth from the mouth of God."

That divine cleansing of the inside of the cup is obtaining that pure Christ-like love which God sheds forth in the hearts of the children of men after they have fulfilled the law. "It is the pure love of Christ which the Father bestows upon all who are *true followers* of His Son Jesus Christ, *after they have prayed for it with all the energy of heart.*" (Moroni 7:47-48). To be a *true follower* means to live literally as He lived—to work as He worked—to do as He did—love as He loved—forgive as He forgave—and believe as He believed.

And the books have been opened and from here on each man will bring his own judgment upon himself—Yea, and "That *all* men might judge between the righteous and the wicked, saith your God."

Yea, the Books have been opened wide, and their hidden treasures revealed that their knowledge might be given to every individual who desires it, and who has prepared himself to receive it—the knowledge of how to open the great Book of Life. The Books of the scripture have been opened for the sole purpose of preparing this people to open that great and glorious Book of Life.

Then if you study carefully that twentieth chapter of Revelations you will say that this record is false—that the Books are to be opened *after* the end of the millennium and the judgment is to come *after* the thousand years of peace. It is true that the great judgment, when men shall have to stand before the throne of God and be judged according to their works will come at the end of that period. But the Books are to be opened at the *beginning* of it. This great truth has been lost in the translations. But ye may know for yourself as to the truth of what is herein written, if you will only pray sincerely, and are willing to turn to the Light of Christ within you, the gift by which ye may judge with a sure knowing. Pray to understand these things. Pray to comprehend the meaning of the Books and the great and glorious Book of Life, which ye are.

Yea, this Book of Life is contained right within man—and man himself must open it, which could only be done after the other Books have been opened, revealing how it is to be done, making manifest the truth that love and perfection in an individual can overcome death. With this knowledge of the laws of perfection, and the laws contained in the Books, the Book of Life can be opened in the hearts of the children of men—and those who open that book need not die nor come into judgment.

Each and every man must open that Book of Life for himself. Those who fail to open it will have to die—and those who die will be brought into the judgment of the Almighty God, for they shall be judged out of the things that are written in the Books—the things they refused to live by after the Books were opened.

"Therefore it is given to abide in you; the record of heaven; the Comforter; the peaceable things of immortal glory; the truth of all things; *that which quickeneth all things, which maketh alive all things;* that which knoweth all things, and hath *all power,* according to wisdom, mercy, truth, justice, and *judgment."* (Moses 6:61).

This record that is given to abide in you is the Book of Life, but of what value is it to you if you fail to open it and to read the glorious things contained therein? Within you is the truth of all things, but if you condemn truth then you have failed to use the power of God within you. Yea, all truth, all knowledge, all power, and the gift of eternal life is contained in the record within you.

Man, you are that Book of Life, and you will have to open it for yourself. If you fail to open it now that the other Books have been opened, revealing to you the knowledge, then you will have to die, and if you die you will pass into judgment, for the Books have now been opened, which are the Word of God, leading to the Tree of Life—the love of God shed forth in the hearts of men.

This is said of those who fail: *"Yea, they are grasped with death,* and hell . . . and all that have been seized therewith must stand before the throne of God, and be judged according to their works." The above states plainly that those who are grasped by death will have to stand before God and be judged.

Then the record goes on to tell who it is who are to receive this great condemnation and judgment!

"Therefore, woe be unto him that is at ease in Zion!

"Woe be unto all that crieth, All is well!

"Yea, woe be unto him *that harkeneth unto the precepts of men, and denieth the power of God,* and the gift of the Holy Ghost!

"Yea, woe be unto him that saith; We have received, and we need no more!

"And in fine, woe be unto all those who tremble, and are angry because of the Truth of God; For behold, he that is built upon the rock receiveth it with gladness; and he that is built upon a sandy foundation trembleth lest he shall fall.

"Woe be unto him that shall say; We have received the word of God, and we need no more of the word of God, for we have enough!

"For behold, thus saith the Lord God: I will give unto the children of men line upon line, precept upon precept, here a little, and there a little; and blessed are those who hearken unto my precepts, and lend an ear unto my counsel, for they shall learn wisdom; *for unto him that receiveth I will give more;* and from them that shall say, we have enough, from them shall be taken away even that which they have.

"Cursed is he that putteth his trust in man, or maketh flesh his arm, or shall hearken unto the precepts of men, save their precepts shall be given by the power of the Holy Ghost." (II Nephi 28:23-31. See also Isa. chapter 28).

"Unto him that receiveth I will give more." "The More" that will be given to those who do not seal their minds against Truth that is revealed by the power of God, will be *power,* as is revealed in the following:

"Now, behold this is wisdom; whoso readeth, let him understand and receive also:

"For unto him that receiveth it shall be given more abundantly, *even power."* (D. & C. 71:5-6).

Yea, they shall receive even power to open the Book of Life. For the Books have been opened and the knowledge made plain whereby man can step into a higher way of life, yea, even beyond death, fulfilling the laws of all righteousness.

Yea, from here on you will be judged according to the great and marvelous truths that are written in the Books— these Books of scripture that are now opened—the Books that reveal the keys to the Book of Life.

Open that Book. Open it, man, for it is yours! Its seal is in your own heart! Open your heart wide to receive the full love of God! Open your heart, your mind, your soul wide to the Spirit of Truth, to the Spirit of Almighty God, to His great, unspeakable love, and to the Light of Christ, then you will have not only power to open that Divine Book of Life, but to read it and fulfill it—and all knowledge will be yours, both in heaven and on earth—and all power.

Speak to God through that glorious instrument of love, your own heart, at all times. Then learn to speak every word you utter through that glorious microphone of perfection. Think through it—and behold you shall walk with God—and the words that you speak will be His words—and your thoughts will be His thoughts—and your power will be His power, for you shall be filled with the Spirit of the Almighty, and receive of His fullness.

The following keys are placed in your hands that you need never fail. Use them. Perfect love! Deep humility! Constant prayer—a prayer that is a song of eternal praise and glory! These keys hold forever the power of light through which the powers of darkness cannot penetrate. Use them! Adore! Worship! Praise and love with every fibre of your being and your prayers will ascend in a flaming glory of everlasting power.

Yea, perfect these keys and use them and the Book of Life will be opened wide to you—and all that it contains, for the Living Book of Life ye are! Yea, the complete record of Life. Man, awake! And know now and forever that you are that sacred Book of Life and if you do not open it no other can. Open that Book of Life and you shall live forever—Yea, open your own soul and read the record written there; open your mind to comprehend the power and strength of your. soul, and the glory of the Spirit of God; open your heart to the great inflow of His everlasting love. Unseal yourself for you are the Book of Life. You are the very glory of God.

CHAPTER XXIII.

THE KEYS OF ALL POWER

You say that you do not comprehend all that is written in this book? Then you must ask, "for everyone who asks receives."

"For behold, my brethren, it is given unto you to judge, that ye may know good from evil, and the way to judge is as plain, that ye may know truth with a perfect knowledge, as the daylight is from the dark night.

"For behold, *the Spirit of Christ is given to every man,* that he may know good from evil; wherefore, I show unto you the way to judge; for everything which inviteth to do good, and to persuade to believe in Christ, is sent forth by the power and gift of Christ; wherefore ye may know with a perfect knowledge it is of God.

"But whatsoever thing persuadeth men to do evil, and believe not in Christ, and deny him, and serve not God, then ye may know with a perfect knowledge it is of the devil; for after this manner doth the devil work, for he persuadeth no man to do good, no, not one; neither do his angels; neither do they who subject themselves unto him.

"And now, my brethren, seeing that ye know the light by which ye may judge, which light is the light of Christ, see that ye judge not wrongfully; for with the same judgment which ye judge ye shall also be judged. (This is perfect in its meaning, for those who reject truth or condemn it have judged themselves unworthy or unprepared to receive it and have thereby sealed their own way of progress).

"Wherefore, I beseech of you, brethren, that ye should search diligently in the light of Christ that ye may know good from evil; and if ye will lay hold upon every good thing, and condemn it not, ye certainly will be a child of Christ." (Moroni 7:15-19).

Paul, writing to the Thessolonians, gave this powerful admonition: "PROVE ALL THINGS, and hold fast to that which is good." He did not say, *"Disprove all things."* Those who seek only to *disprove* everything new they hear are truly judging themselves into darkness. There is an old Hindoo adage on action given as follows: "There are those who *do*; those who *do not*; and those who *undo*!"

This Light of Christ that is given to abide in every man is each man's personal guide and director or savior. Man is saved or redeemed only as he learns to follow that Light within. "This is the Light which shineth, which giveth you light, which is through him who enlighteneth your eyes, which is the same light that quickeneth your understandings!

"Which light proceedeth forth from the presence of God to fill the immensity of space—

"The light which is in all things, which giveth life to all things, which is the law by which all things are governed, even the power of God, who sitteth upon his throne, who is in the bosom of eternity, *who is in the midst of all things."* (D. & C. 88:6-13).

"The light shineth in darkness, and the darkness comprehendeth it not; nevertheless, the day shall come when you shall comprehend even God, being quickened in him and by him.

"Then shall ye know that ye have seen me, that I am, and that *I Am the true light that is in you,* and that you are in me, otherwise ye could not abound." (*Ibid., verses* 49-50).

"And he who accepts not the light is under condemnation," yea for he has rejected the Light of Christ, his own light and glory.

Only those who follow that Light of Christ within themselves are the "True followers of Jesus Christ," for the gift is of Him. Only as man heeds that Light from within his own soul is he a real follower. This is how one takes upon himself the Name of Jesus Christ, and in no other way can it be done. This is how one receives his "Anointing of Light" and finally receives of the "Fullness of the Father." Then that Light is made flesh, for it has become a part of every cell and tissue of his being—yea, his very self.

"And they who accept not that Light are under condemnation."

"For the word of the Lord is truth, and whatsoever is truth is light, and whatsoever is light is Spirit, even the Spirit of Jesus Christ. *And the Spirit giveth light to every man that cometh into the world; and the Spirit enlighteneth every man through the world, that hearkeneth to the voice of the Spirit.* And every one that hearkeneth to the voice of the Spirit cometh unto God, even the Father." (D. & C. 84:45-47).

"And I am the true light that lighteth every man that cometh into the world." (Ibid 93:2).

This Light that is given to abide in each man that cometh into the world is his own record, or Book of Life. "And as the Father hath life in himself, so hath he given to the Son to have Life in himself"—and to every son, and to every daughter is given this gift if they but open their hearts, souls, and hardest of all, their sealed minds, and follow that Light of Christ that is given to abide in them that they judge not wrongfully—that they might "hear the word of God" as it comes to them in time of need—that they might truly "Walk with God." "And He called them Gods unto whom the word of God came."

The Book of Life can only be opened by opening the heart to receive the great love of God, that is shed forth in the hearts of the children of men—the perfect love, the Christlike, divine love of compassion, mercy and forgiveness. The Book of Life can only be opened as man opens His own soul wide to the Spirit of Almighty God—for the record of heaven has been given to abide in man, and is locked as a seed, deep in the center of his soul. The Book of Life can only be opened as man opens his conscious, mortal mind to be taught of the Spirit, and not of man. Man's intellect has nothing whatsoever to do with the great Light of KNOWING, only as he opens his consciousness to become aware of the Light of Christ that is given to abide in him, deep within his own soul. It is only as the mind is brought into subjection, and is trained in its awareness, or consciousness, to comprehend the great power within the soul and its divine contact with Almighty God, and the ability to lay. aside, to some extent, mortal reasoning and step into divine KNOWING that he can bring forth that Light of Christ and use its powers. Those who depend upon their own mortal intellect, their own high "I.Q." abilities, even their own religious training, no matter how high that training has been, cannot reach this great Light of *knowing* unless they set aside the physical and all its learning. Those who depend upon their highly trained religious or scientific minds are often the farthest from the Truth. They "Are ever learning, yet *never able to come to a knowledge of* THE TRUTH."

First there must be developed the ability to believe. One must first believe God when He assures us that He gave this Light of Christ to abide in every man who dwells upon the earth. He must use his intellect to begin, in some measure, to comprehend that that Light of Christ which is given to man, that he might be able to judge good from evil and gradually be led into all truth, is his to use—and that he will be under condemnation if he uses not that light and the power it contains.

After the *believing* that such a Light and power does exist, and after desiring it, and hoping for its complete powers to be unfolded, comes the full *knowing* that it does exist.

This Light that is right within man is most easily developed by first using it as God directed, to judge between good and evil. When in doubt on any subject, on any information, ask the Father in the Name of Jesus Christ to reveal its truth to you by the Light of Christ which He gave to abide in you. Then rely upon that Spirit of Truth within you, or the Light of Christ, for the answer. This will bring it forth and help to develop it.

Then begin to use it with your problems—in the big issues of life—then in all your daily activities. Learn to abide in it at all times. Love it! Glorify God for giving you such a priceless gift, for within that gift is contained all peace, all knowledge, all power; yea, the very gift of life itself. It is yours to use. It has always been yours. All mankind has been struggling under its burdens of human weaknesses, sorrows, difficulties, and darkness and condemnation because it has *rejected* THAT *Light*.

The more you use that great and glorious Light of Christ that has been given to abide in you the greater will be its power in your life. This is the Light of Christ that is in every man who will accept the gift. It is the Light Christ Himself used as He performed His great and mighty works. It is the only possible way one can use the power of Almighty God and fulfill the promises He has given, for this Light is the key to all power.

Turn to this Light of Christ that is given to abide in you. Turn to it under every circumstance in life and rest in the assurance that the Father will perform the works required to glorify His name and to fulfill His promises. This is the only possible way to do the works that Christ did—even the greater works.

Turn to this Light within to solve every difficult situation and begin to glory in its power. This is the gift of God, through His Beloved Son, Jesus Christ, to every one who will accept it and use it. It is all power! All knowing! All peace! All joy! It is glory such as man has never dreamed of, nor been able to conceive with his mortal mind, his conscious intellect. This gift is not a gift of the intellect at all, but a gift of God, and is hidden like a jewel, in the depth of man's soul, or is the precious gem that is buried in a field, which when a man finds, he sells everything that he has to possess that field and own the jewel.

This great gift can only come forth as a power right within man as his mortal intellect is brought into subjection to the Spirit of God. It can only be claimed when one has developed the faith to accept the things that his mortal senses have never seen, felt, heard, smelled or tasted, nor his human mind weighed and measured. This is the great gift beyond mortal concept—the gift of glory and power and light and achievement—Yet it cannot be bought for money, for it is given freely for the use of every man. This is the contact one has with God so that he may never need to walk in his own feeble knowledge and according to his own blind understanding. No matter how much man thinks he knows his learning is foolishness to the Lord. It is impossible to even try to compare the knowledge which man can gather in his mind with the great *Light of All-Knowing power* contained in the Light of Christ that is God's most precious gift to man.

The more one turns to this Light within for help, for information, for guidance, the greater will be its power. Gradually it will come forth in its fulness and man will receive his "Anointing of Light." This great, Holy Anointing does not come to man from without, as many have supposed—it comes forth from within. And man himself must bring it forth. When it has been brought forth by belief, by cultivating, by developing and more and more intense use, man will be filled with light and comprehend all things for he will have learned to abide in the Spirit of Truth, and will become free—free from the shackles of earth.

"And when he was demanded of the Pharisees, when the kingdom of God should come, he answered them and said, the kingdom of God cometh not with observation.

"Neither shall they say, lo here or, lo there! For behold, the kingdom of God is within you." (Luke 17:20-21).

"For the Kingdom of God is not in word, but in power." (I. Cor. 4:20).

"Then said he, unto what is the kingdom of God like? And whereunto shall I resemble it? It is like a grain of mustard seed, which a man took and cast into his garden; and it grew, and waxed a great tree; and the fowls of the air lodged in the branches of it.

"And again he said, whereunto shall I liken the Kingdom of God?

"It is like leaven, which a woman took and hid in three measures of meal, till the whole was leavened." (Luke 13:18-21; Matt. 13:13-33).

The foregoing description of the Kingdom of God is most perfect. It is the tiny seed of Light—the Light of Christ that is given to abide in each and every man who cometh into the world—and it will never grow and mature unless cultivated, cared for, appreciated and loved.

It is also like leaven that must be brought forth right within man, until it fills every cell and fibre of his being.

"Verily, I say unto you, whosoever shall not receive the kingdom of God as a little child shall in nowise enter therein." Yea, he must love it tenderly, even as a little child must be loved. Gather it close into your embrace and feel it grow within you.

This kingdom of heaven is the kingdom within that is finally illuminated by the Light of Christ. It is the Book of Life. It is the power of glory—the gift of God lying dormant in the mortal body of every individual upon this earth.

"He yearns jealously over the Spirit which He made to dwell in us." (James 4:5-6—Emphatic Diaglott translation).

The great Light of Christ can only be developed by those who are willing to submerge the little ego-self. This is the little strutting, pride-filled, bragging, selfish self of man that carries all the sin. The self is sin. The self is the pride that must be conquered. He who loses that little outer, mediocre, mortal-concept-self shall find himself—yea, his own soul. But he who finds that little self-important, ego-self shall lose the great divine self of his soul. It is the little outer, physical mortal self that always desires all the praise, all the honor, all the glory. It hungers for praise and credit above anything else. It wants all the credit possible to receive— and serves only for reward. It often usurps honors in its covetous desire to excel. It is this little mortal self that is the "accuser" of its brethren. It "belittles" the lives and works of others while constantly trying to magnify its own importance.

The divine, glorious Light of Christ from deep within man's soul desires only to glorify God, to give Him all the glory, and to enfold every man in Light and love who will only accept its guidance.

Thus man can be a slave to the little ego-self-important, mortal self, or a true bearer of Light in the realm of the Divine. For he who loses the self shall find it—the greater, divine self of his own soul—the Light of Christ. And he who finds that light and glorifies that light shall become that Light for he shall be filled with it. And it will become a living part of every cell and fibre of his being.

Learn not to follow your own mortal mind with its false

judgments and restricted knowledge, knowing always, "The learning of the world is foolishness to the Lord." Learn to follow that Light within, which is your own individual redeemer, the gift of God, and it will lead you into all Truth. He who fails to accept this gift of the Son, who rejects this light, is under condemnation, for he has sealed his own progress, and "he shall have to stand before the throne of God and be judged according to the works done in the flesh."

The physical mind of man, no matter how well-trained, or how brilliant, has no power to weigh and measure Spiritual evidence. No amount of credits, honors, or degrees can give this power to man. Only the Light of Christ within man's soul has this power. Only that Light of Christ, the "Rock of Revelation" right within man can reveal Spiritual Truth.

Peter gave this bit of information concerning this great gift: "For we did not follow cleverly devised myths when we made known to you the power and coming of the Lord Jesus Christ but we were eye witnesses of his majesty. For when he received honor and glory from God the Father and the voice was born to him by the Majestic Glory, this is my Beloved Son, with whom I am well pleased, we heard the voice born from heaven for we were with him in the holy mount.

"We have also a more sure word of prophecy; whereunto ye do well that ye take heed, as unto a Light that shineth in a dark place, until the day dawn, and the day star arise in your hearts." (II Peter 1:16-19). Here Peter explains that this Light of testimony within was more sure than hearing and seeing, for they had seen Christ ascend. They had heard the voice of God acknowledge and accept Christ, but greater than seeing and hearing was that testimony of Light that bore witness in the darkness of their own hearts, that if they took heed the great day of light should finally arise in their own hearts.

This Light of Christ is the only sure way of judging good and evil. Therefore any man who attempts to judge truth by his own inferior, erring judgment or intelligence will err, for his mortal mind has not that power, unless lighted by that divine contact with the very "Light of Christ" — "The Spirit of Truth." Thus he will "err in vision and stumble in judgment as his words spew forth the great undigested truths to defile the banquet of the Lord." (Isa. 28).

Only as one humbles himself in true and earnest prayer it is possible to *know* Truth. For each Truth that is revealed by the Light of Christ, within, and accepted, another truth will follow. And thus is given the power to grow from grace to grace even to the "Fulness of the Father." This is the law of Christ—the law of eternal progress—the law of eternal life— the law of damnation— "And cursed is he that putteth his trust in man or maketh flesh his arm, or shall harken unto the precepts of men save their precepts shall be given by the power of the Holy Ghost." Yea, cursed is he that putteth his trust in man instead of in the Spirit of Christ, which God has given to each man, that he may judge between truth and error. The only way the glorious power of God can become active on this earth and in the lives of men is as they begin to follow that Light. And no man has the right to take the place of this Light in the life of another, usurping the power of God. Each and every man has the right to walk in the Light of God, and in direct contact with Him.

From the Journal of Discourses, Volume I, page 312 is given this revealing bit of knowledge—"—These glories are called Telestial, Terrestrial and Celestial, which is the highest, these worlds, different apartments, or mansions in our Father's house. Now those men and those women who know no more about the power of God, and the influences of the Holy Spirit, than to be led entirely by another person, suspending their own understanding and pinning their faith on another's sleeve will never be capable of entering into the Celestial kingdom, to be crowned as they anticipate; they will never be capable of becoming Gods. They cannot rule themselves to say nothing of ruling others, but they must be dictated to in every trifle, like a child. They cannot control themselves in the least, but James, Peter, or somebody else must control them. They cannot become Gods, or be crowned as rulers with glory, immortality and eternal lives. They never can hold scepters of glory, majesty and power in the Celestial kingdom. Who will?

Those who are valiant and inspired with the true independence of heaven, who will go forth boldly in the service of their God, leaving others to do as they please." Every man must learn to do his own thinking—and his own searching—and above all, every man must find his own contact with the Almighty through the Light of Christ that is given to abide in him.

Yea, only as he abides in that Light and knows that that Light of Christ abides in him can he KNOW the Truth—The Truth that will "make him free—" And he who is free" shall be free indeed! He shall be redeemed from his weaknesses and also from his sins, cleansed by the power of the Christ within, and the light will grow in his own soul until he is "Anointed with Light"—then shall he receive all power, both in heaven and on earth.

"That which is of God is light; and he that receiveth light, and continueth in God, receiveth more light; and that light groweth brighter and brighter until the perfect day, (or until the day star arise in his heart—or until the fullness is perfected).

"And again, verily I say unto you, and I say it that you may know the truth, that you may chase darkness from among you:

"*He that is ordained of* GOD and sent forth, the same is appointed to be the greatest, notwithstanding he is the least and the servant of all.

"Wherefore, he is possessor of all things for all things are subject unto him, both in heaven and on earth, THE LIFE AND THE LIGHT, THE SPIRIT AND THE POWER, sent forth by the will of the Father through Jesus Christ, His Son.

"But no man is possessor of all things except he be purified and cleansed from all sin." (D. & C. 50:24-28). This purification and cleansing can only come through the power of Jesus Christ, or the Light within each man, as he learns to follow it, to give heed to it, to bring it forth and glorify it. Man must learn of himself to follow that Light into all Truth. He too must live the Life as Christ lived it and that is how Christ lived it. "Christ is the way, the Truth and the Light, and he who trusteth in him shall never fail."

This Light of Christ that God has given to abide in man that he may know how to judge, is the "Rock of Revelation" spoken of in Scripture. It is the very rock upon which a man must build that he may never fall, as is promised—and if he is built upon this rock, and has this light developed in any way whatsoever he shall accept these things with gladness. But if he is not built upon this rock of revelation contained right within himself, he shall rage against these things, "For he shall tremble lest he shall fall." (II Nephi 28:26-29). It is only upon this Light and power of Christ that any individual can possibly understand and fulfill these higher laws.

"And the Father and I are one. I am in the Father and the Father in me; and inasmuch as you have received me, ye are in me and I in you.

"Wherefore, I am in your midst, and I am the good shepherd, and the stone of Israel. He that buildeth upon this rock shall never fall." (D. & C. 50:43-44). Yea, and "The Gates of hell shall not prevail against it."

Yea, this light of Christ that is given as a guide to each and every man who cometh into the world is even more than the "Rock of Revelation" which will reveal good and evil, right and wrong in every move and act of life, so that man need make no mistakes ever if he will only learn to contact this Light, and rely upon it. It is also the "Chief corner stone that was rejected by the builders." Every individual who has built his body, and all have, has rejected this Light. There are a very few exceptions. Yet this Chief-corner-stone, the perfect crowning glory of man's existence has never been placed upon his brow as the great seal of Almighty God—the seal of all-power and all-knowing. This glorious Light enfolded as a seed in each man's soul, the Light of Christ, must be brought forth by desire, by cultivating, by believing, until it grows into a great plant and at last fills the conscious mind of man. Then the Chief corner-stone becomes the head. This is the great seal of God that is to be placed upon the forehead (brought forth into the minds or consciousness of the Saints as given in Rev. 7:3; Rev. 9:4; 14:1) before the work of God can be consummated upon the earth.

Man has waited centuries upon centuries for God to place
that final seal upon his brow, without realizing that he must
himself bring it forth through believing and desiring. He must
place it upon his own brow, or become aware of it in his own
conscious mind. Man is the builder—he has been the one who
rejected the Chief corner-stone that is to become the head—
the crowning light of glory—the very seal of God.

As one receives this Light of Christ into his consciousness,
or permits it to come forth until he is a *true follower* of Jesus
Christ, through this power within his own soul, he will eventually be "Anointed with Light"—for it is when he fully comprehends this great power right within himself and brings it
forth he shall receive his "Anointing" and become powerful.
Then it is that he will receive that *name* of glory, and In that
NAME he shall do all that Christ did. Yea, more. "Take upon
you the NAME of Christ, for it is the only name under heaven
whereby man can be saved." Yea, he shall receive of the "Fullness of the Father" when he has fulfilled that *name,* and he
will become one with Him, and with Christ, and with all mankind, for he will realize that that same light which he has
become and which he has brought forth in his own flesh, is
also in every man. Then the record of heaven which is given
to abide within him will be revealed—yea, the very contents of
the Book of Life—and the last enemy will be conquered—
even death.

"*Therefore it is given to abide in you: the record of heaven;
the Comforter; the peaceable things of immortal glory; the
truth of all things; that which quickeneth all things, which
maketh alive all things; that which knoweth all things, and
hath all power, according to wisdom, mercy, truth, justice and
judgment.*" (Moses 6:61). Read the above. Not with your
eyes, but with your minds, with your souls, and embed it into
every little cell and fibre of your being. Could this power of
heaven, this power which can make alive all things, which
knows all things, and can quicken all things, and which *has all
power* be anything more than the very power of God lying
dormant in you? This very power is given to abide in you.
But of what good is it to you or God or anyone else unless you

bring it forth and use it? It was meant to be used. It is yours
to use. Use it.

How is this Light and power to be brought forth? That is
very simple. First one must believe that it is there because God
said so. Then if he will carefully check back over his life and
remember the emergencies when he was directed into safety,
those high moments of inspiration, those inner promptings, he
will realize that at times it has stepped forth to assist in his
life. Then if that man will only open his mind and soul
to understand and to appreciate this glorious, priceless gift and
will thank God for its help in the past—and open up his soul
so that it can penetrate into his sealed mind he will become
continually more and more aware of its power within his daily
life—until finally he shall speak no word unless it is given to
him of God. First one must begin to use it to judge between
truth and error—he must learn to trust it implicitly instead of
his worldly understanding. Then he gradually begins to feel
the very glory and power of its existence right within himself.
And as he praises it, and thanks God for it, it will become ever
more manifest in his daily activities until he can walk in the
majesty of true assurance, even as Christ did.

The conscious awareness of that "Light of Christ" within is
the contact with God. Keep that awareness always and you
will never walk alone. That awareness is the oneness with the
Almighty. It is the fulfilling of the command, "Be Still, and
know that I Am God." The conscious awareness is the silencing
of the little mortal, ego-self. It is the learning to *listen* as the
voice of the Spirit bears witness to every cell and atom of
one's being that God lives. And most important of all, the
conscious mind must hold that awareness, thus it gradually becomes one with the power of the soul as the soul glories in the
Spirit of God. That awareness is the "Listening", the rejoicing
of the soul as it goes beyond thought. It is this divine, knowing contact that brings "The peace that passeth understanding,"
or the peace that goes beyond the conscious, mortal concept of
thought. This growing awareness of the "Light of Christ" right
within gradually becomes a very part of one's existence and
the physical mind takes hold of it and it becomes *knowledge*

and knowledge is power. Thus the mortal intellect can become one with the Spirit.

"You were bought for a price. Glorify therefore the God in the body of you." (I Cor. 6:20).

"To seek God, if perhaps they might feel (after) him (and find him); though he be not far from any one of us; for in him we live and move and have our being." (Acts 17:27). The original Greek record does not have the word "after" included, nor the words "and find him." It reads quite definitely thus: "That they might *feel* him." Thus the awareness is the "Feeling" Him—the stillness of mind and alertness of soul that will eventually reveal the full power and glory of God.

Those who claim to be highly Spiritual yet have never become aware of that glorious "Light of Christ" right within themselves, and have judged everything according to their mortal intellects have missed the Light completely no matter how sincere they may be. They will never know God for they have never learned to "Be Still" that their souls might *listen* to that voice of all-knowing, all-power and all-truth—the very voice of God.

Become aware of that "Light of Christ within" and hold that awareness and the power of God will become manifest in your life—"Not in words only, but in power." And "He that believeth on me the works that I do shall he do also. And greater works than these shall he do . . ."

"And Christ truly said unto our Fathers, if ye have faith ye can do all things which are expedient unto me.

"And now I speak unto all the ends of the earth—that if the day cometh that the power and gifts of God shall be done away among you, it shall be because of unbelief.

"And woe be unto the children of men if this be the case, for there shall be none that doeth good among you, no, not one. For if there be one among you that doeth good, he shall work by the power and gifts of God.

"And woe unto them who shall do these things away and die, for *they shall die in their sins,* and they cannot be saved in the kingdom of God; and I speak it according to the words of Christ; and I lie not." (Moroni 10:22-26).

"And who shall say that Jesus Christ did not do many mighty miracles? And there were mighty miracles wrought by the hands of his apostles.

"And if there were miracles wrought then, why has God ceased to be a God of miracles and yet be an unchangeable Being? And behold I say unto you he changeth not; if so he would cease to be God; and he ceaseth not to be God, and is a God of miracles.

"And the reason why he ceaseth to do miracles among the children of men is because that they dwindle in unbelief, and depart from the right way, and know not the God in whom they should trust.

"Behold, I say unto you that whoso believeth in Christ, doubting nothing, whatsoever he shall ask the Father in the name of Christ, it shall be granted him; and this promise is to all, even to the ends of the earth." (Mormon 9:17-20—a prophet who lived 400 A. D.)

"And Christ hath said: If ye have faith in me ye shall have power to do whatsoever thing is expedient in me—

". . . And now, my beloved brethren, if this be the case that these things are true which I have spoken unto you, and God will show unto you, with power and great glory at the last day, that they are true, and if they are true has the day of miracles ceased?

"Or have angels ceased to appear unto the children of men? Or has he withheld the power of the Holy Ghost from them? Or will he so long as time shall last, or the earth shall stand, or there shall be one man upon the face thereof to be saved?

"Behold, I say unto you, Nay; for it is by faith that miracles are wrought; and it is by faith that angels appear and minister unto men; *wherefore, if these things have ceased woe be unto the children of men, for it is because of unbelief,* AND ALL IS VAIN." (Moroni 7:33; 35-37).

Yea, "The Light shineth in darkness, and the darkness comprehendeth it not; nevertheless, the day shall come when you shall comprehend even God, being quickened in him, and by him.

"Then shall ye know that ye have seen me, that I Am, and

that I am the true Light that is in you, and that you are in me, otherwise ye could not abound " (or exist). (D. & C. 88:49-50).

When one becomes fully aware of that "Light of Christ" right within himself then he truly realizes that as he holds that constant awareness he is abiding in the Light and power of Christ, and the Light and power of Christ is abiding in him. This "Light of Christ" is the superconscious mind that is right within man. It is a power that lies dormant except in very rare emergencies. It is a power that gives superhuman strength of body, mind or skill to anyone who has ever tapped its unlimited source. Geniuses use this power. But every man has it to use if he only will. It gives according to man's belief, according to his needs, or according to his desires.

When all darkness is completely cast from the mind, all fears and doubts one will have found the Light. This great Light cannot come forth into a mind distraught with darkness and confusion. Cast out the darkness of your own thinking and you will walk forever in the Light, for the little mortal, ego-self will have stepped aside to make way for the divine self of your inner soul—"The Light of Christ that is given to abide in every man that cometh into the world"—the gift of Christ to all men.

This work contains not even a beginning of the great truths to be given when man opens the door—"Behold, I stand at the door and knock, and if any man will hear my voice and open the door, behold, I will come in and feast with him, and he with me." (Rev. 3). He stands knocking on the door of every man's mortal consciousness trying to find admittance into his daily life and affairs.

"And He who knew and brought me up is the Most High in all His perfection. And He glorified me by His kindness, and raised my thoughts to the height of His truth. And from thence He gave me the way of His precepts and I opened the doors that were closed, and I brake in pieces the bars of iron; but my iron melted and dissolved before me; Nothing appeared closed to me; because I was *the door to everything*." (Odes of Solomon 17:7-10). Open that door yourself, your sealed conscious mind, and you will walk with God in eternal glory.

Yes, this work is a very humble work. It only reveals where the great door of Light is, and how it may be opened—the door to the kingdom of heaven—the power of the "Light of Christ" that God has given to abide in every man that cometh into the world, and the power of that Light when man will only begin to use it. But each man must open that door for himself, and of himself, he must step into the great Light that this work only indicates. From here on no man can take you, nor can you take another. You can only prove that the door is there waiting to be opened by entering yourself into the light. It is waiting for you! Open it and enter! You alone can open it. And you can only open it as you *follow the Light of Christ, or the Spirit of Truth that is given to abide in you,* not in someone outside yourself.

And now, a warning, gentle and true. When you begin to bring forth that Light you must never bear witness of its powers within you in such phrases as: "I could actually see Light pouring forth from me"; or "I touched the crippled man by the way and he was healed"; "I laid my hands on the blind and they received their sight." If you thus speak you will lose that power. It must bear witness of you, not you of it, except through the power of your works. It will bear witness by the power that will be manifest in deeds accomplished— "That others *seeing your good works* may glorify your Father which is in heaven." Yea, the works will bear their own witness, even works such as Christ did—and greater works, as you prove yourself worthy to carry such power. And thus the very works will bear witness of the Light within, even as Christ's did. "For my kingdom is not in word, but in power." Christ, after performing a miracle, never again mentioned it. Other men bore witness of it, and the very works bore witness of it. But that is why Christ wrote no record. He would have transgressed the law of the "Light of Christ" for He would have borne witness of Himself. But true to the trust, he proclaimed, "I of myself can do nothing. The Father within me, he doeth the works." Neither did His followers ever testify of the power that God had vested in them. The power itself bore witness. He who transgresses this law can never have the power, for it is the little ego-self that he is seeking to exalt, not God.

"And if your eyes be single to my glory, your whole bodies shall be filled with light, and there shall be no darkness in you; and that body which is filled with light comprehendeth all things.

"Therefore, *sanctify yourselves* that your minds become single to God, and the days will come that you shall see him, for he will unveil his face unto you, and it shall be in his own time, and in his own way, and according to his own will."

"And when you shall receive these things, I would exhort you that ye would ask God, the Eternal Father, in the name of Christ, if these things are not true; and if ye shall ask with a sincere heart, with real intent, having FAITH IN CHRIST, he will manifest the truth of it unto you by the power of the Holy Ghost.

"And by the power of the Holy Ghost ye may know the Truth of all things." (Moroni 10:4-5).

"For Behold, God hath said, a man being evil cannot do that which is good; for if he offereth a gift, or prayeth unto God, except he shall do it with real intent it profiteth him nothing.

"And likewise also is it counted evil unto a man, if he shall pray and not with real intent of heart; yea, and it profiteth him nothing, for God receiveth none such." (Moroni 7:6 and 9).

Only God can reveal truth through that Spirit of Truth or the Light of Christ that is given to abide in man, and by the gift and power of the Holy Ghost. And He only reveals it to those who sincerely ask to KNOW Truth. And only those who will humble themselves in earnest, sincere prayer, and who will rely upon that "Light of Christ" within themselves, will ever be able to KNOW Truth. Belief is not enough for any man. Each person has the right to KNOW for himself. Those who rely on another's opinion are cheating themselves, and failing to glorify the great gift of God within themselves, hence failing to glorify themselves.

It is only by sincere, humble prayer that anyone can judge the works of God, and use that "Light of Christ" within. Or by living the teachings. Any one who will begin to live the teachings of Jesus Christ literally, will know of their truth and their power. This work is for the sole purpose of placing plainly before the understandings of men that they may no longer be passed-over and ignored. There is no new revelation in this work, only the complete unveiling of the great revelations that have been given in the past.

Do not let it worry you because a woman was the scribe. God has said, "I will use the weak and foolish things to confound the wise." He has only kept His word. And since it was a woman who brought darkness into the world a woman will have to assist in rending that veil of darkness. And the veil of darkness is placed as a seal upon the conscious mind to shield or hide the Light of Christ within from those of unholy thoughts or earthly concepts, those wading in bigotry, conceit, lust, avarice, wraths or hurts. Overcome your sins and the veil shall be rent and the glory of His Light shall be forever yours. The time is NOW!

How are these weaknesses to be overcome? It is so easy and so simple. There are just two laws that will fulfill all other laws, keep all other commandments—fulfill all the prophets, glorify God and man and bring to complete perfection all things.

"Thou shalt love the Lord thy God with *all* thy heart, with *all* thy soul, with *all* thy mind, and with *all* thy strength. This is the first and great commandment. And the second is like unto it; thou shalt love thy neighbor as thyself. On these two commandments hang all the laws and the prophets."

Love God with *all* your heart. Concentrate on that great, divine organ of love until you feel love pouring through it in a rhythm of vibrating glory. As you do this it will reveal its secrets, its hidden powers and open wide to receive the great "gift of love which the Lord sheds forth in the hearts of the children of men"—"The love which he bestows upon those who are true followers of His Son, Jesus Christ." Then one learns that the heart is not just a physical organ in a mortal body. He will learn that it is the most divinely constructed microphone ever created, a microphone into which he can speak and God will hear instantly. He can whisper and it will be acknowledged. He can think and it will be understood. If one continues perfecting this glorious gift of love he will learn to speak every word through it, think every thought through it, and thus his words and his thoughts will become divine for he will be thinking as God thinks, loving as God loves—and speaking the language of the angels. He will no longer need to try and reach God through a desperate delay, relay, mislay and waylay system for God will hear instantly—and one will learn of His nearness and His power.

Next, one will learn to "Be Still, and know that I Am, God." One will not only learn to speak through that divine microphone, his heart, but he will learn to *listen*, for it is also a receiving set. And as one learns to *listen* to His voice or to His Word he will learn that His voice is not always expressed in spoken words. His voice may be a soft whisper of peace. It may be a vibration of enfolding confidence—a breath of glory— a feeling of assurance—an inspired thought—a complete revelation of breathtaking unfoldment, an opening of the understanding to grasp and KNOW Truth. And thus by learning to listen and to understand, it is possible to grow into the complete principle of revelation in which one's own mortal knowledge is laid aside to open the heart and soul to the divine wisdom of the Almighty. Ask for Wisdom and it shall be given to you—but remember, ask in faith, without wavering—that it shall be yours.

Then add to the love of your heart *all* the love of your soul, which includes every little cell and atom of your body and Spirit. This expanding love will train every cell and fiber of one's entire being to contain and hold Light—even the Light of Christ—or the Spirit of Almighty God.

As one continues to practice this divine melody of love he will learn that every organ of his body was created Spiritually first and has a Spiritual function to perform. As these organs are awakened to their true Spiritual functions the body will not only be perfected, but actually lifted into a higher spiritual vibration of existence. It will evolve from the mortal concept into the higher or spiritual realm.*

Then as one adds to the love of the heart and the love of the soul *all* the love of the mind he will begin to feel the true glory of this great, unspeakable law. At first it is possible that one may have headaches in the very top of the brain as he practices this love, for it is the highest cells that are prepared to function in the higher spiritual level of devotion, praise, worship and love. These headaches are like hikers cramps when climbing a high mountain after weeks of inactivity. They will soon pass and need not cause any worry. Loving and adoring and giving thanks is the surest way to eliminate them forever.

Then in order to worship or love God with *all* the mind it will be necessary to bring this love into the terrestrial realm of everyday living. And thus everything, every person and every condition will be surrounded and enfolded in this glorifying love of God and one automatically fulfills the Second Great Commandment. It also fulfills the admonition, "And he who is thankful in all things shall be made glorious, and the things of this earth shall be added unto him, an hundred-fold; yea, more." He has reached the place where all things shall be added unto him.

There is still another step to take in order to love God with *all* the mind. It is then necessary to send this love down into the subconscious realm, those dark caverns where nightmares are born, where all hurts lie hidden in their mouldering darkness of corroding evil, where all hates, all fears, all worries and confusion abide. As these realms are opened wide to this glorifying love of God all hurts are healed, forgiven, blotted out; all darkness is banished, and thus one fulfills the admonition "Cast darkness from among you"; all evil is opened to the purifying, cleansing, forgiving rays of the Spirit of God. And one becomes renewed, for the cleansing is glorious and perfect. It is like opening the dank, musty, overcrowded

(*Isa. 16:11; Genesis 43:30; Jer. 4:18-10; Jer. 31:20; Lam. i:20; Lam. 2:11; Phil. 2:1; I. John 3:117; D. & C. Sec. 10:9; sec. 121:3 and verses 45-46. New Testament Apocrypha—Odes of Solomon:26:4; Testament of Simeon 2:10; Testament of Gad 1:34-36.)

cellars wide to the purifying rays of the noonday sun. This is power and joy and glory such as few human beings have experienced for they have not taken this commandment literally. Yet this glory is waiting for any who desire it, that they might be filled with Light.

To love God with *all* one's strength is the most amazing part of this great and glorious commandment. When one becomes angry he flies into a rage with all his strength. The self leaps up like a dragon of destruction and a thousand serpents, spitting fire, strike out as flaming vibrations in every direction to injure and destroy. The *self* is the dragon that each individual must slay before he can be knighted with honor. It is the dragon of the personal little ego-self that guards the cavern containing the priceless jewels locked within. It is truly this dragon of self that is our greatest enemy, and must be slain. And every shooting, hissing vibration of wrath and anger and discord is a snaky lock primed with poison, that must be put down.

When we get angry we put all the strength and power we possess behind our wrath, we become dynamos of energy as we uncoil and lash out in hate—but when we send out love we sit weakly back and expect it to go out on its own.

To love God with *all* our strength we must begin to use the same amount of "umph" and energy to send it out as we do when we hate. Love sent out with all the dynamic energy put behind it brings the most amazing results—those results may not be visible the first day, nor the second—but they will be *felt*. As the same intensity of vibration is placed behind love as one puts behind hate, fear or worries the power of that first and great commandment will begin to reveal the unspeakable magnitude of its divine grandeur. It is then that the world will step aside and let one pass. Yea, it will do more. It will strew the path with roses and palm branches, and crown one's head with honor.

Whenever a discordant, angry thought rears its ugly head it is within the power of every individual to stay it with love. Love quells the vibrations of wrath instantly—and love alone can slay the dragon that lies within each one of us, guarding the entrance to the treasurehouse of Truth—the great jewels

of power, wisdom, understanding, beauty, light and perfection
—the very heaven within, which, when found, will fulfill all
things.

It is when love is sent forth with all the powerful vibrations
of strength that the great and marvelous promises will be fulfilled; "And all things will be subject unto him, both in heaven and on earth, the life and the light, the Spirit and the
power, sent forth by the Father, through Jesus Christ, His Son."
When love is sent forth with all the dynamic strength possible
to command one will be filled with the divine Spirit of the
Almighty—and that Spirit will be subject unto him, for he
will have the power to control it right within his own being.
It is then that he will be able to do the works that Christ did—
even greater works. The door to the storehouse of truth has
been so thoroughly guarded, this kingdom of heaven within,
because none could be entrusted with the ineffable power it
contains without learning the perfect control of his own thoughts
and vibrations first. The great, vibrating love is the gate that is
straight—and the Light of Christ is the path so few have found.

It is most certainly true that the First and Great Commandment fulfills all the laws and all the prophets. If this law
is practiced faithfully until it becomes a vibrating glory in
every cell and fibre one will truly be filled with Light and
comprehend all things.

The great meaning and power of the first and great commandment has never been understood. Behind these commandments, the Sermon on the Mount and these hidden, inner teachings of Jesus Christ is contained all the power of His promises.
It is these unlived, untried teachings and principles that hold
the keys of the way of life. Christ revealed definitely the almost incomprehensible power of His laws when He promised
the power to do all that He did to those who believed. This
was given so that we would understand that we were not to
live on His works, but that *WE SHOULD STEP FORTH AND
DO ALL THAT HE DID—then building upon what He had
accomplished we should go on and do even greater works.*

To sit back and glory in Christ's achievements, to continue
to relive them in sermons only, without having the faith to ful-

fill His words and do His works is a vain and useless thing. His was the example—ours the power to follow and fulfill. Until we take upon ourselves the responsibility of fulfilling His words and doing His works a world will remain in darkness. "His kingdom is not in words, but in power."

That same truth must be applied at all times and in all ages. If we live on the laurels our ancestors won, without adding to the light they held, we are failures and unworthy of the heritage they bequeathed to us. And we are unworthy of the teachings and example of Christ unless we fulfill the very promises He spoke and do the works that He did and then move on to even higher attainments.

These higher attainments can only be reached as one fulfills the laws of righteousness. Thus to love God with all one's heart, soul, mind and strength not only cleanses from *all* sin, but from the very power to sin. Right within itself is contained the keys of utter glory.

To send forth this great and unspeakable love with energy does not mean a tense straining or to over-exert one's nervous system. It means only to let love vibrate within, to keep it vibrating. This is done by being consciously aware of it. Whenever one feels that throbbing vibration of joyous ecstasy within he may begin to comprehend that it is the Light of Christ coming forth into activity. It is this vibration that is most necessary. And in order to get that vibration going and to keep it always one must keep his thoughts and feelings united. This unity is the high point of contact of thought and emotion, or shall we say Spirit, where all real power is generated? This point of contact is that magic switch I had hoped the scientists would find and perfect for us. And now I know that it has alway been ours. This is the point of the "At-one-meant." It is not gained by straining. It is gained by training. Within this point of high vibration and contact lies all the creative power embodied in the souls of men. Keep this point charged with the vibration of eternal love and the universe will lay its powers and its treasures at your feet—and you will have in your hands the very keys of glory, and attain unto the highest mastery. This is the power Christ spoke of, the power He promised to all who would only believe on His words.

Then we make an amazing discovery as we begin to feel the glory and power of this great commandment fulfilled in our lives. We learn that it was not written so much for the glory of God as it was for the glorifying of man. Yet, all commandments were given by God for the progress and development of man. It is he who chooses how fast or how far he will travel. Each man is his own gauge.

As this commandment is practiced faithfully it proves to be the celestial symphony of the spheres, the melody of the universe—and thus man can get into stride with the vibrations of eternity and all life becomes a harmony of pure perfection. Troubles dissolve, darkness is forever banished and light is glorified.

This melody must be practiced not only this day—but tomorrow—and whenever and wherever there is time and opportunity. And very soon it will become a very part of living. Man himself is the musician. He must perfect the glorious, divine, celestial melody that will glorify his soul and his life. He is also the instrument on which the musician plays. In his own being is recorded forever the new song that none can learn except His chosen—or those who have truly chosen Him.

Love is the melody—love unfeigned—love so gentle, so filled with understanding, so pure, so forgiving, so compassionate and so Christ-like it will help to heal a world. "And they sung as it were a new song before the throne, and before the four beasts, and the elders: and no man could learn that song—but those who had the seal of God placed on their foreheads." Only those could vibrate with that glorious song of divine love who had placed that "Light of Christ" or the full knowledge of God within their conscious minds, the seal of God. This love is the very "Light of Christ" as it is brought into manifestation in the lives of men. This is the new song, the divine melody that so few will be able to sing.

This is the only possible way one can become a "True follower of His Son, Jesus Christ." The outer ordinances only cleanse the outside of the cup. The inside of it must be cleansed by a devotion that is perfect, an obedience that leads one into the power to fulfill all things, and the love of God made perfect. Only in this way can one become a "True follower," and receive the gift of perfect, divine, Christ-like love that He sheds forth in the hearts of the children of men.

Hands filled with this divine love and vibrating with the celestial "Christ Light" can bless all that they touch, and the blessing will be acknowledged for they will have overcome darkness and in its place carry divine light, melody of eternal glory. "Such a one is possessor of all things: for all things are subject unto him, both in heaven and on the earth, the life and the light, the Spirit and the power, sent forth by the will of the Father, through Jesus Christ His Son."

This love and "Light of Christ" alone has the power to save the world, redeem man, glorify God and bring light and healing to the earth for it is the very power of God made manifest in the lives of men. And man is permitted to do His works through that "Light of Christ." "Show me thy faith without thy works, and l will show you my faith by my work."

And so the song in the soul is a new song. It is a song of everlasting glory, of divine, perfect love, of light and power and peace—it is truly a new song, and only those can sing it who will eliminate all darkness from them, who will purify themselves and be cleansed from all sin, for the song is pure, celestial, divine love made perfect right within the very being of man. It sings from every cell and fibre of his being—love, adoration, praise, and exaltation.

"After these things I saw four angels standing on the four corners of the earth, holding the four winds of the earth, that the wind shall not blow on the earth, nor on the sea, nor any tree.

"And I saw another angel ascending from the east, having the seal of the living God, and he cried with a loud voice to the four angels, to whom was given to hurt the earth and the sea,

"Saying, Hurt not the earth, neither the sea, nor any trees, till we have sealed the servants of our God in their foreheads.

"And I heard the number of them which were sealed: and

there were sealed an hundred and forty and four thousand of all the tribes of the children of Israel." (Rev. 7:1-4). This amounts to only twelve thousand of each of the twelve tribes —so few out of so many millions.

In chapter nine of Revelations is given a description of the great destructions which are to come upon the earth through airplanes and army tanks, even that "a third part of men will be killed, by the fire, and by the smoke and by the brimstone." But in verse four is given these words: "And it was commanded them that they should not hurt the grass of the earth, neither any green tree; but only those men which have not the seal of God in their foreheads."

"And I looked and lo, a Lamb stood on Mount Zion, and with him an hundred and forty and four thousand, having his Father's name written in their foreheads.

"And I heard a voice from heaven, as the voice of many waters, and as the voice of harpers harping with their harps;

"And they sung as it were a new song before the throne, and before the four beasts, and the elders, and no man could learn the song but the one hundred and forty and four thousand, which were redeemed from the earth.

"These are they which were not defiled with women; for they are virgins. These are they which follow the Lamb (or Light of Christ within) whithersoever *he may lead* (Original Greek). These were redeemed from, among men, being the first fruits unto God and to the Lamb.

"And in their mouth was found no guile; for they were without fault before the throne of God." (Rev. 14:1-5).

These are those who will bring forth the "Light of Christ" from within until their conscious minds are filled with the Light and Glory of God. These are they who will fulfill their part in the New and Everlasting Covenant, and take upon them the Name of Jesus Christ. These are they who have fulfilled or will fulfill the glorious invitation, "Draw near unto me and I will draw near unto you," "Abide in me and I will abide in you." And the New song will be the vibrations of glorifying love that will issue from every cell and fibre of their beings in a rhythm of eternal perfection. And only those who have filled their souls, their hearts and their minds with this glorious love and vibrate with its heavenly adoration of inner praise and rejoicing will be able to send forth this eternal symphony of vibrating light, the new song. The perfect, divine, Christ-like love and praise is the song. "And Charity is the pure love of Christ, and it endureth forever; and whoso is found possessed of it at the last day, it shall be well with him. Wherefore, my beloved brethren, pray unto the Father with all the energy of heart, that ye may be filled with this love, which he hath bestowed upon all who are true followers of his Son, Jesus Christ; that ye may become the sons of God; that when he shall appear we shall be like him, for we shall see him as he is; that we may have this hope; that we may be purified even as he is pure. Amen." (Moroni 7:47-49).

This inward song of gratitude, this divine song of ecstasy singing in the soul is the power of the "Light of Christ" in manifest action as it cleanses one of darkness and fills his entire being with the joy of Light. He who can hold to this divine song of ecstasy for just a few weeks without losing it for a moment will be purified and cleansed from all sin. This glorifying song is the cleansing flame of the Spirit of the Almighty and if one can hold himself, consciously, within that flame he shall be prepared speedily to truly *know* God, for he shall be filled with light and comprehend all things. This is the New Song, this inner song of Spiritual Ecstasy, this song that will glorify God and man, this divine symphony of eternal Love!

Chapter XXIV.

THE NEW AND EVERLASTING COVENANT

A COVENANT is a pledge or a compact between two or more individuals or parties. A covenant has always been considered as an agreement or pledge of sacred power, most binding—a seal of utmost integrity.

God has made many covenants with man, one being the pledge of the rainbow and the promise that the inhabitants of the earth should never again be destroyed by water. Every promise of God is a covenant or pledge that will be fulfilled as we do our part, or keep our side of the compact, for a covenant is binding, and His words cannot fail. If His promises are not fulfilled it is because we have failed to fulfill our part of the stipulations, not because He has forgotten or failed. God never forgets, and He never fails to fulfill His promises.

Of all the covenants God has made there is a very special one, it is known as the "New and Everlasting Covenant." This covenant is above and beyond all other covenants that God has made to man. And Jesus is the mediator of this New and Everlasting Covenant. (Heb. 12:24 and D. & C, 76-69). The above mentioned scripture has been greatly misunderstood. It has been believed that Jesus Christ stands before the throne of God as a mediator, or "go-between", discussing this man's worthiness to recognition or mercy, that man's desires, another's prayers, as he pleads with God to have compassion. It is true that Jesus is the mediator, for in His hands is given the "Light of Christ that is given to abide in every man that cometh into the world." Through the "Light of Christ" within us, he is the mediator, pleading with each man to follow that true Light of unfailing direction, of hope that leads to faith and faith that leads to knowledge and knowledge that leads to power. He is not pleading with God for man—but he is plead-

303

ing with man, for the glory of God. "Behold, I stand at the door and knock, and if any man hear my voice and will open the door, behold, I will come in and feast with him, and he with me."

This New and Everlasting Covenant is the covenant of God with every man that cometh into the world that if he will overcome the self and learn to follow that Light of Christ, or the Spirit, it will lead him to the Christ, and the Christ will then reveal the Father. "And the Father and I are one. I am in the Father and the Father in me; and inasmuch as ye have received me, ye are in me and I in you. Wherefore, I am in your midst, and I am the good shepherd, and the stone of Israel, He that buildeth upon this rock shall never fall." (D. & C. 50:43-44).

"Jesus answered them, I told you, and ye believed not; the works that I do in my Father's name, they bear witness of me.

"But ye believe not, because ye are not of my sheep, and I said unto you,

"My sheep hear my voice, and I know them, and they follow me.

"And I give unto them eternal life; and they shall never perish, neither shall any man pluck them out of my hand.

"My Father, which gave them me, is greater than all: and no man is able to pluck them out of my Father's hand.

"And the Father and I are one." (John 10:25-30).

After one has made the final contact with God, through Jesus Christ, the Mediator, no man or power can ever again take him away from Christ. That one who has made that divine contact will be sealed unto God, or dwelling in His Spirit and abode forever, receiving continual light and knowledge and instruction until he grows into complete perfection, for this is the promise, or the great and everlasting covenant —that He will reveal the Father, and the veil shall be opened and he shall KNOW God.

It is the covenant that every man who seeks God shall find Him. It is the covenant of God in the promise, "Seek me early and ye shall find me," or "Seek me diligently and ye shall find me." "Every one who seeks finds, and he who asks re-

ceives; and he who knocks shall have it opened unto him," or
have the veil parted, the blinding veil of his own mortal understanding. Yea, "Draw near unto me and I will draw near
unto you," "Abide in me and I will abide in you," "For ye
are the temples of the living God." And the covenant stands
forever and it is new for each man who learns to silence that
clamoring, mortal, ego-self and *listens* with his inner ears to
that guiding voice of Light which will lead him to the full
knowledge of God. Thus they learn to hear His voice by listening to that Light of Christ right within their own souls as it
directs them into all righteousness, assisting them to fulfill all
the laws of the kingdom, and perfecting the great, divine gift
of love. And those to whom this voice comes, those who have
learned to listen and to obey the unfailing word of God begin
to fulfill their highest destiny: "And they are called Gods unto
whom the word of God came."

Thus the search for God is not a search into infinitude—
nor a search into far distant spheres, nor a search into foreign
lands. Neither is God found by going from place to place, city
to city, nor up one street and down another, in and out through
buildings, nor by rushing from one church to another. If one
undertakes to find God in this manner he will only get lost
himself, as so many have. The search for God must be right
within man. It is in the depths of his own soul he must seek
for the "Light of Christ" or the "True Way" that will lead to
God, and that *Way* is the continual unfolding or increasing of
Light within, which is the advancing from grace to grace,
which is the gift of God to all men. It is this advancing from
grace to grace, from knowledge to knowledge, light to greater
light that will bring the outer being, the mortal self into complete subjection to the enfolding glory of the Light of the
Spirit of Christ. Such is the redemption of man as he is redeemed from his low, mortal concepts of existence. It is when
one has truly crucified the little, proud, bragging, discordant,
ego-self with its inherent darkness, its fears and its confusion
by holding himself in the purifying rays of the glorious vibrations of Living Light that all things shall be added unto him,
even the power to *comprehend* God. This is heaven. And any

one who can attain unto this condition of perfect, unruffeled peace, glorifying, Christ-like love is abiding in heaven.

"And again, verily I say unto you that it is your privilege and a promise I give unto you that have been ordained unto this ministry, that inasmuch as you strip yourselves from jealousies and fears, and humble yourselves before me, for ye are not sufficiently humble, the veil shall be rent and you shall see me and *know* that I am—*not with the carnal neither natural mind, but with the Spiritual* (mind).

"For no man has seen God at any time in the flesh, *except quickened by the Spirit of God.*

"Neither can any natural man abide the presence of God, neither after the carnal mind."

"Ye are not able to abide the presence of God now, neither the ministering of angels, wherefore, *continue in patience until perfected.*"

The above states most clearly that it is impossible to behold God with the natural or carnal MIND, it does not say *eyes.* Then it states that it is only with the Spiritual (*mind*) that one is able to behold God. Thus the beholding of God is a thing of *comprehension*—"THEY SHALL COMPREHEND EVEN GOD." This is verified in the following:

"The earth rolls upon her wings, and the sun giveth his light by day, and the moon giveth her light by night, and the stars also give their light, as they roll upon their wings in their glory, in the midst of the power of God.

"Unto what shall I liken these kingdoms, that ye may understand?

"Behold, all these are kingdoms, and any man who hath seen any of the least of these *hath* SEEN *God moving in His majesty and power.*

"*I say unto you, he hath seen him; nevertheless,* he who came unto his own was not *comprehended.*

"The light shineth in darkness, and the darkness comprehendeth it not; nevertheless, the day shall come when *you shall comprehend* even God, being quickened in him, and by him.

"Then shall ye know that ye have seen me, that I am, and

that I am the True Light that is in you, and that you are in me, otherwise you could not abound."

It is therefore most definitely true that "No man has seen God at any time in the flesh except quickened by the Spirit of God."

And "Jesus said, At that day ye shall *know* that I am in my Father, and ye in me, and I in you—if a man love me, He will keep my words; and my Father will love Him, and we will come unto him, and make our abode with him."

This is the glory and power of the New and Everlasting Covenant, new because it is new to every individual who fulfills it. Everlasting because it has always been and will always be. It contains a new revelation of utter glory to any individual who partakes of its unspeakable power and who receives of its light—it is truly an everlasting covenant in that it existed before time began for God made it before time was, and it shall endure forever and forever for those who will accept of it and live by it, following the Light of Christ until it leads them to the Father that He might be revealed, and His glory comprehended, and His power made known to those who purify themselves and cleanse themselves from all sin. This is the covenant of Almighty God to all men.

"For He dwelt in him." This is the testimony and the covenant. (See John 14:10-11 also verses 20-23; II. Cor. 6:16; D. & C. 93:17). It contains that divine contact with God that cannot be broken—the promise of eternal progress, of unlimited power and eternal life.

"Wherefore, I will that all men shall repent, for *all* are *under sin*, except those which I have reserved unto myself, holy men that ye know not of.

"Wherefore, I say unto you that I have sent unto you mine everlasting covenant, even that which was from the beginning." (D. & C. 49:8-9).

And you **may be sure that those** righteous men that were reserved unto himself were those who overcame sin through the great and everlasting covenant of that divine, personal contact with Almighty God.

"These are they who are just men made perfect through

Jesus the mediator of the New covenant, who wrought out this perfect atonement." (At-one-meant). Or gave the light which is possible to make man again one with His Maker.

As one begins to comprehend and *feel* the glorious Light of Jesus Christ, which is given by God to abide in every man that cometh into the world, he will begin to develop that light by learning to listen to its voice, and by following its instructions, by praising and giving thanks and glory continually.

Then he will understand the words of Paul: "My little children, of whom I travail in birth until Christ is formed in you." (Gal. 4:19).

He will know with complete knowledge the full import of the words: "I am crucified with Christ; nevertheless I live; yet *not I but Christ liveth in me;* and the life which I now live in the flesh I live by faith of the Son of God, who loved me and gave himself for me." (Gal. 2:20).

"But before faith came, we were kept under the law, shut up unto the faith which should afterwards be revealed.

"Wherefore the law was our schoolmaster to bring us unto Christ, that we might be justified by faith.

"But after the faith is come, we are no longer under the schoolmaster." (Gal. 3:23-25).

"For Christ is the end of the law for righteousness to everyone that believeth." (Rom. 10:4).

Perhaps the above can best be explained by quoting from D. & C. Sec. 84:19-27 and 33: "And this greater priesthood administereth the Gospel and holdeth the mysteries of the kingdom, even the key of the knowledge of God.

20. "Therefore, in the ordinances thereof, the power of godliness is manifest." (If this power is not manifest then it is only manifesting in word and without the power—"And all is vain").

21. "And without the ordinance thereof, and the authority of the priesthood, the power of godliness is not manifest unto men in the flesh.

22. "For without this no man can see the face of God, even the Father, and live." (And unless he fulfills this he has carried this calling in vain—for the purpose of it is to see the

face of God—to know Him, and Jesus Christ whom He has sent—and to have the power to speak in His *Name* and do the works that He did).

23. "Now this Moses plainly taught to the children of Israel in the wilderness, and *sought diligently to sanctify his people that they might behold the face of God.*

24. *"But they hardened their hearts and could not endure His presence; therefore the Lord in his wrath, for his anger was kindled against them* (because they would not purify themselves so that they could behold His face while in this life), swore that they should not enter into his rest while in the wilderness, *which rest is the fullness of his glory."* (The very meaning and purpose of this higher priesthood is to bless and prepare the people to see and *know* God individually and to receive of the fullness of his glory while in the flesh).

25. "Therefore, he took Moses out of their midst, and the Holy Priesthood also;

26. "And the lesser priesthood continued, which priesthood holdeth the key of the ministering of angels and *the preparatory gospel.* (See D. & C. 13).

27. "Which gospel is the gospel of repentance and of baptism, and the remission of sins, and the law of carnal commandments, which the Lord in his wrath caused to continue with the house of Aaron among the children of Israel until John." (Only the first principles of the Gospel remain on the earth, or are active when his people are under condemnation, or "under the wrath of God" because they have refused to live by the higher laws, or take upon them the New and everlasting covenant).

33. "For whoso is faithful unto the obtaining these two priesthoods of which I have spoken, and *the magnifying their calling, are sanctified by the Spirit unto the renewing of their bodies."* And this does not mean just in the resurrection because all the dead, small and great, righteous and wicked shall be resurrected and have their bodies brought forth from their graves.

In verse twenty-six of the foregoing it mentions this preparatory gospel which is to prepare the people to actually *see* and *know* God and to receive of the fullness of His glory.

The above is verified in verses eighteen and nineteen of Section one hundred and seven of the D. & C. as follows:

"The power and authority of the higher or Melchizedek Priesthood is to hold the keys of *all the spiritual blessings* of the church—

"To have the privilege of receiving the mysteries of the kingdom of heaven, to have the heavens opened unto them to commune with the general assembly and church of the First-born, *and to enjoy the communion and presence of God the Father and Jesus Christ the mediator of the New Covenant.*" In other words, the only purpose of the Higher priesthood is to prepare the people to receive the Second Comforter, to know God and to walk in His presence, and this can only be accomplished by being obedient to the direction or voice of Christ as it guides and directs through that divine light within.

A people can pray forever for the power of the Melchizedek priesthood to be upon them, but unless they fulfill the laws of that priesthood, or keep their part of the covenant, sanctifying their souls, and bring forth that Light of Christ from within themselves; relying wholly upon God and upon His promises, "their prayers are vain." Yea, "All is vain." "And there are none that doeth good upon the earth, no not one; for if there be one that doeth good upon the earth he shall work by the power and gifts of God."

It is only by that divine contact within that one can possibly magnify his calling and know God.

"And at that day ye shall know that I am in my Father, and ye in me, and I in you.

"If a man love me he will keep my words; and my Father will love him, and we will come unto him, and make our abode with him." (John 14:20-23).

"Abide in me, and I in you. As the branch cannot bear fruit of itself, except it abide in the vine; no more can ye, except ye abide in me.

"I am the vine, ye are the branches; he that abideth in me,

and I in him, the same bringeth forth much fruit; for without me ye can do nothing." (John 15:5-6).

"Oh righteous Father, the world hath not known thee; but I have known thee, and these have known that thou hast sent me.

"And I have declared unto them thy name, and will declare it; that the love wherewith thou hast loved me may be in them, and I in them." (John 17:25-26).

"And to know the love of Christ, which passeth knowledge, that *ye might be filled with the fullness of God.*

"Now unto him that is able to do exceeding abundantly above all that we ask or think, according to the power that worketh in us." (Eph. 3:19-20).

" . . . Seeing that ye have put off the old man (self) with his deeds.

"And have put on the new man (Christ) which is renewed in knowledge after the image of him that created him;

"Where there is neither Greek nor Jew, circumcision nor uncircumcision, Barbarian, Scythian, bond or free; *But Christ is all and in all."* (Col. 3:9-11).

"But *put ye on the Lord Jesus Christ* and make not provision for the flesh, to fulfill the lusts thereof." (Rom. 13:14).

Thus we understand that the full meaning of the gospel of Jesus Christ, or the gospel of Putting on Christ, is that we might fulfill all its laws, purifying our minds and hearts, sanctifying our souls and abiding in the Light of Christ, which is God's own special gift to every child of earth. When we have, by love and understanding and desire, brought forth this Light of Christ, or the Word and made it flesh, filling every cell and fibre of our beings with this Light, we will receive our *"Anointing of Light."* Then it is that we take upon us that most Holy Name of Jesus Christ and fulfill our part of the New and Everlasting Covenant—for our part of that covenant is that we take upon us that *name.* We must be baptized in that "NAME" as well as in water. We must do all that we do in the name of Christ, and rejoice in the Son forever more.

"Christ is the end of the law for righteousness to everyone that believeth." (Rom. 10:4).

This "Light of Christ," when it has been brought forth completes the fulfillment and is truly the end of the law, and from there on one is no longer under the law, but is abundantly, eternally free—one with God.

Our part of the New and Everlasting Covenant is to take upon us that Name. The Father's part of the covenant is the promise that in that NAME we shall ask anything and have it granted—and in that Name it is possible to fulfill all the laws of righteousness. And the promise of that name is given: "I shall be powerful when I am anointed with light." Or, "I shall be powerful when I have brought forth the Light of Christ from within."

And then we hear the words of the Lord telling why mankind has failed to contact Him—to receive the great promises of power, such as Christ had. "For they have strayed from mine ordinances, and *have broken mine everlasting covenant.*

"They seeketh not the Lord to establish his righteousness, but every man walketh in his own way, and after the image of his own God, whose image is in the likeness of (the things) of the world, and whose substance is that of an idol, which waxeth old and shall perish . . ." (D. & C. 1:16).

"And the weak things of the world shall come forth and break down the mighty and strong ones, that man should not counsel his fellow man, neither trust in the arm of flesh—

"But every man might speak in the name of God the Lord, even the Savior of the world;

"That faith might also be increased in the earth;

"That mine everlasting covenant might be established;

"That the fullness of mine gospel might be proclaimed by the weak and the simple unto the ends of the world, and before kings and rulers." (D. & C. 1:19-23). Here is given the positive information that the time is to come when no man will counsel any other man, for every man shall have that direct contact with God the Father, and will no longer put their trust in the arm of flesh, for the new and everlasting covenant will be established—the covenant of contact that each man will be able to speak the words of God as directed by His voice, even as Christ was.

"For verily I say unto you that I am Alpha and Omega, the beginning and the end, the light and the life of the world, a light that shineth in darkness and the darkness comprehendeth it not.

"I came unto mine own, and mine own received me not; *But unto as many as received me gave I power to do many miracles*" (and unless one can do these miracles they have not yet received Him), "and to become the sons of God; and even unto them that believeth on my name gave I power to obtain eternal life.

"And even so I have sent mine everlasting covenant unto the world, to be a light to the world, and to be a standard for my people, (the light they should follow), *and for the Gentiles to seek to it,* and to be a messenger before my face to prepare the way before me.

"Wherefore, come ye unto it, and with Him that cometh I will reason as with men in days of old, and I will show unto you my strong reasoning." (D. & C. 45:7-10).

This "Light of Christ" that is contained right within man is the power of contact, or the power of the priesthood which Abraham received. ". . . After ye have received my new and everlasting covenant, saith the Lord God; and he that abideth not this law can in nowise enter into my glory, but shall be damned, saith the Lord.

"I am the Lord thy God, and will give unto thee the law of my Holy Priesthood, as was ordained by me and by my Father before the world was.

Now follows just what that covenant or priesthood was: "Abraham *received all things, whatsoever he received, by revelations and commandment, by my Word,* (And that Word is the Spirit of Jesus Christ or Light of Christ), saith the Lord, and he hath entered into his exaltation and sitteth upon his throne."

"Yea, I am the Lord thy God and I give unto you this commandment—that no man shall come unto the Father but by me or by my Word, which is my law, saith the Lord." (D. & C. 132:12).

"And for this cause that men might be made partakers of

the glories which were to be revealed, the Lord sent forth the fullness of his gospel, his everlasting covenant, reasoning in plainness and simplicity—(the instruction from the Light of Christ within).

"To prepare the weak for those things which are coming on the earth, and for the Lord's errand in the day when the weak shall confound the wise, and the little one become a strong nation, and two shall put their tens of thousands to flight." (This indicates the exact time when the *power* shall be given to the weak—the power to confound the wise among men).

"And by the weak things of the earth the Lord shall thrash the nations by the *power of His Spirit.* (And it shall truly be by the very *power* of His Spirit, and not by words only).

"And for this cause these commandments are given: they were commanded to be kept from the world, in the day they were given but NOW are to go forth unto all flesh—

"And this according to the mind and will of the Lord, who ruleth over all flesh.

"And unto him that repenteth and *sanctifieth himself* before the Lord shall be given eternal life.

"And unto them that *harkeneth not to the voice of the Lord* shall be fulfilled that which was written by the Prophet Moses, they shall be cut off from among the people." (D. & C. 133: 57-63).

Yea, "As many as are led by the Spirit of God they are the sons of God." (Rom. 8:14). And unless they are truly led by that divine Spirit in all things they are not His sons regardless of what their claims.

"For you shall live by every word that proceedeth forth from the mouth of God.

"For the word of the Lord is truth, and whatsoever is truth is light, and whatsoever is light is Spirit, even the Spirit of Jesus Christ.

"And the Spirit giveth light to every man that cometh into the world; and the Spirit enlighteneth every man through the world, that *hearkeneth to the voice of the Spirit.* (Which is His word).

"And every one that hearkeneth to the voice of the Spirit cometh unto God, even the Father.

"And the Father teacheth him of the covenant which he has renewed and confirmed upon you . . ."

"And the whole world lieth in sin, and groaneth under darkness and under the bondage of sin.

"And by this you may know they are under the bondage of sin, because they come not unto me.

"For whoso cometh not unto me is under the bondage of sin.

"And whoso receiveth not my voice is not acquainted with my voice, and is not of me." (Every individual who is of God is to learn to hear and be familiar with His divine voice from within, and to keep in contact with it, otherwise he is under sin. D. & C. 84:44-52).

Yes, "My sheep hear my voice, and they know me."

This "Light of Christ" or "Spirit of Christ" that is given to abide within man, can be brought forth to its full perfection by the understanding, obedience and righteous desire of each individual. And with its perfection one receives the fullness of the promise of the *name* of Jesus Christ, and truly takes upon himself that *name*. And then it is that he can ask anything in the *name* of Jesus Christ and have it fulfilled. This *name* contains the everlasting covenant of the Father. It is His covenant that is everlasting, for it is with us forever and forever. It is new because to each individual who fulfills it, it is a new and glorious experience of untold power. As we believe in that *name* and fulfill it we shall be able to do all that Jesus did, and have all that the Father has. The *name* of "Jesus Christ" contains the promise of the Covenant to every child of earth. The *name* "Jehovah" contains the fulfillment of the promise when the covenant is completed.

Pray with all the energy of heart to comprehend what is herein written for it is the Word of God—"And the Word of the Lord is Truth, and whatsoever is truth is Light; and whatsoever is Light is Spirit—even the Spirit of Jesus Christ . . ." And it is the Christ who will reveal the Father—"That you may know the Truth—and the Truth will make you free. And he who is free shall be free indeed."

And again, lest you forget, "Jesus Christ" is the promise. "Jehovah" is the fulfillment of the promise. These words contain unspeakable glory for him who will open his ears to hear and his heart to understand. This is God's covenant, or seal. It is His eternal promise to every man who will fulfill the requirements. It was given as a sacred promise or covenant before time began. It is a covenant of God endless, eternal, Almighty—one with God.

"Ask and ye shall receive. Seek and ye shall find. Knock and it shall be opened unto you."

So be it, for God has spoken, and in the *name* of Jesus Christ it shall be fulfilled unto you according to your faith and understanding—Amen.

Chapter XXV.

"LABOR NOT FOR THAT MEAT THAT PERISHES"

THE TEACHINGS of Jesus Christ contain a true science of life. They are perfect in every detail and mark plainly the pathway of eternal power. His most impractical sounding teachings turn into a revelation of glory when applied under the direction of that living "Light of Christ within."

Few of true integrity and high devotion have fully caught the divine vision of the words, "Labour not for the meat that perisheth." Therefore few have accepted or attempted to follow Him in all things, or become "true followers of His Son, Jesus Christ." But only by living His teachings to the very "letter" can their great dynamic power be known and used.

Most of our modern world ignores completely His instructions to labor not for the food that perishes. His words are scoffed at by the critics, considered impractical by the learned and the wise, explained away by the religious leaders when challenged by them, and used as an excuse for shiftless laziness by those too indolent to work. "The Lord will provide," defends the slothful man, who folding his hands, evades physical responsibility of any kind.

The great vision of a higher way of life has yet to be visioned and then proved practical by the noble and great ones as the only true pattern of life. And no one taking upon himself this pattern can be slothful for one moment. His every thought, every word and every act must be allied with power. He must learn to follow that divine Light of Christ within, by overcoming the self, and be willing to serve God with a greater intensity than he could possibly put into any job, position, business enterprise or any physical labor on this earth. This way is truly not for the slothful, lazy individual, for this is the path of selfless devotion which demands a constant awareness, an ever-watchful alertness of soul and heart, an untiring,

burning desire, a vision of utter glory that weaves it into tangible reality for the glory of God and the benefit of man.

The following is from the original Greek Text of Matt.
6:24:

"No one is able two lords to serve; either the one he will
hate, and the other he will love; or one he will cling to, and
the other he will slight. Not are you able to serve God and
mammon." Mammon is the personification of worldly wealth.

"Lay not up for yourselves treasures upon earth, where
moth and rust doth corrupt, and where thieves break through
and steal;

"But lay up for yourselves treasures in heaven, where neither moth nor rust doth corrupt, and where thieves do not
break through and steal.

"For where your treasure is, there will your heart be also."
(Matt. 6:19-21).

To most individuals this means something entirely different
than Christ intended it to mean. It does not mean to plod
miserably through a dreary life of suffering and poverty in
the hope of a great reward in some far-off heaven. It means
literally to open your heart to that divine kingdom of heaven
that is *within you*. Fill that kingdom with your desires, with
love, mercy, compassion, unselfish service and loving devotion to the Most High God. These treasures will cleanse and
purify the soul, right here on earth, and thus one may enter
and abide in that true kingdom of heaven, walking in majesty
and power, doing the very works that Christ did.

"Therefore I say unto you, take no thought for your life,
what ye shall eat, or what ye shall drink, nor yet for your
body, what ye shall put on. Is not the life more than meat, and
the body than raiment?

"Therefore take no thought saying, what shall we eat? or,
What shall we drink, or Wherewithal shall we be clothed?

"For after these things do the Gentiles seek; for the heavenly Father knoweth that ye have need of all these things.

"*But seek ye* FIRST *the kingdom of God, and his righteousness;* AND ALL THESE THINGS SHALL BE ADDED UNTO YOU."
(Matt. 6:24-26 and verses 31-33).

Then Christ went on to explain that he who seeks to live by these higher laws must never let fear enter the heart, fear of what will happen tomorrow, but with absolute confidence in the power of God, and an implicit trust in His promises, live today in a perfect faith that can know no fear.

Then is given the warning that in the last days men would worship the works of their own hands instead of God.

This was also given in Jeremiah as follows: "And go not after other gods to serve them, and to worship them, and provoke me not to anger with the works of your hands . . .

"Ye have not hearkened unto me, saith the Lord; that ye might provoke me to anger with the works of your hands, to your own hurt." (Jer. 25:6-7).

Then again Christ gave the definite command: "Labor not for the meat which perisheth, but for that meat which endureth unto life, which the Son of man shall give unto you." (John 6:27).

When the multitude asked how they could have the power to do the works that He did, namely, feed five thousand with practically nothing and a prayer of sure knowing, the answer was:

"This is the work of God, that ye believe on him whom he hath sent."

And if one truly believes on Jesus Christ then he must believe in the *power of His name.* One must also believe on every word He has spoken, and every word that He may speak through that divine "Light of Christ" that has been given to abide in every individual who has come into the world. If one does not live by *every* word that has proceeded out of His mouth then he has failed—consequently is walking in his own strength—and if in his own strength then he is walking in darkness.

Then comes the glorious invitation from the Son of God: "Come unto me, all ye that labour and are heavy laden, and I will give you rest." This invitation is to every man, woman and child upon this earth. If you are serving the world, laboring with all your strength to make a living, or are laboring to get gain, or great wealth, or for any other purpose than to glorify God, you may go to Christ and find rest. Yea, you may turn to that Light of Christ within and be directed into the divine, glorious reality of His nearness and power, which is described as follows: *"Which rest is the fullness of my glory."* Could any promise be greater?

Yea, "Put on the Lord Jesus Christ and make not provisions for the flesh, to fulfill the lusts thereof." (Rom. 13:14).

The Lord's Prayer also contains the truth of this higher law: "Give us this day our daily bread . . ." By trusting implicitly in the power of God faith becomes knowing, and one becomes wholly obedient to the voice of the Father, as he permits God to direct him in all things, until he himself emerges into that power. As one learns to follow that divine voice he drops his fears, his worries, his grudges and confusion. He lives a higher law than that followed by the multitude. He no longer labors for the food that perishes but will receive sufficient for his needs, whatever they are—yea, more than enough, "For there will not be room enough to receive." He will no longer work to acquire large bank accounts, great stores of wealth that can be destroyed in an instant's flash, or be left behind by death. One who has wealth depends for his strength upon that wealth and neglects those greater treasures locked within his own soul. But he who trusts in the power of God for his strength will accumulate a wealth that is far beyond anything that mortal mind has yet contemplated. His wealth will be that peace that passeth understanding, the power of God in action in every move of his life, the power to still the storms, to walk above trials and temptations, the power to live in majesty and eternal light, freed from darkness, fears, confusion and wrath.

Yea, "Because thou sayest, I am rich, and increased with goods and have need of nothing; and knowest not that thou art wretched, and miserable, and poor and blind, and naked:

"I counsel thee to buy of me gold tried in the fire, that thou mayest be rich; and white raiment, that thou mayest be clothed, and that the shame of thy nakedness do not appear; and anoint thine eyes with eyesalve, that thou mayest see." (Rev. 3:17-18).

"And lo, one coming, said to him: O teacher good what good must I do, that I have life age-lasting?

"He said to him; why me askest thou concerning the good? One is the Good (or God). If but thou wishest to enter into the life, keep strictly the commandments.

"He says to him: Which? Then Jesus said, Not thou shalt kill; Not thou shalt commit adultery; Not thou shalt steal; Not thou shalt testify falsely;

"Honor the father and the mother, and thou shalt love the neighbor of thee as thyself.

"Says to him the young man; All these I kept from childhood of me; what more do I want?

"Said to him the Jesus; If thou wishest perfect to be, go, sell thee the possessions, and give to the poor, and thou shalt have treasures in heaven; and follow me.

"Having heard and the young man the word, went away sorrowing; he was for having possessions many.

"And Jesus said to the disciples of himself: Indeed I say to you, that with difficulty a rich man shall enter into the kingdom of heaven.

"Again I say to you, easier it is a camel through the eye of a needle to pass than a rich man into the kingdom of God to enter." (Matt. 19:16-24—Original Greek translation).

The above is most explicit. If the rich young man could have made that last step he could have received the greater treasures. No one ever gave up a fault without being rewarded with a virtue. Every achievement of devotion and every sacrifice brings strength and character. And these higher virtues become the man, strong, majestic and wise as he grows from grace to grace. In order to receive "all that the Father has" it is necessary to give all that one possesses.

These higher laws of glory are only for those who are willing to sell all that they have that they might purchase the field containing the great hidden treasure. They have to be willing to give up all the lesser treasures they possess in order to purchase that one precious pearl of great price—the kingdom of heaven.

One truly has to give up his mortal, earthly kingdom in or-

der to purchase the greater kingdom in which all things will
be added. One has to be willing to give up all that he has of a
temporal nature in order to enter in at the straight gate, for it
is the "Needle's Eye." And it is as difficult for a rich man
to enter the higher realm of power as it is for the camel to
go through the eye of the needle.

At night the great wide gates of the city of Jerusalem were
closed to the caravans and only a small pedestrian gate, known
as the "needle's eye" remained open. Sometimes a lone traveler, coming to the city by night, could enter that gate with his
camel. But only after the camel had been stripped of its load,
and then upon its knees it could crawl through that small doorway. But there was still another consideration, the camel had
to be *willing*. But as a rule camels are very obstinate beasts.
Camels are never affectionate animals, never devoted to a
master, and are usually stubborn and vicious. And no amount
of pulling or dragging could force a camel through that small
gate without its full co-operation—and only the power of God
could give it that willingness.

And no man can enter that straight and narrow gate unless
he is willing and desires it. He must be willing to unload his
possessions, his bigotry, his self, his pride and prejudices.
Then and then only can he enter that gate into the Holy City
of Jerusalem—the city of eternal light where there is no more
darkness either in his surroundings or within himself. Then it
is that he comprehends all things—the glory of his own heaven
—and he need go no more out into the confusion of a discordant world. And this does not mean that he need become a
recluse. It means that he can walk this earth in majesty and
power, with complete understanding of the path he treads.

Yea, "Straight is the gate and narrow is the way, and few
there be who find it" for those who are too overburdened
with their mortal accumulations must unload.

This straight and narrow way of divine light belongs to
the one who will strip himself of his worldly accumulations of
thoughts and things, discarding the external impermanence for
the glory of the permanent, eternal values. Such a one will find
the true gifts, the deeper, unspeakable power, the great joy,

the peace that passeth understanding, perfect health, happiness, eternal light, all-wisdom, all-knowing—and all things will be subject unto him, both in heaven and on earth: the life and the light, the Spirit and the power, sent forth by the will of the Father through Jesus Christ, the Son, through that contact with the "Light of Christ within" which is the gate—the door upon which Christ knocks—the door that man himself must open—and enter. To enter that gate his eyes must be truly single to the glory of God.

"He commandeth that there shall be no priestcrafts; for behold, priestcrafts are that men preach and set themselves up for a light unto the world, that they may get gain and praise of the world; but they seek not the welfare of Zion (the pure in heart).

"Behold, the Lord hath forbidden this thing; wherefore, the Lord hath given a commandment, that all men shall have charity, which charity is love, and except they shall have charity they are nothing. Wherefore, if they have charity they would not suffer the laborer in Zion to perish.

"But the laborer in Zion shall labor for Zion; for *if they labor for money they shall perish.*"

"And when thou prayest, not thou shalt be like the hypocrites, for they love in the synagogues and in the corners of the wide places standing to pray, *that they may appear to the men.* Indeed I say to you, that they have in full the reward of them." Yea there is no reward from God for such public prayers that are offered to be heard of men.

"But thou, when thou prayest, enter into the retired place of thee, and locking the door of thee, pray thou to the Father of thee, in the secret; and the Father of thee who seeing in the secret place, will give to thee in the clear light." (Matt. 6:5-6 —Original Greek translation).

The foregoing pattern of prayer has been with us for two thousand years yet very few have understood its true meaning. It is revealing in another way the command, "Be Still, and know that I am, God." It is revealing the sacred information of how to contact God. Enter into the secret place, the holy of holies within your own soul, the very center of that "Light of Christ," then close the doors of consciousness to all outside things, to men, to worldly thoughts and influences. Then make known to God your desires, not with much "babbling" as the original gives it, but with loving faith and devotion. Then "believe" and "know that you receive" and you shall have whatsoever you ask. Praise and give thanks and know that the Father who heareth in secret shall truly reward you openly, or bring into manifest, visible form the fulfillment of your requests. It is the Father who doeth the works, and you need not worry as to how it is to be accomplished. Only *know* that if your desires are not vainglorious and will harm no man they will be fulfilled. It is the law. Just praise and give thanks and you fulfill the law.

"Ask, and it shall be given you; seek, and ye shall find; knock, and it shall be opened unto you:

"For everyone that asketh receiveth; and he that seeketh findeth; and to him that knocketh it shall be opened.

"Or what man is there of you, whom if his son ask bread, will he give him a stone?

"Or if he ask a fish, will he give him a serpent?

"If ye then, being evil, know how to give good gifts unto your children, how much more shall your Father which is in heaven give good things to them that ask him?"

"He that asketh in Spirit, asketh according to the will of God, and he shall have whatsoever he asketh."

If we ask our earthly parents anything we ask them according to the power of our flesh, our physical voice. But when we make a request of God it is quite necessary that we ask through the Spirit, for He is the Father of our Spirits.

"And this is the confidence that we have in him, that, if we ask anything according to his will, he heareth us:

"And if we know that he hear us, whatsoever we ask, we know that we have the petitions that we desired of him." (I John 5:14-15).

"Draw nigh unto God, and he will draw nigh to you; Cleanse your hands—and purify your hearts, ye double minded." This is referring definitely to those who are trying to serve both God and the world with its wealth and mortal desires. (James 4:8).

This drawing near to God is drawing near to him in Spirit, or through the Spirit seek to know him. One's requests, in order to be granted, must be made through the Spirit, or through that silent chamber in the depths of his own soul, not through loud shouting in public places, not through many words—but in the secret, silent place where the "Light of Christ" abides.

If one understands this method of prayer he can truly approach the Father in heaven, and "asking according to the Spirit, he shall have whatsoever he saith," for his requests shall be fulfilled and brought forth into manifest form—thus the very substance of things hoped for becomes a reality. As one prays in this true pattern of prayer it matters not whether his prayers be offered in a church, in his family, or silently in his own sacred room, just so long as he is not making a prayer to be heard of men, but is truly speaking to God from the very center of his soul, with all the world locked out.

This perfect method of prayer opens wide the heart to receive the divine benediction of a loving, gracious Father. It opens every cell of the body to receive His light. It brings the mind into subjection to the Spirit and fulfills the first and great commandment. It is the purification of the mortal self with its burden and weaknesses, its shames and failures.

These greater blessings can come only through that divine contact with God. No one on earth can give this contact to another. Each must do his own praying, his own asking, his own seeking and searching. "And to know the love of Christ, which passeth knowledge," (a love that reaches beyond the power of mind and thought into the feelings, the very depth of one's being), "That ye might *be filled with all* THE FULLNESS OF GOD."

"Now unto him that is able to do exceeding abundantly above all that we ask or think, according to the power that worketh in us." (Eph. 3:19-20).

This again proclaims the truth of the Sermon on the Mount, there where earthly parents give good gifts to their children who ask them—the heavenly Father will give so much greater

gifts to those who ask, and the asking must be through the
Spirit.

The Light of Christ that is given to abide in each man that
cometh into the world must be contacted, loved, developed,
acknowledged and followed so that it can become an everlasting power and glory right within man. Love must be perfected
—love for God—love for God's children—for His world and
the greatness of His creations. And as surely as one desires
this divine, pure Christ-like love it will grow within him—a
love so tender, so compassionate, so forgiving it will help to
glorify a world. Then the little mortal self is forgotten and left
behind and one steps into that great spiritual self and the
divinity of his own soul becomes manifest.

With such a vision and such divine love one understands the
truth of the words of Enoch as given in the New Testament
Apocrypha: "Cursed every man who opens his lips for the
bringing into contempt and calumny of his neighbor, because
he brings God into contempt."

And, "He who works crookedly or speaks evil against any
soul, will not make justice for himself for all time." (Secrets
of Enoch LII:2 and LX:4). Then it becomes apparent that
any individual, or any unauthorized group who goes forth to
execute justice upon any man becomes lost in a great and
shameful injustice.

With these higher laws of love and devotion and true prayer
one treads a sacred highway of divine light—the straight and
narrow way, walking hand in hand with God, growing from
grace to grace until he is filled with light, or is "Anointed
with Light" and finally receives of the "Fullness of the
Father" and has all that the Father has.

This is a road no lazy man can possibly tread. It is paved
with flaming desire, lighted by high vision and traveled with a
constant alertness of soul and mind. It is a road of unfolding,
of developing, of evolving from a common mediocre mortal
into a being of majesty and power, filled with light. It is the
road that fulfills the *name* of Jesus Christ and bestows the
power of that *name*. It is the road that fulfills every promise
and one does not need to labor for the things that perish for

he will be able to use the great atomic law in its true form and bring forth an abundance of all things to supply all his needs direct from the great universal source of eternal energy or Spirit.

Thus the following may be completely fulfilled:

"That which is of God is light; and he that receiveth light, and continueth in God, receiveth more light; and that light groweth brighter until the perfect day (or until he is perfected).

"And again, verily I say unto you, and I say it that you may *chase darkness from among you*:

"He that is ordained of God and sent forth (or he who receives his anointing of Light), the same is appointed to be the greatest, notwithstanding he is the least and the servant of all.

"Wherefore, he is possessor of all things; for all things are subject unto him, both in heaven and on earth, the life and the light, the Spirit and the power, sent forth by the will of the Father through Jesus Christ, his Son.

"But no man is possessor of all things except he be purified from all sin.

"And if ye are purified and cleansed from all sin, ye shall ask whatsoever you will in the *name* of Jesus and it shall be done." (D. & C. 50:24-29).

This great, unspeakable power mentioned, that will be able to command the life, the light and even the very Spirit of God, both in heaven and on earth and have it obey, comes to man when he has brought forth that "Light of Christ from within." This is his "Anointing of Light." It is the power of Almighty God in action. It is the very power of creation—the power that can form atoms out of pure, original energy and multiply them into tangible substance, for "Faith is the substance of things hoped for; the evidence of things not seen." Then when faith becomes perfect it turns into knowledge and the things hoped for become a living, tangible reality, whether it be the restoring of one's eyes or hearing, the renewing of flesh or bones, or strength or understanding, it shall be fulfilled.

It is then that the prayers offered in the secret of one's own closet, or soul, are fulfilled openly. Even one's daily needs can be supplied from this unlimited storehouse of eternal abundance and dynamic power. Anything that is needed for satisfaction, progress and happiness either for oneself or for his neighbor, can be brought forth for the use of those who will fulfill the law. This is the contact Christ had with the Father. The power He used. It is the power of creation which He tried so hard to teach mankind about, proclaiming its existence and that it was for all to use who would only believe —yea, the power to raise the dead—move mountains—supply all one's needs and to perform the miracles that were promised should follow those who believe. This is the power God promised to those who would only believe on the *name* of Jesus Christ. It is the power of that *name*. It is God's power as He is permitted to work through His chosen instrument, man. It is the power of divine love, eternal light, wisdom and majesty fulfilled and brought forth in the life of every individual who will only believe and then follows that belief through to its ultimate perfection. Thus faith becomes knowing—and knowing is power. "Faith promises all things; and it fulfills all things."

These great promises, as they are brought forth in the lives of men, contain the fullness of the Everlasting Gospel of Jesus Christ—"a gospel of power, not of words."

These promises are of God. They are sacred and true. And they fail not. This dynamic power belongs to him who will only believe on the *name* of Jesus Christ, and then take upon him that *name*. It is the power that belongs to him who will fulfill the New and Everlasting Covenant, and Christ is its mediator through that divine "Light of Christ that is given to abide in every man that cometh into the world." This is the power of God that becomes active in the lives of men when they live by every Word that proceeds forth from the mouth of God until they themselves become that Word. And God speaks His Words only through the purified hearts of men.

Oh glorious children, arise and put off thy dark grave clothes of death and old age and array thyselves in eternal light. And Christ is the way, the Truth, and the Light. Follow that Light that is within your own souls and you need never walk in darkness for you shall walk with God. And "Thou shalt have dominion over the earth and all things therein" "for in the similitude of God art thou made." "Yea, all that the Father has is yours." You shall be one with Him in power, in understanding and in love and majesty. This is the only meaning of the words: "Be one with God."

"Come unto Me all ye ends of the earth! Come! And I will gather you tenderly as a hen gathers her chickens under her wings that you might escape the great wrath that is to be poured out upon all nations. Come unto me, and I will give you rest—yea, even the rest of the fullness of my glory. The time is now! My arms are outstretched, and my voice is unto all men! Come!

"And no man shall ever read this record who shall not know of its truth through the power of the Holy Ghost, if he will only ask in the *name* of Jesus Christ; praying with a sincere heart and an open mind. Yea, through the Light of Christ abiding within him he may know the truth of this work—and by this Light he may know the truth of all things.

"So be it."

CHAPTER XXVI.

THE SEAL

THIS BOOK was written and its covers closed. Then came the command to reopen it, for the great quest for which the work was begun was not fully revealed. The quest was for a complete understanding and revelation of that small word FAITH—faith to move mountains, dissolve misfortunes and endow man with its infinite power. Yes, for the promises are that those who believe shall have power to restore, to heal, to create and to fulfill all things. And "these promises are unto *all*, even unto the ends of the earth." And though the book was written this power still remains just beyond reach. That must never be, lest the purpose of the book be in vain and its revealed truths remain fruitless in your hands, or worse still, only words written upon many pages.

For this reason the command has been given to open again the covers of the book and the doors of the universe and let the great, breath-taking power of eternal creation pour itself out upon these final pages that all-power might be placed in your hands.

"Faith is the substance of things hoped for." Just words? Oh no! Listen carefully and they will be endowed with everlasting life.

Yes, "Faith is the substance of things hoped for"—and the *substance* of things *hoped* for is the great spiritual energy out of which all things are composed, all things which do or can exist in the thoughts of man or in either the tangible realm of earth or the intangible realm of spirit.

With this knowledge it is now possible to comprehend that faith is an ELEMENT. It is the greatest of all elements for it is the mother of all others. It is as definite as radium, or air,

330

or water. It is truly the mother substance or element out of which all existing things are composed. To mortal eyes it is not tangible in its true, original state. It is as intangible as hydrogen or oxygen or many of the other elements that have been discovered in recent years. But when this greatest of all elements is combined in the right proportions it becomes as definitely tangible to the physical senses as H^2O combined as water.

This greatest of all elements, this substance or Spiritual material of everlasting creation, boundless energy, Almighty power can become tangible in newly created forms, or as renewed cells and tissues of a worn-out body, or in any form that substance can possibly assume through the simple combination of hope, or thought, or deep desire, blended with the inner emotions or feelings of the soul. As thought and emotion, or feeling, or belief blend in the magic combination of united strength, it is the power of creation and FAITH, or the great spiritual, mother element of substance which is given the pattern it must fill. This mother element, or Spirit substance, or eternal energy fills all space, composes all matter, manifests all life and all existence.

"And Jesus said unto him, if thou canst believe, all things are possible to him that believeth." (Mark 9:23)

"For verily I say unto you, that whosoever shall say unto this mountain, Be thou cast into the sea; *and shall not doubt in his heart,* but shall believe that those things which he saith shall come to pass, he shall have whatsoever he saith.

"Therefore, I say unto you, what things soever ye desire when ye pray, believe that ye receive them and ye shall have them." (Mark 11: 23-24; Matt. 17:20)

There is an ancient record as old as the earth itself; at least it is as old as the Great Pyramid of Egypt, which reveals the principle of faith without ever profaning the word as we have done, for it never even mentions the word "faith". It uses instead the word "matter" and reads as follows:

"O my son, matter becomes; formerly it was, for matter is the vehicle of becoming. Becoming is the mode of activity of the uncreate and foreseeing God. Having been endowed with the germ of becoming" (through desire, thought or deep hope) "matter is brought into BIRTH, for the creative force (of thought) fashions it according to the ideal forms. Matter not yet engendered has no form; it becomes when it is put into operation"—by the mind of man.

As one opens his mind to comprehend the dynamic meaning of the great substance or eternal element of existence, he realizes how we have profaned, even blasphemed the word FAITH in our profound ignorance.

Through endless centuries Christians have claimed it as their special gift in vain. They have boasted of its powers in words but their works are dead. James has been quoted from pulpits by the score; "Show me your faith without your works and I will show you my faith by my works;" and the works have been interpreted as meaning some small service rendered, some position or office held in some church or congregation, or some donation or contribution or alms-giving. And the very translation has been a vain and perverse one. These words of James mean only one thing, the showing of one's faith by one's WORKS OF FAITH with the dynamic power of creation and fulfilment bearing continual witness as it becomes active and is brought into life. Without the faith to perform the miracles and signs which Christ promised should follow those who profess to believe, all things are vain. No doctrine, no matter how true, or how divine, no authority, no formulas, no rituals nor words can justify a lack of this power in any professing Christian's life. "*MY* Kingdom is not in word, but in POWER."

And when THAT power is in action it can neither be bought nor sold. No one can charge for it and escape the wrath of God for that power is God's power and His gifts cannot be bought, nor the benefits of them. "Freely ye received, freely ye must give." Those who seek to sell the gifts and powers of God shall perish from the earth, and on the day of Judgment when they are called forth and in their boasting testify that in His Name they did many mighty miracles and many wonderful works their rebuke shall rob them forever after of any powers or rights or claims upon the mercy of God—"Depart from me ye accursed, I know ye not." It is true that he who serves God is

worthy of his hire—Yea, his *higher* reward of complete understanding and all-power. And as he rises to be the greatest he
must also become more literally the very servant of all, freely
and without price, even as the Son of the Living God. And then
all things will be added unto him, and all powers.

This dynamic element of eternal creation has always been.
It will always be. Man has not comprehended it. A few have
sought desperately for its unlimited powers that they might sell
them at a price or glorify themselves above their fellow man,
but few have realized that this gift of everlasting Faith belongs
to all. It is a divine gift and is free for the use of every man.
No individual can monopolize this infinite power of Almighty
God. It is a principle as eternal as eternity. It fills the universe
and is as free as the air itself. It is illimitable, yet it is subject
unto the mind of mortal man.

We have used it, to be sure. Everyone who thinks, who desires, who hates or envies or hopes uses it, or mis-uses it, for
we have used it in such blind ignorance that the world itself is
on the very verge of utter ruin because of our *mis*-use of it.
It had been mis-used to bring forth the dark, hidden lusts of
men's depraved desires, their dreams of conquest, personal
power or revenge. It has been mis-used to fulfill hates and fears
and greed and selfish ambitions. Used in this manner it brings
naught but dire calamities, misery and eventually death.

FAITH, the great mother element, the dynamic, Spiritual
substance which fills all space, all time and composes all things
is surrounding us always. We are literally immersed in it, composed of it, and have complete control over it as we work in
accordance with the law of the universe—the law of love—love
for God, for our fellowman, for all created things and love for
this infinite substance of everlasting power and intelligence as
our mortal fingers reach out to take hold of it.

After one is purified and cleansed from all sin, having cast
out darkness completely that its destructive vibrations can never
again touch him, nor be sent out from him by negative thinking
or negative emotions, then will be fulfilled the almost incomprehensible promise of Almighty God: "Wherefore he is possessor of all things; for all things will be subject unto him,

both in heaven and on earth, the Light and the Life, the Spirit and the power sent forth by the will of the Father, through Jesus Christ, His Son."

This very principle of Faith which reaches out into infinitude as the greatest element or Spiritual substance waiting to be taken hold of and acted upon and brought forth into tangible fulfilment of hopes, or dreams, or prayers, or desires, is the very Spirit and power which will become subject unto all who desire to use it according to the universal law—for the benefit of all. It is the great principle upon which heaven and earth are founded, and this principle of unlimited power will be subject unto all who will purify themselves from all sin as they use the dynamic "Light of Christ which is given to abide in every man who cometh into the world."

This divine Light of Christ within man, when brought forth to its infinite perfection of complete fulfilment, IS LOVE— love eternal and divine. It is the very power of life, for it is life. It is this Light and this life that will also be subject unto those who fulfill the laws. And they who reject this Light are truly under condemnation. And though they may have faith to move mountains, to raise the dead, to give all that they possess to the poor, and their bodies to be burned, yet have not this love their works are empty and as sounding brass and tinkling symbols. It is only love that gives meaning to the power and glorifies it with divine purpose.

Combine this divine, Christ-like love with a knowledge and understanding of the great principle of faith and the keys of the universe and of eternal life will be placed in your hands and no power in existence will ever be able to take them from you. This Light or Spirit of Christ is the Living Word of God as it bears witness in your own soul, or is spoken through your own heart. "And they were called Gods unto whom the word of God came," for to such is given the keys of all-power and divine majesty.

"The weak things of the world shall come forth and break down the mighty and strong ones, that man should not counsel his fellow man, neither trust in the arm of flesh—

"But that EVERY man might speak in the Name of God the Lord, even the Savior of the world;

"That faith also might increase in the earth;

"That mine everlasting covenant might be established;" in the souls of the children of men, that they might find that divine contact with Me through the Light of Christ in their own souls.

For this purpose was this book written, and for this purpose it has come forth—that the Spirit of God might begin to be poured out upon all flesh, and that a knowledge of God might cover the earth as the waters cover the sea, that the bigotry and pride and self-righteousness and arrogance and monopolies might cease and the power of God be made manifest in the lives of all men.

Take hold of the Light that has been inborn within your own soul, the Light of Christ within you, and you will be given the powers of the universe, for all things will become subject unto you, both in heaven and on earth, the Light and the life, the Spirit and the power of creation and of eternal life. Nothing will be impossible unto you. Know this, O man, whatsoever has been accomplished in times past can and must be accomplished again. And greater things than have ever been accomplished are waiting for fulfilment as YOU take hold of the ineffable power of faith. "All that the Father has is yours." Yes, the very powers of creation are waiting but the touch of your hand, the opening of your mind. Step forth and claim your birthright, for God is your Sire. "For everyone who loveth *is* BORN OF GOD, AND KNOWETH GOD." (I. John 4:7, 8 and 16; see also Rom. 13:7 and 1, and Gal. 5:13-14 and 18 and verses 22-23.)

If this power of faith is used to bring forth first the fulfilment of one's personal, temporal desires for outward show, or for display or personal lust then the greater powers and the glory of the Kingdom are never made manifest. "Seek first the Kingdom of God and HIS righteousness, or seek to become as righteous as He is righteous, and all else will be added unto you."

This is the record of the blessings and the powers of Almighty God which are offered to the race of men—

Yes, ". . . Has the day of miracles ceased?

"Or have angels ceased to appear unto the children of men? Or has He withheld the power of the Holy Ghost from them? Or will He so long as time shall last, or the earth shall stand, or there shall be one man upon the face thereof to be saved?

"Behold I say unto you, Nay; for it is by faith that miracles are wrought; and it is by faith that angels appear and minister unto men; wherefore, if these things have ceased woe be unto the children of men, for it is because of unbelief, and all is vain," or completely in vain.

Yes, this is the record of the blessings and the powers of Almighty God which are offered freely to the race of men, and the Seal of God is upon it and none can destroy it. He who lifts his hand or his voice to destroy it shall himself reap destruction, for God has spoken. And His words shall be witnessed by His Son through the Light in the souls of men, and through the Holy Ghost to all who will only humble themselves and ask with sincere hearts to know the Truth of this work for it has come forth through the power of Almighty God, through the name of His Son, Jesus Christ, and by the power of the Holy Ghost it shall stand.   Amen.

INDEX

Abide—102, 107.
Accuser—147.
Acorn—108.
Aimlessness—57.
Alchemy—137.
"All is well"—86.
All-knowledge—278.
All-peace—278.
All-truth—229.
Alma—182.
Alone—167.
Angel of death—181.
Angels—25, 105, 164, 289.
Angels in disguise—164.
Animals—17.
Anointed—209, 210, 213, 219, 222, 260, 262, 284.
Anointing—28, 221, 231, 280, 327.
Apocrypha—79, 88, 218, 223, 326.
Approval—203.
Arm of flesh—312.
"As a man thinketh"—53.
Asleep—32.
Ask—72, 95, 104, 129, 134, 190, 221, 228, 324.
Atomic Power—8, 32, 64, 191.
Atonement—70.
Attention—93.
Attribute—187.
Awake—233.
Awaken—192.
Awareness—128, 287.
Awe—112.

Balance—12.
Banish darkness—128.
Baptized—212.
Battlefield—123.

Believe—39.
"Be Still - -"—106, 107, 132, 227, 287.
Blasphemed—165, 170.
Blasphemy—166.
Blessings—21, 22.
Blindness of mind—170.
Blues—96.
Book of life—146, 270, 271, 273.
Books opened—271.
Born of the Spirit—212.
Born again—192.
Bosom of eternity—248.
Braggarts—155.
Broadcast—96.
Broken heart—84, 90.
Bulb—108.
By the finger of God—236.

Calamities—157.
Calling—20.
Capital and labor—152.
Captive daughters—234.
Carnally minded—189.
Caught up—85.
Caverns—78.
Celestial realm—157.
Celestial symphony—299.
Celestial Glory—59, 96, 253, 283, 299.
Center of Soul—105.
Charity—178.
Chatters—141.
Cheats—155.
Cheerfulness—224.
Chemistry—18, 136, 138, 139.
Christianity—105, 110.
Christians—104.

Christ's power—193, 194.
Circulatory—8.
City of Enoch—149, 182.
Cleansed—149, 166.
Cleanse hands—324.
Clothe—11.
Columbus—40, 204.
Come—134, 329.
Come Unto Me—329.
Comforter—208, 272.
Compassion—99.
Comprehend—305.
Comprehend all things—100, 119, 305.
Comprehendeth—86, 100, 117, 119.
Confusion—107.
Congregation of the mighty—251.
Conscious—128, 253.
Conquest of self—161, 317.
Conscience—201, 202, 203, 205.
Consciousness—253.
Contribute—17.
Control—57.
Cosmic rays—120, 125.
Courage—30, 203.
Covenant, The—164, 303, 304, 305, 307, 310, 312, 313, 315.
Covereth the earth—188.
Create—9, 11, 15.
Created—9.
Criminals—23, 50, 205.

Dam—89.
Damn—89.
Damned—158.
Darkness—165, 233, 290, 327.
Daughter—42.
David's prayer—113.
Death—10, 12, 183, 184, 189, 190, 272, 288.
Deep Sleep—166.
Depression—26.
Designer—8.
Desire—17, 63, 93.
Despair—225.
Destiny—20, 27, 54, 159, 199.

Die in sins—288.
Diligently—133.
Divinity—175.
Doctors—155.
Domineering—150.
Door, The—218, 225, 226, 228, 290.
Doubting—79, 81, 223.
Dreams—37.

Earth—17.
Earthquake—122.
Ecstasy—138, 222, 223, 302.
Education—56, 204.
Electricity—4.
Elements—243.
Elijah—182.
Emotions—69, 70, 157.
End, The—250.
Ends of earth—288.
Energy—4, 5, 8, 64, 125, 159.
Enjoyments—85.
Enoch—182.
Entities—60, 61.
Equal with God—188.
Error of boasting—291.
Eternal life—170, 185, 232.
Ether—182.
Everyone who asks—130 .
Evolve—261.
Exercise—28, 64, 81, 109.
Eyes to see—138.

Face unveiled—127.
Faculty—85.
Faith—24, 26, 27, 28, 29, 34, 39, 64, 65, 66, 67, 79, 81, 108, 207, 233, 328.
Falsehood—257.
Fanatics—99.
Fantasy—58.
Father, The—228.
Father doeth—101.
Fear—112, 222, 319.
Feast—127.
Feel Him—132, 288.

Few chosen—163.
Filthy—96.
Flesh—169, 178, 253.
Forgive—172, 174.
Forgiveness—167, 173.
Forgiving—171.
Foundation—84, 191.
Fourth dimension—100, 191.
Free agency—129.
Free-doom—150, 208.
Fruit of Spirit—225.
Fulfills—227.
Fulness—88, 119, 180, 209, 211, 231, 240, 241, 243, 248, 274, 283, 311, 320, 325.
Future—72.

Get understanding—180.
Gifts—91, 132, 140, 288.
Glorified in truth—269.
Glorify the day—142.
Glorious—21.
Glory—143.
God—7, 10.
God, Concerning
  Comprehend God—117, 118, 119, 128.
  Day of God—124.
  Equal with God—188.
  Every man speak in name of God—312, 335.
  Gifts of God—173, 207, 288.
  Glory of God—50.
  God dwelleth in midst—19.
  God's promises—268.
  I Am, God—116.
  Integrity of God—96.
  Kingdom of God—97, 281.
  Know God—111, 117, 134.
  Love God—293, 294, 295.
  Light of God—175.
  Love of God—130.
  Seal of God—286.
  Seek God—131.
  Seen God—117, 242, See God 310.
  Spirit of God—188, 253.
  Word of God—217, 252.
Gods—9, 251, 262, 283, 305.
Go on to perfection—186.

Grace—84, 85, 87, 305, 326.
Great Commandments—98, 171, 174, 293.
Great volume—236.
Greater works—104, 110, 297.

Hate—4, 5, 158, 172.
Healed—26.
Hermas—79, 224.
Hid—84, 191, 257, 264.
Hidden treasures—266, 269.
His Name—319.
Holy Ghost—87, 90, 187, 292.
Holy men—307.
Holy of Holies—202, 215, 216, 323.
Holy Spirit—126, 223, 224, 226.
Hopelessness—26, 207.
How to judge truth—270, 275, 276.
How to pray—323.
Human nature—147.
Humility—161, 188, 227, 283, 293.
Hypnotism—73, 74.

Ills—75.
Imagination—36.
Imagine—12.
Immortality—20, 190.
Incorruption—218.
India—39.
Infallible Guide—207.
In Him we live—134.
Inside of the cup—78.
Inspired—127.
Instinct—10.
Instruction—85.
Instrument—176.
Intelligence—8, 18, 57, 255.
Intelligences—19.
In the Father—102.
Inventions—93.

James Allen—53.
Jealousy—158.
Jehoshaphat—125.
Jehovah—114, 115, 315.

Jesus—210.
Jewels—235.
Joan of Arc—204.
Job—15.
John the Beloved—183.
Joint-heirs—213, 253.
Judge—81, 275.
Justify—50.
Just men made perfect—307.

Keys—159, 230.
Kingdom—78, 86, 195.
Kingdom of heaven—195, 267.
Kingdoms—242.
Knowing—207, 277.
Knowledge—155, 239, 272.

Labor not—98, 317.
Lamentations—165.
Language of soul—141.
Law—35, 36, 47, 71.
Laws of righteousness—167.
Lay hold of—188.
Lazy—317.
Learning of world—282.
Learn to listen—294.
Lepers—25, 26.
Letter, The—236.
Liars—186, 258.
Lied—158.
Life—198.
Light—106, 107, 119, 122, 125, 151,
    175, 176, 198, 204, 211, 230, 242,
    247, 255, 256, 257, 276, 277, 278,
    279, 284, 288, 290, 328.
Light of Christ—198, 204, 211, 240,
    256, 276, 278, 279, 282, 284, 288.
    290, 313, 328.
Light of sun—122.
Light shines—151.
Light within—210, 233.
Lips—99, 141, 142, 262.
Live the laws—192.
Loaves—81.
Lord's Prayer—174.

Love—5, 6, 31, 72, 83, 85, 90, 98,
    128, 139, 158, 161, 168, 171, 173,
    176, 177, 179, 180, 225, 263, 264,
    270, 297, 298, 302, 326.
Love of God—91.
Love thy neighbor—174.
Lucifer—181.
Lust—156.

Machine—93.
Maker—85.
Mammon—318.
Man—65.
Many called—163.
Marden—49.
Martyrs—189.
Marvelous—84, 191.
Matchmaking—150.
Matter—64.
Maturity—56.
Mediator, The—303.
Mediocre—75, 168.
Melchizedek—165.
Melody—174.
Microphone—132, 293.
Miracles—24, 25, 89, 288, 289, 313.
Monopolized—130.
Monopoly—131, 132, 161.
Moses—114, 115, 182.
Music—6.
Musician—59, 176.
Musty past—111.
My sheep—315.
Mysteries—83, 165, 239, 248, 266.
Mystery of Godliness—170.

Name, The—210, 211, 213, 215, 217,
    220, 221, 259, 301, 315, 319, 326.
Narrow Way—205.
Necessities—26.
Needle's eye, The—321.
Negatives—504.
Nephi—182.
New Covenant—310.

New song, The—300, 301.
Noble—16, 17.
Not robbery—188.
Not under the law—225, 246, 308, 312.

Obedience—110.
Obtain—34.
Odes of Solomon—218, 236.
Offend—85.
Oil—229, 230.
Opportunity—21.
Ordained—18, 210, 284.
Orthodox—32, 75.
Outside, The—228.
Outer darkness—233.
Outside of cup—78, 91, 207.
Overcome—173, 184, 191, 223, 225, 257, 260, 261.
Overcoming self—317.

Parents—9, 18.
Passivity—32, 94.
Passover, The—226.
Pattern—22, 23, 32, 199, 200, 206, 210, 212, 216, 230, 244.
Peace—124, 234, 235, 278.
Pearls—22, 44, 45.
Pearly gates—263.
Perfect—50, 254, 260.
Perfection—59, 68, 85, 132, 158, 169, 178, 186, 244.
Perish—49.
Personality—13.
Petition—81.
Pioneering—100.
Plant—206.
Planting—38, 69.
Pliable—57.
Possessor—245, 285.
Possessor of all things—269.
Power—8, 22, 24, 28, 32, 33, 67, 71, 77, 86, 90, 106, 109, 110, 111, 128, 131, 160, 173, 177, 179, 183, 184, 193, 232, 241, 273, 296, 312, 328.

Power over death—184, 185.
Practical—8.
Pray—86, 323.
Prayer—92, 132, 142, 158, 174, 188, 283, 293, 320, 325.
Prayeth continually—188.
Precepts of men—86, 272.
Predecessors—76.
Preparation—228.
Priestcrafts—323.
Present—58.
Price—31.
Principle—28.
Prison house—181.
Probation—261.
Production—35, 46, 72.
Progress—17, 20.
Promise—89, 190, 192, 316, 319, 328.
Promises of faith—108.
Promises, The—328.
Prove all things—270, 275, 276.
Purification—216, 245, 251.
Purified—230, 245, 327.
Purify—22, 82, 83, 99.

Quest—29, 32.
Quickened—127, 214, 244, 306.
Quickeneth—33, 205, 208, 242, 247, 272, 286.

Reach—188.
Reaching—17.
Reach into heaven—250.
Realities—1, 3, 6, 8, 157.
Record of heaven—204, 208, 247, 286.
Reign—92.
Repentance—152, 199.
Restricted powers—116.
Reveal—87, 188.
Revealed—87.
Revelation—88, 252.
Rewards—202.
Rhythm—12.

Rich—255, 320, 321.

Rich young man—162, 321.

Righteousness—90, 161, 164, 167.

Rituals—91.

Robert Henri—204.

Rock of Revelation—285.

Royal household—234.

Russia—123.

Sacrament—185, 259.

Sadness—223, 224.

Saints—172.

Sanctification—221.

Sanctified—127, 309.

Scientists—65.

Seal—21, 330, 336.

Sealed—32, 286.

Sealed mind—112.

Second Comforter—82, 83, 164, 165, 168, 308, 309, 310.

Seeds—37, 38, 69.

Seek—63, 89, 90, 95, 114, 129, 133, 190, 228, 318.

Seek ye first—318.

Self-pity—97.

Self-righteousness — 147, 160, 161, 258.

Self, The—161, 281, 292, 317.

Sermon on Mount—104, 171.

Servant—90.

Service—154.

Shall be delivered—124.

Shall see God—310.

Signs—24, 109.

Sin—108, 196.

Sinned—50.

Sins as scarlet—260.

Sneer—156.

Song of ecstasy, The—302.

Sons—229.

Sons of God—313.

Sorrows—21.

Soul—13, 21, 30, 105,

Souls cheated—86.

Soul, With all the—294.

Sparrow—129.

Sphinx—147.

Spirit—7, 70, 129, 193, 219, 277, 314.

Spirit of Christ—87, 120, 211, 275, 278, 282, 284, 288, 290, 312, 313, 328.

Spirit of Revelation—87, 88.

Spirit of Truth—177, 200, 209, 241, 268, 328.

Spirit teacheth—187.

Spiritual realm—97.

State of wickedness—265.

Steward—162.

Still small voice—208, 215.

Storehouse—34, 94.

Strong, The—239.

Strange Act—238.

Subconscious—74.

Subject unto you—229, 245, 269, 284, 327.

Substance—64.

Sun darkened—122.

Sup—127, 140.

Symbolism—166.

Symbols—145, 164.

Talents—30.

Tangible—4, 14, 65, 93, 144.

Telestial—95.

Temperature—11.

Temples—216.

Tempted—53.

Terrestial—95.

Testing—166, 250.

Tests—160, 164, 166.

Test truth—270, 275, 276.

Thankfulness—17, 21, 72, 97, 136, 226.

Think—54.

Thinking—62, 94.

Thoughts—5, 7, 38, 52, 60, 67, 68, 70, 85.

Three Nephites—182.

Three tests—160.

Today—73.
Tongue—85.
Transmutation—140, 143.
Transmute—152.
Transmuted—137.
Treasures—87, 266, 269.
Treasures in heaven—318.
Tree of Life—189, 194, 195, 196, 265, 266.
True followers—300.
Trust arm of flesh—253, 312.
Truth—31, 33, 243, 249.
Truth-All—169, 227.

Unbelief—84, 173.
Uncontrolled—51.
Under condemnation—201.
Unhappy still—96.
Unlived—167.
Unorthodox—192.
Unseal—75.
Untried—167.
Upon my house—165.

Vain—25, 104, 289, 310.
Veil—38.
Veil rent—62, 166, 222, 264.
Vengeance—82, 165.
Vibrations—69, 72, 145, 146, 151, 159, 167, 226, 297.
Views—85.
Vine, The—103, 108, 310.
Virgins—301.
Vision—49, 192.
Visualize—37, 47, 48, 94.

Voice—202, 203, 205, 208, 225, 262.
Volume—236.

Wage slaves—142.
Way of Holiness—235.
Way, The—206.
Weak and foolish things—293, 312, 314, 334.
Weaknesses—258.
Wealth—151, 160, 164, 320.
Weeds—55, 71.
What we are—158.
Wickedness—82.
Will—12.
Wisdom—22, 52, 87.
With all the heart—293.
With all the mind—295.
With all the soul—294.
Within, The—212.
Without sin—258.
Without vision—192.
Witness—25.
Woman—293.
Word—91, 195, 218, 220, 248, 249, 252.
Word made flesh—178.
Works—84, 172, 228, 297.
Worry—58.

Yoke—255.
You—3, 12.

Zion—234, 323.
"Zion prospers"—86.